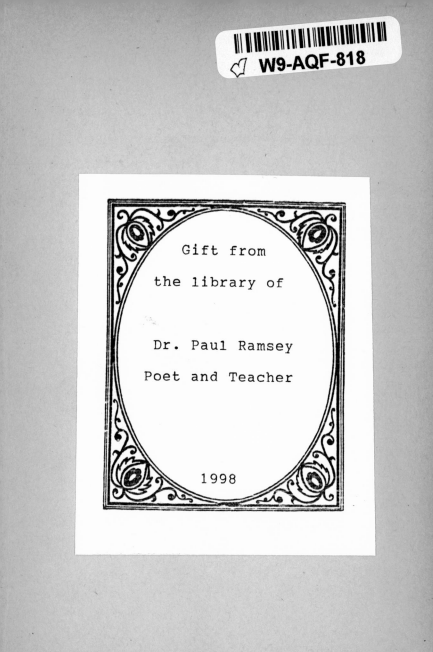

A
STUDY OF POETRY

BY

BLISS PERRY

Professor of English Literature in Harvard University

AUTHOR OF "A STUDY OF PROSE FICTION," "WALT WHITMAN,"
"THE AMERICAN MIND," ETC.

BOSTON NEW YORK CHICAGO

HOUGHTON MIFFLIN COMPANY

The Riverside Press Cambridge

137924

The Riverside Press
CAMBRIDGE . MASSACHUSETTS
U . S . A

TO
M. S. P.

PREFACE

THE method of studying poetry which I have followed in this book was sketched some years ago in my chapter on "Poetry" in *Counsel Upon the Reading of Books*. My confidence that the genetic method is the natural way of approaching the subject has been shared by many lovers of poetry. I hope, however, that I have not allowed my insistence upon the threefold process of "impression, transforming imagination, and expression" to harden into a set formula. Formulas have a certain dangerous usefulness for critics and teachers, but they are a very small part of one's training in the appreciation of poetry.

I have allotted little or no space to the specific discussion of epic and drama, as these types are adequately treated in many books. Our own generation is peculiarly attracted by various forms of the lyric, and in Part Two I have devoted especial attention to that field.

While I hope that the book may attract the traditional "general reader," I have also tried to arrange it in such a fashion that it may be utilized in the classroom. I have therefore ventured, in the Notes and Illustrations and Appendix, to suggest some methods and material for the use of students.

I wish to express my obligations to Professor R. M. Alden, whose *Introduction to Poetry* and *English Verse* I have used in my own Harvard courses in poetry. His views of metre have probably influenced mine even more than I am aware. The last decade, which has witnessed such an extraordinary revival of interest in poetry, has produced many valuable contributions to poetic theory. I have found Professor Fairchild's *Making of Poetry* particularly suggestive. Attention is called, in the Notes and Bibliography, to many other recent books on the subject.

' Professors A. S. Cook of Yale and F. B. Snyder of Northwestern University have been kind enough to read in manuscript certain chapters of this book, and Dr. P. F. Baum of Harvard has assisted me most courteously. I am indebted to several fellow-writers for their consent to the use of extracts from their books, particularly to Brander Matthews for a passage from *These Many Years* and to

Henry Osborn Taylor for a passage from his *Classical Heritage of the Middle Ages*.

I wish also to thank the publishers who have generously allowed me to use brief quotations from copyrighted books, especially Henry Holt & Co. for permission to use a quotation and drawing from William James's *Psychology*, and The Macmillan Company for permission to borrow from John La Farge's delightful *Considerations on Painting*.

B. P.

CONTENTS

CONTENTS

A STUDY OF POETRY

PART I

POETRY IN GENERAL

"Sidney and Shelley pleaded this cause. Because they spoke, must we be dumb?"

GEORGE E. WOODBERRY, A New Defense of Poetry

A STUDY OF POETRY

. .

CHAPTER I

A GLANCE AT THE BACKGROUND

It is a gray day in autumn. I am sitting at my desk, wondering how to begin the first chapter of this book about poetry. Outside the window a woman is contentedly kneeling on the upturned brown earth of her tulip-bed, patting lovingly with her trowel as she covers the bulbs for next spring's blossoming. Does she know Katharine Tynan's verses about "Planting Bulbs"? Probably not. But I find myself dropping the procrastinating pen, and murmuring some of the lines:

"Setting my bulbs a-row
   In cold earth under the grasses,
Till the frost and the snow
   Are gone and the Winter passes —

.   .   .   .

"Turning the sods and the clay
   I think on the poor sad people
Hiding their dead away
   In the churchyard, under the steeple.

"All poor women and men,
    Broken-hearted and weeping,
Their dead they call on in vain,
    Quietly smiling and sleeping.

"Friends, now listen and hear,
    Give over crying and grieving,
There shall come a day and a year
    When the dead shall be as the living.

"There shall come a call, a foot-fall,
    And the golden trumpeters blowing
Shall stir the dead with their call,
    Bid them be rising and going.

"Then in the daffodil weather,
    Lover shall run to lover;
Friends all trooping together;
    Death and Winter be over.

"Laying my bulbs in the dark,
    Visions have I of hereafter.
Lip to lip, breast to breast, hark!
    No more weeping, but laughter!"

Yet this is no way to start your chapter,
suggests Conscience. Why do you not write
an opening paragraph, for better for worse, instead of looking out of the window and quoting Katharine Tynan? And then it flashes
over me, in lieu of answer, that I have just
discovered one way of beginning the chapter,

after all! For what I should like to do in this book is to set forth in decent prose some of the strange potencies of verse: its power, for instance, to seize upon a physical image like that of a woman planting bulbs, and transmute it into a symbol of the resurrection of the dead; its capacity for turning fact into truth and brown earth into beauty; for remoulding the broken syllables of human speech into sheer music; for lifting the mind, bowed down by wearying thought and haunting fear, into a brooding ecstasy wherein weeping is changed into laughter and autumnal premonitions of death into assurance of life, and the narrow paths of individual experience are widened into those illimitable spaces where the imagination rules. Poetry does all this, assuredly. But how? And why? That is our problem.

"The future of poetry is immense," declared Matthew Arnold, and there are few lovers of literature who doubt his triumphant assertion. But the past of poetry is immense also: impressive in its sheer bulk and in its immemorial duration. At a period earlier than any recorded history, poetry seems to have occupied the attention of men, and some of the finest spirits in every race that has attained to civilization have devoted themselves to its production, or at least given themselves freely to the enjoyment of reciting and reading verse, and of meditating upon its significance. A consciousness of this rich human background should accompany each new endeavor to examine the facts about poetry and to determine its essential nature. The facts are indeed somewhat complicated, and the nature of poetry, in certain aspects of it, at least, will remain as always a mystery. Yet in that very complication and touch of mystery there is a fascination which has laid its spell upon countless generations of men, and which has been deepened rather than destroyed by the advance of science and the results of scholarship. The study of folklore and comparative literature has helped to explain some of the secrets of poetry; the psychological laboratory, the history of criticism, the investigation of linguistics, the modern developments in music and the other arts, have all contributed something to our intelligent enjoyment of the art of poetry and to our sense of its importance in the life of humanity. There is no field of inquiry where the interrelations of knowledge are more acutely to be perceived. The beginner in the study of poetry may at once comfort himself and increase his zest by remembering that any real training which he has already had in scientific observation, in the habit of analysis, in the study of races and historic periods, in the use of languages, in the practice or interpretation of any of the fine arts, or even in any bodily exercise that has developed his sense of rhythm, will be of ascertainable value to him in this new study.

But before attempting to apply his specific knowledge or aptitude to the new field for investigation, he should be made aware of some of the wider questions which the study of poetry involves. The first of these questions has to do with the relations of the study of poetry to the general field of Æsthetics.

1. The Study of Poetry and the Study of Æsthetics

The Greeks invented a convenient word to describe the study of poetry: "Poetics." Aristotle's famous fragmentary treatise bore that title, and it was concerned with the nature and laws of certain types of poetry and with the relations of poetry to the other arts. For the Greeks assumed, as we do, that poetry is an art: that it expresses emotion through words rhythmically arranged. But as soon as they began to inquire into the particular kind of emotion which is utilized in poetry and the various rhythmical arrangements employed by poets, they found themselves compelled to ask further questions. How do the other arts convey feeling? What arrangement or rhythmic ordering of facts do they use in this process? What takes place in us as we confront the work of art, or, in other words, what is our reaction to an artistic stimulus?

For an answer to such wider questions as these, we moderns turn to the so-called science of Æsthetics. This word, derived from the Greek *aisthanomai* (to perceive), has been defined as "anything having to do with perception by the senses." But it was first used in its present sense by the German thinker Baumgarten in the middle of the eighteenth century. He meant by it "the theory of the fine arts." It has proved a convenient term to describe both "The Science of the Beautiful" and "The Philosophy of Beauty"; that is, both the analysis and classification of beautiful things as well as speculation as to the origin and nature of Beauty itself. But it should be borne in mind that æsthetic inquiry and answer may precede by thousands of years the use of the formal language of æsthetic theory. Mr. Kipling's "Story of Ung" cleverly represents the cave-men as discussing the very topics which the contemporary studio and classroom strive in vain to settle, — in vain, because they are the eternal problems of art. Here are two faces, two trees, two colors, one of which seems preferable to the other. Wherein lies the difference, as far as the objects themselves are concerned? And what is it which the preferable face or tree or color stirs or awakens within us as we look at it? These are what we call æsthetic questions, but a man or a race may have a delicate and sure sense of beauty without consciously asking such questions at all. The awareness of beautiful objects in nature, and even the ability to create a beautiful work of art, may not be accompanied by any gift for æsthetic speculation. Conversely, many a Professor of æsthetics has contentedly lived in an ugly house and you would not think that he had ever looked at river or sky or had his pulses quickened by a tune. Nevertheless, no one can turn the pages of a formal History of Æsthetics without being reminded that the oldest and apparently the most simple inquiries in this field may also be the subtlest and in a sense the most modern. For illustration, take the three philosophical contributions of the Greeks to æsthetic theory, as they are stated by Bosanquet:[1] (1) the conception that art deals with images, not realities, i.e. with æsthetic "semblance" or things as they appear to the artist; (2) the conception that art consists in "imitation," which they carried to an absurdity, indeed, by arguing that an imitation must be less "valuable" than the thing imitated; (3) the conception that beauty consists in certain formal relations, such as symmetry, harmony of parts — in a word, "unity in variety."

Now no one can snap a Kodak effectively without putting into practice the first of these conceptions: nor understand the "new music" and "free verse" without reckoning with both the second and the third. The value to the student of poetry of some acquaintance

---

[1] Bosanquet, *History of Æsthetic*, chap. 3.

with æsthetic theory is sometimes direct, as
in the really invaluable discussion contained
in Aristotle's *Poetics*, but more often, perhaps,
it will be found in the indirect stimulus to
his sympathy and taste. For he must survey
the widespread sense of beauty in the ancient
world, the splendid periods of artistic creation in the Middle Ages, the growth of a new
feeling for landscape and for the richer and
deeper human emotions, and the emergence
of the sense of the "significant" or individ-
ually "characteristic" in the work of art.
Finally he may come to lose himself with
Kant or Hegel or Coleridge in philosophical
theories about the nature of beauty, or to
follow the curious analyses of experimental
æsthetics in modern laboratories, where the
psycho-physical reactions to æsthetic stimuli
are cunningly registered and the effects of
lines and colors and tones upon the human
organism are set forth with mathematical
precision. He need not trouble himself over-
much at the outset with definitions of Beauty.
The chief thing is to become aware of the long
and intimate preoccupation of men with
beautiful objects and to remember that any
inquiry into the nature and laws of poetry

will surely lead him into a deeper curiosity as to the nature and manifestations of æsthetic feeling in general.

2. *The Impulse to Artistic Production*

Furthermore, no one can ask himself how it is that a poem comes into being unless he also raises the wider question as to the origin and working of the creative impulse in the other arts. It is clear that there is a gulf between the mere sense of beauty — such as is possessed by primitive man, or, in later stages of civilization, by the connoisseur in the fine arts — and the concrete work of art. Thousands enjoy the statue, the symphony, the ode; not one in a thousand can produce these objects. Mere connoisseurship is sterile. "The ability to produce one fine line," said Edward FitzGerald, "transcends all the Able-Editor ability in this ably-edited universe." What is the impulse which urges certain persons to create beautiful objects? How is it that they cross the gulf which separates the enjoyer from the producer?

It is easier to ask this question than to find a wholly satisfactory answer to it. Plato's explanation, in the case of the poet, is simple enough: it is the direct inspiration of the divinity, — the "god" takes possession of the poet. Perhaps this may be true, in a sense, and we shall revert to it later, but first let us look at some of the conditions for the exercise of the creative impulse, as contemporary theorists have endeavored to explain them.

Social relations, surely, afford one of the obvious conditions for the impulse to art. The hand-clapping and thigh-smiting of primitive savages in a state of crowd-excitement, the song-and-dance before admiring spectators, the chorus of primitive ballads, — the crowd repeating and altering the refrains, — the rhythmic song of laboring men and of women at their weaving, sailors' "chanties," the celebration of funeral rites, religious processional and pageant, are all expressions of communal feeling, and it is this communal feeling — "the sense of joy in widest commonalty spread" — which has inspired, in Greece and Italy, some of the greatest artistic epochs. It is true that as civilization has proceeded, this communal emotion has often seemed to fade away and leave us in the presence of the individual artist only. We see

Keats sitting at his garden table writing the "Ode to Autumn," the lonely Shelley in the Cascine at Florence composing the "West Wind," Wordsworth pacing the narrow walk behind Dove Cottage and mumbling verses, Beethoven in his garret writing music. But the creative act thus performed in solitude has a singular potency, after all, for arousing that communal feeling which in the moment of creation the artist seems to escape. What he produces in his loneliness the world does not willingly let die. His work, as far as it becomes known, really unites mankind. It fulfills a social purpose. "Its function is social consolidation."

Tolstoy made so much of this "transmission of emotion," this "infectious" quality of art as a means of union among men, that he reduced a good case to an absurdity, for he argued himself into thinking that if a given work of art does not infect the spectator — and preferably the uneducated "peasant" spectator — with emotion, it is therefore not art at all. He overlooked the obvious truth that there are certain types of difficult or intricate beauty — in music, in architecture, and certainly in poetry — which so tax the attention and the analytical and reflective powers of the spectator as to make the inexperienced, uncultured spectator or hearer simply unaware of the presence of beauty. Debussy's music, Browning's dramatic monologues, Henry James's short stories, were not written for Tolstoy's typical peasant. They would "transmit" to him nothing at all. But although Tolstoy, a man of genius, overstated his case with childlike perversity, he did valuable service in insisting upon emotion as a basis for the art-impulse. The creative instinct is undeniably accompanied by strong feeling, by pleasure in the actual work of production and in the resultant object, and something of this pleasure in the harmonious expression of emotion is shared by the competent observer. The permanent vitality of a work of art does consist in its capacity for stimulating and transmitting pleasure. One has only to think of Gray's "Elegy" and the delight which it has afforded to generations of men.

Another conception of the artistic impulse seeks to ally it with the "play-instinct." According to Kant and Schiller there is a free "kingdom of play" between the urgencies of

necessity and of duty, and in this sphere of
freedom a man's whole nature has the chance
to manifest itself. He is wholly man only
when he "plays," that is, when he is free to
create. Herbert Spencer and many subsequent theorists have pointed out the analogy
between the play of young animals, the free
expression of their surplus energy, their organic delight in the exercise of their muscles,
and that "playful" expenditure of a surplus
of vitality which seems to characterize the
artist. This analogy is curiously suggestive,
though it is insufficient to account for all the
phenomena concerned in human artistic
production.

The play theory, again, suggests that old
and clairvoyant perception of the Greeks that
the art-impulse deals with æsthetic appear-
ances rather than with realities as such. The
artist has to do with the semblance of things;
not with things as they "are in themselves"
either physically or logically, but with things
as they appear to him. The work of the impressionist painter or the imagist poet illustrates this conception. The conventions of
the stage are likewise a case in point. Stage
settings, conversations, actions, are all af-

fected by the *"optique du théâtre,"* they are composed in a certain "key" which seeks to give a harmonious impression, but which conveys frankly semblance and not reality. The craving for "real" effects upon the stage is anti-æsthetic, like those gladiatorial shows where persons were actually killed. I once saw an unskilful fencer, acting the part of Romeo, really wound Tybalt: the effect was lifelike, beyond question, but it was shocking.

From this doctrine of æsthetic semblance or "appearance" many thinkers have drawn the conclusion that the pleasures afforded by art must in their very nature be disinterested and sharable. Disinterested, because they consist so largely in delighted contemplation merely. Women on the stage, said Coquelin, should afford to the spectator "a theatrical pleasure only, and not the pleasure of a lover." Compare with this the sprightly egotism of the lyric poet's

> "If she be not so to me,
> What care I how fair she be?"

A certain aloofness is often felt to characterize great art: it is perceived in the austerity and reserve of the Psyche of Naples and the Venus of Melos:

"And music pours on mortals
Its beautiful disdain."

The lower pleasures of the senses of taste and touch, it is often pointed out, are less pleasurable than the other senses when revived by memory. Your dinner is *your* dinner — your exclusive proprietorship of lower pleasure — in a sense in which the snowy linen and gleaming silver and radiant flowers upon the table are not yours only because they are sharable. If music follows the dinner, though it be your favorite tune, it is nevertheless not yours as what you have eaten is yours. Acute observers like Santayana have denied or minimized this distinction, but the general instinct of men persists in calling the pleasures of color and form and sound "sharable," because they exist for all who can appreciate them. The individual's happiness in these pleasures is not lessened, but rather increased, by the coexistent happiness of others in the same object.

There is one other aspect of the artistic impulse which is of peculiar importance to the student of poetry. It is this: the impulse toward artistic creation always works along lines of order. The creative impulse may re-

main a mystery in its essence, the play of
blind instinct, as many philosophers have
supposed; a portion of the divine energy
which is somehow given to men. All sorts of
men, good and bad, cultured and savage, have
now and again possessed this vital creative
power. They have been able to say with
Thomas Lovell Beddoes:

> "I have a bit of fiat in my soul,
>   And can myself create my little world."

The little world which their imagination has
created may be represented only by a totem
pole or a colored basket or a few scratches on
a piece of bone; or it may be a temple or a
symphony. But if it be anything more than
the mere whittling of a stick to exercise surplus energy, it is ordered play or labor. It
follows a method. It betrays premeditation.
It is the expression of something in the mind.
And even the mere whittler usually whittles
his stick to a point: that is, he is "making"
something. His knife, almost before he is
aware of what he is doing, follows a pattern —
invented in his brain on the instant or remembered from other patterns. He gets
pleasure from the sheer muscular activity,

and from his tactile sense of the bronze or steel as it penetrates the softer wood. But he gets a higher pleasure still from his pattern, from his sense of making something, no matter how idly. And as soon as the pattern or purpose or "design" is recognized by others the maker's pleasure is heightened, sharable. For he has accomplished the miracle: he has thrown the raw material of feeling into form — and that form itself yields pleasure. His "bit of fiat" has taken a piece of wood and transformed it: made it expressive of something. All the "arts of design" among primitive races show this pattern-instinct.

But the impulse toward an ordered expression of feeling is equally apparent in the rudimentary stages of music and poetry. The striking of hands or feet in unison, the rhythmic shout of many voices, the regular beat of the tom-tom, the excited spectators of a college athletic contest as they break spontaneously from individual shouting into waves of cheering and of song, the quickened feet of negro stevedores as some one starts a tune, the children's delight in joining hands and moving in a circle, all serve to illustrate the law that as feeling gains in intensity it tends toward ordered expression. Poetry, said Coleridge, in one of his marvelous moments of insight, is the result of "a more than usual state of emotion" combined "with more than usual order."

What has been said about play and sharable pleasure and the beginning of design has been well summarized by Sidney Colvin:[1]

"There are some things which we do because we must; these are our necessities. There are other things which we do because we ought; these are our duties. There are other things which we do because we like; these are our play. Among the various kinds of things done by men only because they like, the fine arts are those of which the results afford to many permanent and disinterested delight, and of which the performance, calling for premeditated skill, is capable of regulation up to a certain point, but that point passed, has secrets beyond the reach and a freedom beyond the restraint of rules."

3. "Form" and "Significance" in the Arts

If the fine arts, then, deal with the ordered or harmonious expression of feeling, it is clear that any specific work of art may be regarded, at least theoretically, from two

[1] Article on "The Fine Arts" in *Encyclopædia Britannica*.

points of view. We may look at its "outside"
or its "inside"; that is to say at its ordering
of parts, its pattern, its "form," or else at the
feeling or idea which it conveys. This distinction between form and content, between
expression and that which is expressed, is
temptingly convenient. It is a useful tool of
analysis, but it is dangerous to try to make
it anything more than that. If we were looking at a water-pipe and the water which
flows through it, it would be easy to keep a
clear distinction between the form of the iron
pipe, and its content of water. But in certain
of the fine arts very noticeably, such as
music, and in a diminished degree, poetry,
and more or less in all of them, the form *is*
the expression or content. A clear-cut dis-
section of the component elements of outside
and inside, of water-pipe and water within it,
becomes impossible. Listening to music is like
looking at a brook; there is no inside and
outside, it is all one intricately blended complex of sensation. Music is a perfect example
of "embodied feeling," as students of æsthetics term it, and the body is here inseparable
from the feeling. But in poetry, which is likewise embodied feeling, it is somewhat easier

to attempt, for purposes of logical analysis, a separation of the component elements of thought (i.e. "content") and form. We speak constantly of the "idea" of a poem as being more or less adequately "expressed," that is, rendered in terms of form. The actual form of a given lyric may or may not be suited to its mood,[1] or the poet may not have been a sufficiently skilful workman to achieve success in the form or "pattern" which he has rightly chosen.

Even in poetry, then, the distinction between inside and outside, content and form, has sometimes its value, and in other arts, like painting and sculpture, it often becomes highly interesting and instructive to attempt the separation of the two elements. The French painter Millet, for instance, is said to have remarked to a pupil who showed him a well-executed sketch: "You can paint. But what have you to *say?*" The pupil's work had in Millet's eyes no "significance." The English painter G. F. Watts often expressed himself in the same fashion: "I paint first of all because I have something to say. . . . My

[1] Certainly not, for instance, in Wordsworth's "Reverie of Poor Susan."

intention has not been so much to paint pictures that will charm the eye as to suggest great thoughts that will appeal to the imagination and the heart and kindle all that is best and noblest in humanity. . . . My work is a protest against the modern opinion that Art should have nothing to say intellectually."

On the other hand, many distinguished artists and critics have given assent to what has been called the "Persian carpet" theory of painting. According to them a picture should be judged precisely as one judges a Persian rug — by the perfection of its formal beauty, its harmonies of line, color and texture, its "unity in variety." It is evident that the men who hold this opinion are emphasizing form in the work of art, and that Millet and Watts emphasized significance. One school is thinking primarily of expression, and the other of that which is expressed. The important point for the student of poetry to grasp is that this divergence of opinion turns upon the question of relative emphasis. Even pure form, or "a-priori form" as it has sometimes been called, — such as a rectangle, a square, a cube, — carries a certain element of association which gives it a degree of sig-

nificance. There is no absolutely bare or
blank pattern. "Four-square" means something to the mind, because it is intimately
connected with our experience.[1] It cannot be
a mere question of balance, parallelism and
abstract "unity in variety." The acanthus
design in architectural ornament, the Sara-
cenic decoration on a sword-blade, aim indeed
primarily at formal beauty and little more.
The Chinese laundryman hands you a red
slip of paper covered with strokes of black ink
in strange characters. It is undecipherable to
you, yet it possesses in its sheer charm of
color and line, something of beauty, and the
freedom and vigor of the strokes are expressive of vitality. It is impossible that Maud's
face should really have been

"Faultily faultless, icily regular, splendidly null,
  Dead perfection, no more."

Nevertheless, though absolutely pure decorative beauty does not exist, the artist may
push the decorative principle very far, so
far, indeed, that his product lacks interest
and proves tedious or nonsensical. There is
"nonsense-verse," as we shall see later, which

[1] See Bosanquet, *Three Lectures on Æsthetic*, pp. 19, 29, 39,
and Santayana, *The Sense of Beauty*, p. 83.

fulfills every condition for pure formal beauty in poetry. Yet it is not poetry, but only nonsense-verse.

Now shift the interest from the form to the meaning contained in the work of art, that is, to its significance. An expressive face is one that reveals character. Its lines are suggestive of something. They are associated, like the lines of purely decorative beauty, with more or less obscure tracts of our experience, but they arouse a keen mental interest. They stimulate, they are packed closely with meaning, with fact, with representative quality. The same thing is true of certain landscapes. Witness Thomas Hardy's famous description of Egdon Heath in *The Return of the Native*. It is true of music. Certain modern music almost breaks down, as music, under the weight of meaning, of fact, of thought, which the composer has striven to make it carry.

There is no question that the principle of significance may be pushed too far, just as the principle of decorative or purely formal beauty may be emphasized too exclusively. But is there any real antagonism between the elements of form and significance, beauty and expressiveness? This question has been

debated ever since the time of Winckelmann
and Lessing. The controversy over the work
of such artists as Wagner, Browning, Whitman, Rodin has turned largely upon it.
Browning himself strove to cut the difficult
æsthetic knot with a rough stroke of common
sense:

> "Is it so pretty
> You can't discover if it means hope, fear,
> Sorrow or joy? Won't beauty go with these?" [1]

He tried again in the well-known passage
from *The Ring and the Book*:

> "So may you paint your picture, twice show truth,
> Beyond mere imagery on the wall, —
> So note by note bring music from your mind
> Deeper than ever e'en Beethoven dived, —
> So write a book shall mean beyond the facts,
> Suffice the eye and save the soul beside."

How Whistler, the author of *Ten O'Clock*
and the creator of exquisitely lovely things,
must have loathed that final line! But Bosanquet's carefully framed definition of the beautiful, in his *History of Æsthetic*, endeavors,
like Browning, to adjust the different claims
of form and significance: "The beautiful is
that which has characteristic or individual

[1] "Fra Lippo Lippi."

expressiveness for sense-perception or imagination, subject to the conditions of general or abstract expressiveness in the same medium." That is to say, in less philosophical language, that as long as you observe the laws of formal beauty which belong to the medium in which you are working, you may be as expressive or significant as you like. But the artist must be obedient to the terms of his chosen medium of expression; if he is composing music or poetry he must not break the general laws of music or poetry in order to attempt that valiant enterprise of saving a soul.

4. The Man in the Work of Art

Though there is much in this matter of content and form which is baffling to the student of general æsthetic theory, there is at least one aspect of the question which the student of poetry must grasp clearly. It is this: there is nothing in any work of art except what some man has put there. *What he has put in* is our content question; *what shape he has put it into* is our form question. In Bosanquet's more technical language: "A man is the middle term between content and expression." There is doubtless some element of mystery in what we call creative power, but this is a part of man's mystery. There is no mystery in the artist's material as such: he is working in pigments or clay or vibrating sound or whatever other medium he has chosen. The qualities and possibilities of this particular medium fascinate him, preoccupy him. He comes, as we say, to think in terms of color or line or sound. He learns or may learn in time, as Whistler bade him, "never to push a medium further than it will go." The chief value of Lessing's epoch-making discussion of "time-arts" and "space-arts" in his *Laokoon* consisted in the emphasis laid upon the specific material of the different arts, and hence upon the varying opportunities which one medium or another affords to the artist. But though human curiosity never wearies of examining the inexhaustible possibilities of this or that material, it is chiefly concerned, after all, in the use of material as it has been moulded by the fingers and the brain of a particular artist. The material becomes transformed as it passes through his "shop," in some such way as iron is transformed into steel in a blast furnace. An apparatus called a "transformer" alters the wavelength of an electrical current and reduces high pressure to low pressure, or the reverse. The brain of the artist seems to function in a somewhat similar manner as it reshapes the material furnished it by the senses, and expresses it in new forms. Poetry furnishes striking illustrations of the transformations wrought in the crucible of the imagination, and we must look at these in detail in a subsequent chapter. But it may be helpful here to quote the testimony of two or three artists and then to examine the psychological basis of this central function of the artist's mind.

"Painting is the expression of certain sensations," said Carolus Duran. "You should not seek merely to copy the model that is posed before you, but rather to take into account the impression that is made upon the mind. . . . Take careful account of the substances that you must render — wood, metal, textures, for instance. When you fail to reproduce nature *as you feel it*, then you falsify it. *Painting is not done with the eyes, but with the brain*."

W. W. Story, the sculptor, wrote: "Art is art because it is not nature. . . . The most perfect imitation of nature is therefore not

art. *It must pass through the mind of the artist
and be changed.* Art is nature reflected through
the spiritual mirror, and tinged with all the
sentiment, feeling, passion of the spirit that
reflects it."

In John La Farge's *Considerations on Painting,* a little book which is full of suggestiveness to the student of literature, there are
many passages illustrating the conception of
art as "the representation of the artist's view
of the world." La Farge points out that
"drawing from life is an exercise of memory.
It might be said that the sight of the moment
is merely a theme upon which we embroider
the memories of former likings, former as-
pirations, former habits, images that we have
cared for, and through which we indicate to
others our training, our race, the entire educated part of our nature."

One of La Farge's concrete examples must
be quoted at length: [1]

"I remember myself, years ago, sketching with
two well-known men, artists who were great
friends, great cronies, asking each other all the
time, how to do this and how to do that; but absolutely different in the texture of their minds and
in the result that they wished to obtain, so far as

[1] *Considerations on Painting,* pp. 71–73. Macmillan.

the pictures and drawings by which they were well known to the public are concerned.

"What we made, or rather, I should say, what we wished to note, was merely a memorandum of a passing effect upon the hills that lay before us. We had no idea of expressing ourselves, or of studying in any way the subject for any future use. We merely had the intention to note this affair rapidly, and we had all used the same words to express to each other what we liked in it. There were big clouds rolling over hills, sky clearing above, dots of trees and water and meadow-land below us, and the ground fell away suddenly before us. Well, our three sketches were, in the first place, different in shape; either from our physical differences, or from a habit of drawing certain shapes of a picture, which itself usually indicates — as you know, or ought to know — whether we are looking far or near. Two were oblong, but of different proportions; one was more nearly a square; the distance taken in to the right and left was smaller in the latter case, and, on the contrary, the height up and down — that is to say, the portion of land beneath and the portion of sky above — was greater. In each picture the clouds were treated with different precision and different attention. In one picture the open sky above was the main intention of the picture. In two pictures the upper sky was of no consequence — it was the clouds and the mountains that were insisted upon. The drawing was the same, that is to say, the general make of things; but each man had involuntarily looked upon what was most interesting to him in the whole sight; and though the whole sight was what he meant to represent, he had unconsciously preferred a beauty or an interest of things different from what his neighbour liked.

"The colour of each painting was different — the vivacity of colour and tone, the distinctness of each part in relation to the whole; and each picture would have been recognized anywhere as a specimen of work by each one of us, characteristic of our names. And we spent on the whole affair perhaps twenty minutes.

"I wish you to understand, again, that we each thought and felt as if we had been photographing the matter before us. We had not the first desire of expressing *ourselves*, and I think would have been very much worried had we not felt that each one was true to nature. And we were each one true to nature. . . . If you ever know how to paint somewhat well, and pass beyond the position of the student who has not yet learned to use his hands as an expression of the memories of his brain, you will always give to nature, that is to say, what is outside of you, the character of the lens through which you see it — which is yourself."

Such bits of testimony from painters help us to understand the brief sayings of the critics, like Taine's well-known "Art is nature seen through a temperament," G. L. Raymond's "Art is nature made human," and Croce's "Art is the expression of impressions." These painters and critics agree, evidently, that the mind of the artist is an

organism which acts as a "transformer." It
receives the reports of the senses, but alters
these reports in transmission and it is precisely in this alteration that the most personal and essential function of the artist's
brain is to be found.

Remembering this, let the student of
poetry now recall the diagram used in handbooks of psychology to illustrate the process of sensory stimulus of a nerve-centre and
the succeeding motor reaction. The diagram
is usually drawn after this fashion:

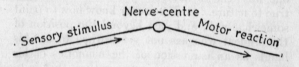

The process is thus described by William
James:[1]

"The afferent nerves, when excited by some
physical irritant, be this as gross in its mode of
operation as a chopping axe or as subtle as the
waves of light, convey the excitement to the
nervous centres. The commotion set up in the
centres does not stop there, but discharges through
the efferent nerves, exciting movements which vary
with the animal and with the irritant applied."

[1] *Psychology, Briefer Course,* American Science Series, p. 91.
Henry Holt.

The familiar laboratory experiment irritates with a drop of acid the hind leg of a frog. Even if the frog's brain has been removed, leaving the spinal cord alone to represent the nervous system, the stimulus of the acid results in an instant movement of the leg. Sensory stimulus, consequent excitement of the nerve centre and then motor reaction is the law. Thus an alarmed cuttlefish secretes an inky fluid which colors the sea-water and serves as his protection. Such illustrations may be multiplied indefinitely.[1] It may seem fanciful to insist upon the analogy between a frightened cuttlefish squirting ink into sea-water and an agitated poet spreading ink upon paper, but in both cases, as I have said elsewhere, "it is a question of an organism, a stimulus and a reaction. The image of the solitary reaper stirs a Wordsworth, and the result is a poem; a profound sorrow comes to Alfred Tennyson, and he produces *In Memoriam*."[2]

In the next chapter we must examine this

---

[1] See the extremely interesting statement by Sara Teasdale, quoted in Miss Wilkinson's *New Voices*, p. 199. Macmillan, 1919.

[2] *Counsel upon the Reading of Books*, p. 219. Houghton Mifflin Company.

process with more detail. But the person who asks himself how poetry comes into being will find a preliminary answer by reflecting upon the relation of "impression" to "expression" in every nerve-organism, and in all the arts. Everywhere he must reckon with this ceaseless current of impressions, "the stream of consciousness," sweeping inward to the brain; everywhere he will detect modification, selections, alterations in the stream as it passes through the higher nervous centres; everywhere he will find these transformed "impressions" expressed in the terms of some specific medium. Thus the temple of Karnak expresses in huge blocks of stone an imagination which has brooded over the idea of the divine permanence. The Greek "discus-thrower" is the idealized embodiment of a typical kind of athlete, a conception resulting from countless visual and tactile sensations. An American millionaire buys a "Corot" or a "Monet," that is to say, a piece of colored canvas upon which a highly individualized artistic temperament has recorded its vision or impression of some aspect of the world as it has been interpreted by Corot's or Monet's eye and brain and hand. A certain stimulus or "impression," an organism which reshapes impressions, and then an "expression" of these transformed impressions into the terms permitted by some specific material: that is the threefold process which seems to be valid in all of the fine arts. It is nowhere more intricately fascinating than in poetry.

CHAPTER II

THE PROVINCE OF POETRY

"The more I read and re-read the works of the great poets, and the more I study the writings of those who have some Theory of Poetry to set forth, the more am I convinced that the question What is Poetry? can be properly answered only if we make What it does take precedence of How it does it."

J. A. STEWART, *The Myths of Plato*

IN the previous chapter we have attempted a brief survey of some of the general æsthetic questions which arise whenever we consider the form and meaning of the fine arts. We must now try to look more narrowly at the special field of poetry, asking ourselves how it comes into being, what material it employs, and how it uses this material to secure those specific effects which we all agree in calling "poetical," however widely we may differ from one another in our analysis of the means by which the effect is produced.

Let us begin with a truism. It is universally admitted that poetry, like each of the fine arts, has a field of its own. To run a surveyor's line accurately around the borders of this field, determining what belongs to it rather than to the neighboring arts, is always difficult and sometimes impossible. But the field itself is admittedly "there," in all its richness and beauty, however bitterly the surveyors may quarrel about the boundary lines. (It is well to remember that professional surveyors do not themselves own these fields or raise any crops upon them!) How much map-making ingenuity has been devoted to this task of grouping and classifying the arts: distinguishing between art and fine art, between artist, artificer and artisan; seeking to arrange a hierarchy of the arts on the basis of their relative freedom from fixed ends, their relative complexity or comprehensiveness of effect, their relative obligation to imitate or represent something that exists in nature! No one cares particularly to-day about such matters of precedence — as if the arts were walking in a carefully ordered ecclesiastical procession. On the other hand, there is ever-increasing recognition of the soundness of the distinction made by Lessing in his *Laokoon: or the Limits of Painting and Poetry;* namely, that the fine arts differ, as media of expression, according to the nature of the material which they employ. That is to say, the "time-arts" — like poetry and music — deal primarily with actions that succeed one another in time. The space-arts — painting, sculpture, architecture — deal primarily with bodies that coexist in space. Hence there are some subjects that belong naturally in the "painting" group, and others that belong as naturally in the "poetry" group. The artist should not "confuse the genres," or, to quote Whistler again, he should not push a medium further than it will go. Recent psychology has more or less upset Lessing's technical theory of vision,[1] but it has confirmed the value of his main contention as to the fields of the various arts.

1. The Myth of Orpheus and Eurydice

An illustration will make this matter clear. Let us take the Greek myth of Orpheus and Eurydice, which has been utilized by many artists during more than two thousand years assuredly, and how much longer no one knows. Virgil told it in the *Georgics* and Ovid in the *Metamorphoses*. It became a favorite theme of medieval romance, and whether told in a French *lai* or Scottish ballad like "King

[1] F. E. Bryant, *The Limits of Descriptive Writing*, etc. Ann Arbor, 1906.

Orfeo," it still keeps, among all the strange transformations which it has undergone, "the freshness of the early world." Let us condense the story from King Alfred's Anglo-Saxon version of Boethius's *De Consolatione Philosophiæ:* "There was once a famous Thracian harper named Orpheus who had a beautiful wife named Eurydice. She died and went to hell. Orpheus longed sorrowfully for her, harping so sweetly that the very woods and wild beasts listened to his woe. Finally, he resolved to seek her in hell and win her back by his skill. And he played so marvelously there that the King of Hell to reward him gave him back his wife again, only upon the condition that he should not turn back to look at her as he led her forth. But, alas, who can constrain love? When Orpheus came to the boundary of darkness and light, he turned round to see if his wife was following — and she vanished."

Such was the myth in one of its manifold European forms. It deals obviously with a succession of events, with actions easily narratable by means of a "time-art" like poetry. The myth itself is one of fascinating human interest, and if a prose writer like Hawthorne had chosen to tell it in his *Wonder-Book*, we should doubtless speak of it as a "poetic" story. We should mean, in using that adjective, that the myth contained sentiment, imagination, passion, dramatic climax, pathos — the qualities which we commonly associate with poetry — and that Hawthorne, although a prose writer, had such an exquisite sympathy for Greek stories that his handling of the material would be as delicate, and the result possibly as lovely, as if the tale had been told in verse. But if we would realize the full value of Lessing's distinction, we must turn to one of the countless verse renderings of the myth. Here we have a succession of actions, indeed, quite corresponding to those of the prose story. But these images of action, succeeding one another in time, are now evoked by successive musical sounds, — the sounds being, as in prose, arbitrary word-symbols of image and idea, — only that in poetry the sounds have a certain ordered arrangement which heightens the emotional effect of the images evoked. Prose writer and poet might mean to tell precisely the same tale, but in reality they cannot, for one is composing, no matter how cunningly, in the tunes of prose and the other in the tunes of verse. The change in the instrument means an alteration in the mental effect.

Now turn to Lessing's other exemplar of the time-arts, the musician — for musicians as well as poets, painters and sculptors have utilized the myth of Orpheus and Eurydice. What can the musician do with the theme? Gluck's opera may serve for answer. He cannot, by the aid of music alone, call up very definite ideas or images. He cannot tell the Orpheus story clearly to one who has never heard it. But to one who already knows the tale, a composer's overture — without stage accessories or singing actors or any "operatic" devices as such — furnishes in its successions and combinations of musical sound, without the use of verbal symbols, a unique pleasurable emotion which strongly and powerfully reinforces the emotions suggested by the Orpheus myth itself. Certain portions of the story, such as those relating to the wondrous harping, can obviously be interpreted better through music than through the medium of any other art.

What can Lessing's "space-arts," sculpture and painting, do with the material furnished by the Orpheus myth? It is clear that they cannot tell the whole story, since they are dealing with "bodies that coexist" rather than with successive actions. They must select some one instant of action only, and preferably the most significant moment of the whole, the parting of husband and wife. In the museum at Naples there is the wonderful Greek treatment of this theme, in sculptured high relief. The sculptor has chosen the moment of parting. Hermes, the messenger of the gods to recall Eurydice, has twined his hand gently around the left hand of the woman. With her right hand she still touches her husband, but the dread instant is upon them all. The sculptor, representing the persons in three dimensions, as far as high relief allows, has sufficiently characterized their faces and figures, and with exquisite sense of rhythm and balance in his composition has fulfilled every requirement of formal beauty that marble affords.

In Sir Frederick Leighton's painting of Orpheus and Eurydice and in many another less famous painter's rendering of the theme, there is likewise the portrayal of an arrested moment. But the painter represents the per-

sonages and the background in two dimensions. He can separate his figures more completely than the sculptor, can make their
instant of action more "dramatic," can
portray certain objects, such as the diapha-
nous robe of Eurydice as she vanishes into
mist, which are beyond the power of the
sculptor to represent, and above all he can
suggest the color of the objects themselves,
the degree of light and shade, the "atmosphere" of the whole, in a fashion unap-
proachable by the rival arts.

The illustration need not be worked out
more elaborately here, though the student
may profitably reflect upon the resources of
the modern moving picture — which is a novel
combination of the " time " and "space" arts
— and of the mimetic dance, as affording
still further opportunities for expressing the
artistic possibilities of the Orpheus story.
But the chief lesson to be learned by one who
is attempting in this way to survey the provinces of the different arts is this: no two of all
the artists who have availed themselves of
the Orpheus material have *really had the same
subject*, although the title of each of their
productions, if catalogued, might conven-

iently be called "Orpheus and Eurydice."
Each has had his own conception of the theme,
each his own professional technique in handling his chosen medium, each his own habits
of brain, each, in a word, has found his own
subject. "Are these children who are playing
in the sunlight," said Fromentin, "or is it a
place in the sunlight in which children are
playing?" One is a "figure" subject, that is
to say, while the other is a landscape subject.

The whole topic of the "provinces" of the
arts becomes hopelessly academic and sterile
if one fails to keep his eye upon the individual
artist, whose free choice of a subject is conditioned solely by his own artistic interest in
rendering such aspects of any theme as his
own medium of expression will allow him to
represent. Take one of the most beautiful
objects in nature, a quiet sea. Is this a
"painter-like" subject? Assuredly, yet the
etcher has often rendered the effect of a quiet
sea in terms of line, as a pastellist has rendered it in terms of color, and a musician in
terms of tone-feeling, and a poet in terms of
tone-feeling plus thought. Each one of them
finds something for himself, selects his own
"subject," from the material presented by

the quiet sea, and whatever he may find belongs to him. We declaim against the confusion of the genres, the attempt to render in the terms of one art what belongs, as we had supposed, to another art, and we are often right in our protest. Yet artists have always been jumping each other's claims, and the sole test of the lawfulness of the procedure is the success of the result. If the border-foray of the impressionist or imagist proves successful, well and good, but a triumphant raid should not be mistaken for the steady lines of the main campaign.

2. The Special Field

What then do we mean by the province of poetry? Simply that there is a special field in which, for uncounted centuries, poets have produced a certain kind of artistic effect. Strictly speaking, it is better to say "poets" rather than "the poet," just as William James confesses that strictly speaking there is no such thing as "the Imagination," there are only imaginations. But "the poet" is a convenient expression to indicate a man functioning *qua* poet — i.e. a man poetizing; and we shall continue to use it. When we say that "the poet" in Sir Walter Scott inspires this or that utterance, while "the novelist" or "the historian" or "the critic" in him has prompted this or that other utterance, we are within our rights.

The field of poetry, as commonly understood, is that portion of human feeling which expresses itself through rhythmical and preferably metrical language. In this field "the poet" labors. The human feeling which he embodies in verse comes to him originally, as feeling comes to all men, in connection with a series of mental images. These visual, auditory, motor or tactile images crowd the stream of consciousness as it sweeps inward to the brain. There the images are subjected to a process of selection, modification, transformation.[1] At some point in the process the poet's images tend to become verbal, — as the painter's or the musician's do not, — and these verbal images are then discharged in rhythmical patterns. It is one type of the threefold process roughly described at the close of Chapter I. What is peculiar to the poet as compared with other men or other

[1] "The finest poetry was first experience; but the thought has suffered a transformation since it was an experience." Emerson, *Shakespeare: The Poet.*

artists is to be traced not so much in the peculiar nature of his visual, auditory, motor
or tactile images — for in this respect poets
differ enormously among one another — as
in the increasingly verbal form of these
images as they are reshaped by his imagination, and in the strongly rhythmical or
metrical character of the final expression.

Let carbon represent the first of the stages,
the excited feeling resulting from sensory
stimulus. That is the raw material of poetic
emotion. Let the diamond represent the
second stage, the chemical change, as it were,
produced in the mental images under the
heat and pressure of the imagination. The
final stage would be represented by the cut-
ting, polishing and setting of the diamond, by
the arrangement of the transformed and now
purely verbal images into effective rhythmical or metrical designs.

Wordsworth once wrote of true poets who
possessed
"The vision and the faculty divine,
  Though wanting the accomplishment of verse."
Let us venture to apply Wordsworth's
terminology to the process already described.
The "vision" of the poet would mean his

sense-impressions of every kind, his experience, as Goethe said, of "the outer world,
the inner world and the other world." The
"faculty divine," into which vision blends
insensibly, would mean the mysterious change
of these sense-impressions — as they become
subjected to reflection, comparison, memory,
"passion recollected in tranquillity," — into
words possessing a peculiar life and power.
The "accomplishment of verse" is easier to
understand. It is the expression, by means of
these words now pulsating with rhythm —
the natural language of excitement — of whatever the poet has seen and felt, modified by
his imagination. The result is a poem: "embodied feeling."

Browning says to his imaginary poet:

"Your brains beat into rhythm — you tell
        What we felt only."

There is much virtue, for us, in this rudely
vigorous description of "the poet." Certainly
all of us feel, and thus far we are all potential
poets. But according to Browning there is,
so to speak, a physiological difference between the poet's brain and ours. His brain
beats into rhythm; that is the simple but
enormous difference in function, and hence it

is that he can tell what we only feel. That is, he becomes a "singer" as well as "maker," while we, conscious though we may be of the capacity for intense feeling, cannot embody our feelings in the forms of verse. We may indeed go so far as to reshape mental images in our heated brains — for all men do this under excitement, but to sing what we have thus made is denied to us.

3. An Illustration from William James

No one can be more conscious than the present writer of the impossibility of describing in plain prose the admittedly complicated and mysterious series of changes by which poetry comes into being. Those readers who find that even the lines just quoted from Wordsworth and Browning throw little new light upon the old difficulties, may nevertheless get a bit of help here by turning back to William James's diagram of the working of the brain. It will be remembered that in Chapter I we used the simplest possible chart to represent the sensory stimulus of a nerve-centre and the succeeding motor reaction, and we compared the "in-coming" and "out-going" nerve processes with the function of

Impression and Expression in the arts. But to understand something of what takes place in the making of poetry we must now substitute for our first diagram the slightly more complicated one which William James employs to represent, not those lower nerve-centres which "act from present sensational stimuli alone," but the hemispheres of the human brain which "act from considerations." [1] Considerations are images constructed out of past experience, they are reproductions of what has been felt or witnessed.

" They are, in short, *remote* sensations; and the main difference between the hemisphereless animal and the whole one may be concisely expressed by saying that *the one obeys absent, the other only present, objects. The hemispheres would then seem to be the chief seat of memory.*"

Then follows the accompanying diagram and illustration.

" If we liken the nervous currents to electric currents, we can compare the nervous system, C, below the hemispheres to a direct circuit from sense-organ to muscle along the line $S...C...M$. The hemisphere, H, adds the long circuit or loopline through which the current may pass when for any reason the direct line is not used.

"Thus, a tired wayfarer on a hot day throws

[1] *Psychology, Briefer Course*, pp. 97, 98.   Henry Holt.

himself on the damp earth beneath a maple-tree. The sensations of delicious rest and coolness pouring themselves through the direct line would naturally discharge into the muscles of complete extension: he would abandon himself to the dangerous repose. But the loop-line being open, part of the current is drafted along it, and awakens rheumatic or catarrhal reminiscences, which prevail over the instigations of sense, and make the man arise and pursue his way to where he may enjoy his rest more safely."

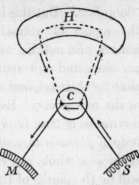

William James's entire discussion of the value of the hemisphere "loop-line" as a reservoir of reminiscences is of peculiar suggestiveness to the student of poetry. For it is along this loop-line of "memories and ideas of the distant" that poetry wins its generalizing or universalizing power. It is here that the life of reason enters into the life of mere sensation, transforming the reports of the nerves into ideas and thoughts that have coherence and general human significance. It is possible, certainly, as the experiments of contemporary "imagists" prove, to write poetry of a certain type without employing the "loop-line." But this is pure sensorium verse, the report of retinal, auditory or tactile images, and nothing more. "Response to impressions and representation of those impressions in their *original isolation* are the marks of the new poetry. Response to impressions, *correlation of those impressions into a connected body of phenomena,* and final interpretation of them as a whole are, have been, and always will be the marks of the enduring in all literature, whether poetry or prose."[1] To quote another critic: "A rock, a star, a lyre, a cataract, do not, except incidentally and indirectly, owe their command of our sympathies to the bare power of evoking reactions in a series of ocular envelopes or auditory canals. Their power lies in their freightage of association, in their tactical position at the focus of converging experience, in the number and vigor of the occasions in which they have crossed and recrossed the palpitating thoroughfares of life. . . . Sense-impressions are poetically valuable

[1] Lewis Worthington Smith, "The New Naïveté," *Atlantic,* April, 1916.

only in the measure of their power to procreate or re-create experience." [1]

One may give the fullest recognition to the delicacy and sincerity of imagist verse, to its magical skill in seeming to open new doors of sense experience by merely shutting the old doors of memory, to its naïve courage in rediscovering the formula of "Back to Nature." [2] Like "free verse," it has widened the field of expression, although its advocates have sometimes forgotten that thousands of "imagist" poems lie embedded in the verse of Browning and even in the prose of George Meredith. [3] We shall discuss some of its tenets later, but it should be noted at this point that the radical deficiency of imagist verse, as such, is in its lack of general ideas. Much of it might have been written by an infinitely sensitive decapitated frog. It is "hemisphereless" poetry.

4. *The Poet and Other Men*

The mere physical vision of the poet may or may not be any keener than the vision of

[1] O. W. Firkins, "The New Movement in Poetry," *Nation*, October 14, 1915.

[2] See the discussion of imagist verse in chap. III.

[3] J. L. Lowes, "An Unacknowledged Imagist," *Nation*, February 24, 1916.

other men. There is an infinite variety in the bodily endowments of habitual verse-makers: there have been near-sighted poets like Tennyson, far-sighted poets like Wordsworth, and, in the well-known case of Robert Browning, a poet conveniently far-sighted in one eye and near-sighted in the other! No doubt the life-long practice of observing and recording natural phenomena sharpens the sense of poets, as it does the senses of Indians, naturalists, sailors and all outdoors men. The quick eye for costume and character possessed by a Chaucer or a Shakspere is remarkable, but equally so is the observation of a Dickens or a Balzac. It is rather in what we call psychical vision that the poet is wont to excel, that is, in his ability to perceive the meaning of visual phenomena. Here he ceases to be a mere reporter of retinal images, and takes upon himself the higher and harder function of an interpreter of the visible world. He has no immunity from the universal human experiences: he loves and he is angry and he sees men born and die. He becomes according to the measure of his intellectual capacity a thinker. He strives to see into the human heart, to comprehend the working of the human mind. He reads the divine justice in the tragic fall of Kings. He penetrates beneath the external forms of Nature and perceives her as a "living presence." Yet the faculty of vision which the poet possesses in so eminent a degree is shared by many who are not poets. Darwin's outward eye was as keen as Wordsworth's; St. Paul's sense of the reality of the invisible world is more wonderful than Shakspere's. The poet is indeed first of all a seer, but he must be something more than a seer before he is wholly poet.

Another mark of the poetic mind is its vivid sense of relations. The part suggests the whole. In the single instance there is a hint of the general law. The self-same Power that brings the fresh rhodora to the woods brings the poet there also. In the field-mouse, the daisy, the water-fowl, he beholds types and symbols. His own experience stands for all men's. The conscience-stricken Macbeth is a poet when he cries, "Life is a walking shadow," and King Lear makes the same pathetic generalization when he exclaims, "What, have his daughters brought him to this pass?" Through the shifting phenomena of the present the poet feels the sweep of the universe; his mimic play and "the great globe itself" are alike an "insubstantial pageant," though it may happen, as Tennyson said of Wordsworth, that even in the transient he gives the sense of the abiding, "whose dwelling is the light of setting suns."

But this perception of relations, characteristic as it is of the poetic temper, is also an attribute of the philosopher. The intellect of a Newton, too, leaps from the specific instance to the general law; every man, in proportion to his intelligence and insight, feels that the world is one; while Plato and Descartes play with the time and space world with all the grave sportiveness of Prospero.

Again, the poets have always been the "genus irritabile" — the irritable tribe. They not only see deeply, but feel acutely. Often they are too highly sensitized for their own happiness. If they receive a pleasure more exquisite than ours from a flower, a glimpse of the sea, a gracious action, they are correspondingly quick to feel dissonances, imperfections, slights. Like Lamb, they are "rather squeamish about their women and children." Like Keats, they are "snuffed out by an

article." Keener pleasures, keener pains, this
is the law of their life; but it is applicable to
all persons of the so-called artistic temperament. It is one of the penalties of a fine organism. It does not of itself describe a poet.[1]

The real difference between "the poet" and
other men is rather to be traced, as the
present chapter has tried to indicate, in his
capacity for making and employing verbal
images of a certain kind, and combining these
images into rhythmical and metrical designs.
In each of his functions — as "seer," as
"maker," and as "singer" — he shows himself a true creator. Criticism no longer attempts to act as his "law-giver," to assert
what he may or may not do. The poet is free,
like every creative artist, to make a beautiful
object in any way he can. And nevertheless
criticism — watching countless poets lovingly for many a century, observing their
various endowments, their manifest endeavors, their victories and defeats, observing likewise the nature of language, that
strange medium (so much stranger than any
clay or bronze!) through which poets are

[1] I have here utilized a few paragraphs from my chapter on
"Poetry" in *Counsel upon the Reading of Books*, Houghton
Mifflin Company.

compelled to express their conceptions —
criticism believes that poetry, like each of
the sister arts, has its natural province, its
own field of the beautiful. We have tried in
this chapter to suggest the general direction
of that field, without looking too narrowly for
its precise boundaries. In W. H. Hudson's
Green Mansions the reader will remember
how a few sticks and stones, laid upon a hill-
top, were used as markers to indicate the
outlines of a continent. Criticism, likewise,
needs its poor sticks and stones of commonplace, if it is to point out any roadway. Our
own road leads first into the difficult territory
of the poet's imaginings, and then into the
more familiar world of the poet's words.

CHAPTER III

THE POET'S IMAGINATION

"The essence of poetry is *invention;* such invention as, by producing something unexpected, surprises and delights."

SAMUEL JOHNSON

"The singers do not beget, only the Poet begets."

WALT WHITMAN

WE must not at the outset insist too strongly upon the radical distinction between "the poet" — as we have called him for convenience — and other men. The common sense of mankind asserts that this distinction exists, yet it also asserts that all children are poets after a certain fashion, and that the vast majority of adult persons are, at some moment or other, susceptible to poetic feeling. A small girl, the other day, spoke of a telegraph wire as "that message-vine." Her father and mother smiled at this naïve renaming of the world of fact. It was a child's instinctive "poetizing" imagination, but the father and mother, while no longer capable, perhaps, of such daring verbal magic, were conscious that they had too often played with the world of fact, and, for the instant at least, remoulded it into something nearer the heart's desire. That is to say, they could still feel "poetically," though their wonderful chance of making up new names for everything had gone as soon as the gates were shut upon the Paradise of childhood.

All readers of poetry agree that it originates somehow in feeling, and that if it be true poetry, it stimulates feeling in the hearer. And all readers agree likewise that feeling is transmitted from the maker of poetry to the enjoyer of poetry by means of the imagination. But the moment we pass beyond these accepted truisms, difficulties begin.

1. Feeling and Imagination

What is feeling, and exactly how is it bound up with the imagination? The psychology of feeling remains obscure, even after the labors of generations of specialists; and it is obvious that the general theories about the nature of imagination have shifted greatly, even within the memory of living men. Nevertheless there are some facts, in this constantly contested territory, which now seem indisputable. One of them, and of peculiar significance to students of poetry, is this: in the stream of objects immediately present to consciousness there are no images of feeling itself.[1]

"If I am asked to call up an image of a rose, of a tree, of a cloud, or of a skylark, I can readily do it; but if I am asked to feel loneliness or sorrow, to feel hatred or jealousy, or to feel joy on the return of spring, I cannot readily do it. And the reason why I cannot do it is because I can call up no image of any one of these feelings. For everything I come to know through my senses, for everything in connection with what I do or feel I can call up some kind of mental image; but for no kind of feeling itself can I ever possibly have a direct image. The only effective way of arousing any particular feeling that is more than mere bodily feeling is to call up the images that are naturally connected with that feeling." [2]

If then, "the raw material of poetry," as Professor Fairchild insists, is "the mental image," we must try to see how these images are presented to the mind of the poet and in turn communicated to us. Instead of asserting, as our grandfathers did, that the imagi-

[1] This point has been elaborated with great care in Professor A. H. R. Fairchild's *Making of Poetry*. Putnam's, 1912.
[2] Fairchild, pp. 24, 25.

nation is a "faculty" of the mind, like "judgment," or accepting the theory of our fathers that imagination "is the whole mind thrown into the process of imagining," the present generation has been taught by psychologists like Charcot, James and Ribot that we are chiefly concerned with "imaginations," that is, a series of visual, auditory, motor or tactile images flooding in upon the mind, and that it is safer to talk about these "imaginations" than about "the Imagination." Literary critics will continue to use this last expression — as we are doing in the present chapter — because it is too convenient to be given up. But they mean by it something fairly definite: namely, the images swarming in the stream of consciousness, and their integration into wholes that satisfy the human desire for beauty. It is in its ultimate aim rather than in its immediate processes that the "artistic" imagination differs from the inventor's or scientist's or philosopher's imagination. We no longer assert, as did Stopford Brooke some forty years ago, that "the highest scientific intellect is a joke compared with the power displayed by a Shakespeare, a Homer, a Dante." We are inclined

rather to believe that in its highest exercise
of power the scientific mind is attempting
much the same feat as the highest type of
poetic mind, and that in both cases it is a
feat of imaginative energy.

2. Creative and Artistic Imagination

The reader who has hitherto allowed himself to think of a poet as a sort of freak of
nature, abnormal in the very constitution of
his mind, and achieving his results by methods
so obscure that "inspiration" is our helpless
name for indicating them, cannot do better
than master such a book as Ribot's *Essay on
the Creative Imagination.*[1] This famous psy-
chologist, starting with the conception that
the raw material for the creative imagination
is images, and that its basis lies in a motor
impulse, examines first the emotional factor
involved in every act of the creative imagination. Then he passes to the unconscious factor, the involuntary "coming" of the idea,
that "moment of genius," as Buffon called it,
which often marks the end of an unconscious
elaboration of the idea or the beginning of

[1] Th. Ribot, *Essai sur l'Imagination créatrice.* Paris, 1900.
English translation by Open Court Co., Chicago, 1906.

conscious elaboration.[1] Ribot points out that certain organic changes, as in blood circulation — the familiar rush of blood to the head — accompany imaginative activity. Then he discusses the inventor's and artist's "fixed idea," their "will that it shall be so," "the motor tendency of images engendering the ideal." Ribot's distinction between the animal's revival of images and the true creative combination of images in the mental life of children and of primitive man bears directly upon poetry, but even more suggestive to us is his diagram of the successive stages by which inventions come into being. There are two types of this process, and three stages of each: (A) the "idea," the "discovery" or invention, and then the verification or application; or else (B) the unconscious preparation, followed by the "idea" or "inspiration," and then by the "development" or construction. Whether a man is inventing a safety-pin or a sonnet, the series of imaginative processes seems to be much the same. There is of course a typical difference between the "plastic" imagination, dealing with clear

[1] See the quotation from Sir William Rowan Hamilton, the mathematician, in the "Notes and Illustrations" for this chapter.

images, objective relations, and seen at its best in the arts of form like sculpture and architecture, and that "diffluent" imagination which prefers vaguely outlined images, which is markedly subjective and emotional, and of which modern music like Debussy's is a good example. But whatever may be the specific type of imagination involved, we find alike in inventor, scientist and artist the same general sequence of "germ, incubation, flowering and completion," and the same fundamental motor impulse as the driving power.

Holding in mind these general characteristics of the creative imagination, as traced by Ribot, let us now test our conception of the distinctively artistic imagination. Countless are the attempts to define or describe it, and it would be unwise for the student, at this point, to rest satisfied with any single formulation of its functions. But it may be helpful to quote a paragraph from Hartley B. Alexander's brilliant and subtle book, *Poetry and the Individual*: [1]

"The energy of the mind or of the soul — for it welds all psychical activities — which is the agent of our world-winnings and the procreator of

[1] Putnam's, 1906.

our growing life, we term imagination. It is distinguished from perception by its relative freedom from the dictation of sense; it is distinguished from memory by its power to acquire — memory only retains; it is distinguished from emotion in being a force rather than a motive; from the understanding in being an assimilator rather than the mere weigher of what is set before it; from the will, because the will is but the wielder of the reins — the will is but the charioteer, the imagination is the Pharaoh in command. It is distinguished from all these, yet it includes them all, for it is the full functioning of the whole mind and in the total activity drives all mental faculties to its one supreme end — the widening of the world wherein we dwell. Through beauty the world grows, and it is the business of the imagination to create the beautiful. The imagination synthesises, humanises, personalises, illumines reality with the soul's most intimate moods, and so exalts with spiritual understandings."

The value of such a description, presented without any context, will vary with the training of the individual reader, but its quickening power will be recognized even by those who are incapable of grasping all the intellectual distinctions involved.

3. Poetic Imagination in Particular

We are now ready, after this consideration of the creative and artistic imagination, to look more closely at some of the qualities of the poetic imagination in particular. The specific formal features of that imagination lie, as we have seen, in its use of verbal imagery, and in the combination of verbal images into rhythmical patterns. But are there not functions of the poet's mind preceding the formation of verbal images? The psychology of language is still unsettled, and whether a man can think without the use of words is often doubted. But a painter can certainly "think" in terms of color, as an architect or mathematician can "think" in terms of form and space, or a musician in terms of sound, without employing verbal symbols at all. And are there not characteristic activities of the poetic imagination which antedate the fixation and expression of images in words? Apparently there are.

The reader will find, in the "Notes and Illustrations" for this chapter, a quotation from Mr. Lascelles-Abercrombie, in which he refers to the "region where the outward radiations of man's nature combine with the irradiations of the world." That is to say, the inward-sweeping stream of consciousness is instantly met by an outward-moving activity

of the brain which recognizes relationships
between the objects proffered to the senses
and the personality itself. The "I" projects
itself into these objects, claims them, ap-
propriates them as a part of its own nature.
Professor Fairchild, who calls this self-pro-
jecting process by the somewhat ambiguous
name of "personalizing," rightly insists, I believe, that poets make a more distinctive use
of this activity than other men. He quotes
some of the classic confidences of poets themselves: Keats's "If a sparrow come before my
window I take part in its existence and pick
about the gravel"; and Goethe on the sheep
pictured by the artist Roos, "I always feel
uneasy when I look at these beasts. Their
state, so limited, dull, gaping, and dreaming,
excites in me such sympathy that I fear I shall
become a sheep, and almost think the artist
must have been one." I can match this Goethe
story with the prayer of little Larry H., son
of an eminent Harvard biologist. Larry, at
the age of six, was taken by his mother to the
top of a Vermont hill-pasture, where, for the
first time in his life, he saw a herd of cows and
was thrilled by their glorious bigness and
nearness and novelty. When he said his

prayers that night, he was enough of a poet
to change his usual formula into this:

> "Jesus, tender Shepherd, hear me,
> Bless thy little *cow* to-night" —

Larry being the cow.

> "There was a child went forth every day,"

records Walt Whitman,

> "And the first object he look'd upon that object
> he became."

Professor Fairchild quotes these lines from
Whitman, and a few of the many passages of
the same purport from Coleridge and Wordsworth.   They are all summed up in Coleridge's
heart-broken

> "Oh, Lady, we receive but what we give,
> And in our life alone does Nature live."

This "animism," or identifying imagination, by means of which the child or the primitive man or the poet transfers his own life into
the unorganic or organic world, is one of the
oldest and surest indications of poetic faculty,
and as far as we can see, it is antecedent to
the use of verbal images or symbols.

Another characteristic of the poetic temperament, allied with the preceding, likewise
seems to belong in the region where words are

not as yet emerging above the threshold of consciousness. I mean the strange feeling, witnessed to by many poets, of the fluidity, fusibility, transparency — the infinitely changing and interchangeable aspects — of the world as it appears to the senses. It is evident that poets are not looking — at least when in this mood — at our "logical" world of hard, clear fact and law. They are gazing rather at what Whitman called "the eternal float of solution," the "flowing of all things" of the Greeks, the "river within the river" of Emerson. This tendency is peculiarly marked, of course, in artists possessing the "diffluent" type of imagination, and Romantic poets and critics have had much to say about it. The imagination, said Wordsworth, "recoils from everything but the plastic, the pliant, the indefinite." [1] "Shakespeare, too," says Carlyle,[2] "does not look *at* a thing, but into it, through it; so that he constructively comprehends it, can take it asunder and put it together again; *the thing melts as it were, into light under his eye, and anew creates itself before him.* That is to say, he is a Poet. For Goethe,

---

[1] Preface to 1815 edition of his *Poems*.
[2] Essay on "Goethe's Works."

as for Shakespeare, *the world lies all translu-
cent, all fusible* we might call it, encircled with
Wonder; the Natural in reality the Supernatural, for to the seer's eyes both become one."

In his essay on Tieck Carlyle remarks again
upon this characteristic of the mind of the
typical poet: "He is no mere observer and
compiler; rendering back to us, with additions
or subtractions, the Beauty which existing
things have of themselves presented to him;
but a true Maker, to whom the actual and
external is but the excitement for ideal creations representing and ennobling its effects."

Coleridge's formula is briefer still; the imagination "dissolves, diffuses, dissipates, in
order to re-create." [1]

Such passages help us to understand the
mystical moments which many poets have recorded, in which their feeling of "diffusion"
has led them to doubt the existence of the
external world. Wordsworth grasping " at a
wall or tree to recall myself from this abyss
of idealism to the reality," and Tennyson's
"weird seizures" which he transferred from
his own experience to his imaginary Prince in
The Princess, are familiar examples of this

---

[1] *Biographia Literaria.*

type of mysticism. But the sense of the infinite fusibility and change in the objective world is deeper than that revealed in any one type of diffluent imagination. It is a profound characteristic of the poetic mind as such. Yet it should be remembered that the philosopher and the scientist likewise assert that ours is a vital, ever-flowing, onward-urging world, in the process of "becoming" rather than merely "being." "We are far from the noon of man" sang Tennyson, in a late-Victorian and evolutionary version of St. John's "It doth not yet appear what we shall be." "The primary imagination," asserted Coleridge, "is a repetition in the finite mind of the eternal act of creation in the infinite *I am*." [1] Here, evidently, unless the "God-intoxicated" Coleridge is talking nonsense, we are in the presence of powers that do not need as yet any use of verbal symbols.

4. Verbal Images

The plasticity of the world as it appears to the mind of the poet is clearly evidenced by the swarm of images which present themselves to the poet's consciousness. In the re-presen-

[1] *Biographia Literaria*, chap. 13.

tation of these pictures to us the poet is
forced, of course, to use verbal images. The
precise point at which he becomes conscious
of employing words no doubt varies with the
individual, and depends upon the relative
balance of auditory, visual or tactile images in
his mind. Swinburne often impresses us as
working primarily with the "stuff" of word-
sounds, as Browning with the stuff of sharp-
cut tactile or motor images, and Victor Hugo
with the stuff of visual impressions. But in
each case the poet's sole medium of *expression
to us* is through verbal symbols, and it is hard
to get behind these into the real workshop of
the brain where each poet is busily minting
his own peculiar raw material into the current
coin of human speech.

Nevertheless, many poets have been sufficiently conscious of what is going on within
their workshop to tell us something about it.
Professor Fairchild has made an interesting
collection [1] of testimony relating to the tu-
multuous crowding of images, each clamoring,
as it were, for recognition and crying "take
me!" He instances, as other critics have done,
the extraordinary succession of images by

[1] *The Making of Poetry*, pp. 78, 79.

which Shelley strives to portray the spirit of the skylark. The similes actually chosen by Shelley seem to have been merely the lucky candidates selected from an infinitely greater number. In Francis Thompson's captivating description of Shelley as a glorious child the reader is conscious of the same initial rush of images, although the medium of expression here is heightened prose instead of verse: [1]

"Coming to Shelley's poetry, we peep over the wild mask of revolutionary metaphysics, and we see the winsome face of the child. Perhaps none of his poems is more purely and typically Shelleian than *The Cloud*, and it is interesting to note how essentially it springs from the faculty of make-believe. The same thing is conspicuous, though less purely conspicuous, throughout his singing; it is the child's faculty of make-believe raised to the nth power. He is still at play, save only that his play is such as manhood stops to watch, and his playthings are those which the gods give their children. The universe is his box of toys. He dabbles his fingers in the day-fall. He is gold-dusty with tumbling amidst the stars. He makes bright mischief with the moon. The meteors nuzzle their noses in his hand. He teases into growling the kennelled thunder, and laughs at the shaking of its fiery chain. He dances in and out of the gates of heaven: its floor is littered with his broken fancies. He runs wild over the fields of

[1] *Dublin Review*, July, 1908.

ether. He chases the rolling world. He gets between the feet of the horses of the sun. He stands
in the lap of patient Nature, and twines her loosened tresses after a hundred wilful fashions, to see
how she will look nicest in his song."

5. The Selection and Control of Images

It is easier, no doubt, to realize something
of the swarming of images in the stream of
consciousness than it is to understand how
these images are selected, combined and controlled. Some principle of association, some
law governing the synthesis, there must be;
and English criticism has long treasured some
of the clairvoyant words of Coleridge and
Wordsworth upon this matter. The essential
problem is suggested by Wordsworth's phrase
"the manner in which we associate ideas in a
state of excitement." Is the "excitement,"
then, the chief factor in the selection and combination of images, and do the "feelings," as
if with delicate tentacles, instinctively choose
and reject and integrate such images as blend
with the poet's mood?

Coleridge, with his subtle builder's instinct,
uses his favorite word "synthesis" not
merely as applied to images as such, but to
all the faculties of the soul:

"The poet, described in ideal perfection, brings the whole soul of man into activity, with the subordination of its faculties to each other according to their relative worth and dignity. He diffuses a tone and a spirit of unity, that blends, and as it were fuses, each into each, by that synthetic and magical power to which I would exclusively appropriate the name of Imagination." "Synthetic and magical power," indeed, with a Coleridge as Master of the Mysteries! But the perplexed student of poetry may well wish a more exact description of what really takes place.

An American critic, after much searching in recent psychological explanations of artistic creation, attempts to describe the genesis of a poem in these words: [1]

"The poet concentrates his thought on some concrete piece of life, on some incident, character, or bit of personal experience; because of his emotional temperament, this concentration of interest stirs in him a quick play of feeling and prompts the swift concurrence of many images. Under the incitement of these feelings, and in accordance with laws of association that may at least in part be described, these images grow bright and clear,

[1] Lewis E. Gates, *Studies and Appreciations*, p. 215. Macmillan, 1900.

take definite shapes, fall into significant groupings, branch and ramify, and break into sparkling mimicry of the actual world of the senses — all the time delicately controlled by the poet's conscious purpose and so growing intellectually significant, but all the time, if the work of art is to be vital, impelled also in their alert weaving of patterns by the moods of the poet, by his fine instinctive sense of the emotional expressiveness of this or that image that lurks in the background of his consciousness. For this intricate web of images, tinged with his most intimate moods, the poet through his intuitive command of words finds an apt series of sound-symbols and records them with written characters. And so a poem arises through an exquisite distillation of personal moods into imagery and into language, and is ready to offer to all future generations its undiminishing store of spiritual joy and strength."

A better description than this we are not likely to find, although some critics would question the phrase, "all the time delicately controlled by the poet's conscious purpose." [1] For sometimes, assuredly, the synthesis of images seems to take place without the volition of the poet. The hypnotic trance, the

[1] "Poetry is not like reasoning, a power to be exerted according to the determination of the will. A man cannot say, 'I will compose poetry.' . . . It is not subject to the control of the active powers of the mind. . . . Its birth and recurrence have no necessary connection with the consciousness or will." Shelley, *A Defense of Poetry.*

narcotic dream or revery, and even our experience of ordinary dreams, provide abundant examples. One dreams, for instance, of a tidal river, flowing in with a gentle full current which bends in one direction all the water-weeds and the long grasses trailing from the banks; then somehow the tide seems to change, and all the water and the weeds and grasses, even the fishes in the stream, turn slowly and flow out to sea. The current synthesizes, harmonizes, moves onward like music, — and we are aware that it is all a dream. Coleridge's "Kubla Khan," composed in a deep opium slumber, moves like that, one train of images melting into another like the interwoven figures of a dance led by the "damsel with a dulcimer." There is no "conscious purpose" whatever, and no "meaning" in the ordinary interpretation of that word. Nevertheless it is perfect integration of imagery, pure beauty to the senses. Something of this rapture in the sheer release of control must have been in Charles Lamb's mind when he wrote to Coleridge about the "pure happiness" of being insane. "Dream not, Coleridge, of having tasted all the grandeur and wildness of fancy till you have gone mad! All

now seems to me vapid, comparatively so."
(June 10, 1796.)

If "Kubla Khan" represents one extreme,
Poe's account of how he wrote "The Raven"[1]
— incredible as the story appears to most of us
— may serve to illustrate the other, namely,
a cool, conscious, workmanlike control of
every element in the selection and combination of imagery. Wordsworth's naïve explanation of the task performed by the imagination
in his "Cuckoo" and "Leech-Gatherer"[2]
occupies a middle ground. We are at least
certain of his entire honesty — and incidentally of his total lack of humor!

> "'Shall I call thee Bird,
>   Or but a wandering Voice?'

"This concise interrogation characterizes the
seeming ubiquity of the voice of the cuckoo, and
dispossesses the creature almost of a corporeal
existence; the Imagination being tempted to this
exertion of her power by a consciousness in the
memory that the cuckoo is almost perpetually
heard throughout the season of spring, but seldom
becomes an object of sight. . . .

> "'As a huge stone is sometimes seen to lie
> Couched on the bald top of an eminence,
> Wonder to all who do the same espy

[1] *The Philosophy of Composition.*
[2] Preface to poems of 1815–1845.

By what means it could thither come, and whence,
So that it seems a thing endued with sense,
Like a sea-beast crawled forth, which on a shelf
Of rock or sand reposeth, there to sun himself.

Such seemed this Man; not all alive or dead
Nor all asleep, in his extreme old age.
.   .   .   .
Motionless as a cloud the old Man stood,
That heareth not the loud winds when they call,
And moveth altogether if it move at all.'

"In these images, the conferring, the abstracting, and the modifying powers of the Imagination,
immediately and mediately acting, are all brought
into conjunction. The stone is endowed with something of the power of life to approximate it to the
sea-beast; and the sea-beast stripped of some of
its vital qualities to assimilate it to the stone;
which intermediate image is thus treated for the
purpose of bringing the original image, that of the
stone, to a nearer resemblance to the figure and
condition of the aged man; who is divested of so
much of the indications of life and motion as to
bring him to the point where the two objects unite
and coalesce in just comparison."

Wordsworth's analysis of the processes of
his own imagination, like Poe's story of the
composition of "The Raven," is an analysis
made after the imagination had functioned.
There can be no absolute proof of its correctness in every detail. It is evident that we

have to deal with an infinite variety of normal
and abnormal minds. Some of these defy
classification; others fall into easily recognized types, such as "the lunatic, the lover and
the poet," as sketched by Theseus, Duke of
Athens. How modern, after all, is the Duke's
little lecture on the psychology of imagination!

"The lunatic, the lover and the poet
  Are of imagination all compact;
  One sees more devils than vast hell can hold,
  That is, the madman: the lover, all as frantic,
  Sees Helen's beauty in a brow of Egypt:
  The poet's eye, in a fine frenzy rolling,
  Doth glance from heaven to earth, from earth to
            heaven;
  And as imagination bodies forth
  The forms of things unknown, the poet's pen
  Turns them to shapes and gives to airy nothing
  A local habitation and a name.
  Such tricks hath strong imagination,
  That, if it would but apprehend some joy,
  It comprehends some bringer of that joy;
  Or in the night, imagining some fear,
  How easy is a bush supposed a bear!"[1]

Shakspere, it will be observed, does not
hesitate to use that dangerous term "the
poet!" Yet as students of poetry we must
constantly bring ourselves back to the recorded experience of individual men, and

[1] *Midsummer Night's Dream*, v, i, 7-22.

from these make our comparisons and generalizations. It may even happen that some readers will get a clearer conception of the selection and synthesis of images if they turn for the moment away from poetry and endeavor to realize something of the same processes as they take place in imaginative prose. In Hawthorne's *Scarlet Letter*, for example, the dominant image, which becomes the symbol of his entire theme, is the piece of scarlet cloth which originally caught his attention. This physical object becomes, after long brooding, subtly changed into a moral symbol of sin and its concealment. It permeates the book, it is borne openly upon the breast of one sufferer, it is written terribly in the flesh of another, it flames at last in the very sky. All the lesser images and symbols of the romance are mastered by it, subordinated to it; it becomes the dominant note in the composition. The romance of *The Scarlet Letter* is, as we say of any great poem or drama, an "ideal synthesis"; i.e. a putting together of images in accordance with some central idea. The more significant the idea or theme or master image, the richer and fuller are the possibilities of beauty in detail.

Apply this familiar law of complexity to a poet's conscious or unconscious choice of images. In the essay which we have already quoted [1] Lewis Gates remarks:

" In every artist there is a definite mental bias, a definite spiritual organization and play of instincts, which results in large measure from the common life of his day and generation, and which represents this life — makes it potent — within the individuality of the artist. This so-called 'acquired constitution of the life of the soul' — it has been described by Professor Dilthey with noteworthy acuteness and thoroughness — determines in some measure the contents of the artist's mind, for it determines his interests, and therefore the sensations and perceptions that he captures and automatically stores up. It guides him in his judgments of worth, in his instinctive likes and dislikes as regards conduct and character, and controls in large measure the play of his imagination as he shapes the action of his drama or epic and the destinies of his heroes. Its prejudices interfiltrate throughout the molecules of his entire moral and mental life, and give to each image and idea some slight shade of attractiveness or repulsiveness, so that when the artist's spirit is at work under the stress of feeling, weaving into the fabric of a poem the competing images and ideas in his consciousness, certain ideas and images come more readily and others lag behind, and the resulting work of art gets a colour and an emotional tone and suggestions of value that subtly reflect the genius of the age."

[1] *Studies and Appreciations,* p. 216.

6. "Imagist" Verse

Such a conception of the association of images as reflecting not only this "acquired constitution of the soul" of the poet but also the genius of the age is in marked contrast to some of the theories held by contemporary "imagists." As we have already noted, in Chapter II, they stress the individual reaction to phenomena, at some tense moment. They discard, as far as possible, the long "loop-line" of previous experience. As for diction, they have, like all true artists, a horror of the *cliché* — the rubber-stamp word, blurred by use. As for rhythm, they fear any conventionality of pattern. In subsequent chapters we must look more closely at these matters of diction and of rhythm, but they are both involved in any statement of the principles of Imagist verse. Richard Aldington sums up his article on "The Imagists" [1] in these words:

"Let me resume the cardinal points of the Imagist style: 1. Direct treatment of the subject. 2. A hardness and economy of speech. 3. Individuality of rhythm; vers libre. 4. The exact word. The Imagists would like to possess 'le mot

[1] "Greenwich Village," July 15, 1915.

qui fait image, l'adjectif inattendu et précis qui
dessine de pied en cap et donne la senteur de la
chose qu'il est chargé de rendre, la touche juste,
la couleur qui chatoie et vibre.'"

In the preface to *Imagist Poets* (1915), and
in Miss Amy Lowell's *Tendencies in Modern
American Poetry* (1917) the tenets of imagism
are stated briefly and clearly. Imagism, we
are told, aims to use always the language of
common speech, but to employ always the
exact word, not the nearly-exact nor the
merely decorative word; to create new
rhythms — as the expression of new moods —
and not to copy old rhythms, which merely
echo old moods; to allow absolute freedom in
the choice of a subject; to present an image,
rendering particulars exactly; to produce
poetry that is hard and clear, never blurred or
indefinite; to secure condensation.

It will be observed that in the special
sort of picture-making which Imagist poetry
achieves, the question of free verse is merely
incidental. "We fight for it as a principle
of liberty," says Miss Lowell, but she does
not insist upon it as the only method of
writing poetry. Mr. Aldington admits frankly
that about forty per cent of *vers libre* is prose.

Mr. Lowes, as we have already remarked, has printed dozens of passages from Meredith's novels in the typographical arrangement of free verse so as to emphasize their "imagist" character. One of the most effective is this:

> "He was like a Tartar
> Modelled by a Greek:
> Supple
> As the Scythian's bow,
> Braced
> As the string!"

Suppose, however, that we agree to defer for the moment the vexed question as to whether images of this kind are to be considered prose or verse. Examine simply for their vivid picture-making quality the collections entitled *Imagist Poets* (1915, 1916, 1917), or, in the *Anthology of Magazine Verse* for 1915, such poems as J. G. Fletcher's "Green Symphony" or "H. D.'s" "Sea-Iris" or Miss Lowell's "The Fruit Shop." Read Miss Lowell's extraordinarily brilliant volume *Men, Women and Ghosts* (1916), particularly the series of poems entitled "Towns in Colour." Then read the author's preface, in which her artistic purpose in writing "Towns in Col-

our " is set forth: "In these poems, I have en-
deavoured to give the colour, and light, and
shade, of certain places and hours, stressing
the purely pictorial effect, and with little or no
reference to any other aspect of the places described. It is an enchanting thing to wander
through a city looking for its *unrelated beauty*,
the beauty by which it captivates the sensuous sense of seeing." [1]

Nothing could be more gallantly frank than
the phrase "unrelated beauty." For it serves
as a touchstone to distinguish between those
imagist poems which leave us satisfied and
those which do not. Sometimes, assuredly,
the insulated, unrelated beauty is enough.
What delicate reticence there is in Richard
Aldington's "Summer":

> "A butterfly,
> Black and scarlet,
> Spotted with white,
> Fans its wings
> Over a privet flower.
>
> "A thousand crimson foxgloves,
> Tall bloody pikes,
> Stand motionless in the gravel quarry;
> The wind runs over them.

[1] Italics mine.

> "A rose film over a pale sky
> Fantastically cut by dark chimneys;
> Across an old city garden."

The imagination asks no more.

Now read my friend Baker Brownell's "Sunday Afternoon":

> "The wind pushes huge bundles
> Of itself in warm motion
> Through the barrack windows;
> It rattles a sheet of flypaper
> Tacked in a smear of sunshine on the sill.
> A voice and other voices squirt
> A slow path among the room's tumbled sounds.
> A ukelele somewhere clanks
> In accidental jets
> Up from the room's background."

Here the stark truthfulness of the images does not prevent an instinctive "Well, what of it?" "And afterward, what else?" Unless we adopt the Japanese theory of "stop poems," where the implied continuation of the mood, the suggested application of the symbol or allegory, is the sole justification of the actual words given, a great deal of imagist verse, in my opinion, serves merely to sharpen the senses without utilizing the full imaginative powers of the mind. The making of images is an essential portion of the poet's task, but in memorably great poetry it is only a detail in a larger whole. Miss Lowell's "Patterns" is one of the most effective of contemporary poems, but it is far more than a document of imagism. It is a triumph of structural imagination.

7. *Genius and Inspiration*

Whatever may be the value, for students, of trying to analyse the image-making and image-combining faculty, every one admits that it is a necessary element in the production of poetry. Let Coleridge have the final statement of this mystery of his art: "The power of reducing multitude into unity of effect, and modifying a series of thoughts by some one predominant thought or feeling, may be cultivated and improved, but can never be learnt. It is in this that *Poeta nascitur non fit*." We cannot avoid the difficulties of the question by attributing the poet's imagination to "genius." Whether genius is a neurosis, as some think, or whether it is sanity at perfection, makes little difference here. Both a Poe and a Sophocles are equally capable of producing ideal syntheses. Nor does the old word "inspiration" help much either. Whatever we mean by inspiration — a something not ourselves, supernatural or sub-liminal — a "vision" of Blake, the "voices" of Joan of Arc, the "god" that moved within the Corybantian revelers — it is an excitement of the image-making faculty, and not that faculty itself. Disordered "genius" and inspiration undisciplined by reason are alike powerless to produce images that permanently satisfy the sense of beauty. Tolstoy's common-sense remark is surely sound: "One's writing is good only where the intelligence and the imagination are in equilibrium. As soon as one of them over-balances the other, it's all up." [1]

8. A Summary

Let us now endeavor to summarize this testimony which we have taken from poets and critics. Though they do not agree in all details, and though they often use words that are either too vague or too highly specialized, the general drift of the testimony is fairly clear. Poets and critics agree that the imagination is something different from the mere memory-image; that by a process of selection and combination and re-presentation of

[1] Compare W. A. Neilson's chapter on "The Balance of Qualities" in *Essentials of Poetry*. Houghton Mifflin Company, 1912.

images something really new comes into being, and that we are therefore justified in using the term *constructive*, or *creative* imagination.   This imagination embodies, as we say,
or "bodies forth," as Duke Theseus said, "the
forms of things unknown."   It ultimately becomes the poet's task to "shape" these forms
with his "pen," that is to say, to suggest them
through word-symbols, arranged in a certain
fashion.   The selection of these word-symbols
will be discussed in Chapter IV, and their
rhythmical arrangement in Chapter V.   But
we have tried in the present chapter to trace
the functioning of the poetic imagination in
those stages of its activity which precede the
definite shaping of poems with the pen.   If we
say, with Professor Fairchild,[1] that "the central processes or kinds of activity involved in
the making of poetry are three: personalizing,
combining and versifying," it is obvious that
we have been dealing with the first two.   If we
prefer to use the famous terms employed by
Ruskin in *Modern Painters*, we have been
considering the penetrative, associative and
contemplative types of imagination.   But
these Ruskinian names, however brilliantly

Making of Poetry, p. 34.

and suggestively employed by the master, are dangerous tools for the beginner in the study of poetry.

If the beginner desires to review, at this point, the chief matters brought to his attention in the present chapter, he may make a real test of their validity by opening his senses to the imagery of a few lines of poetry. Remember that poets are endeavoring to convey the "sense" of things rather than the knowledge of things. Disregard for the moment the precise words employed in the following lines, and concentrate the attention upon the images, as if the image were not made of words at all, but were mere naked sense-stimulus.

In this line the poet is trying to make us *see* something ("visual" image):

> "The bride hath paced into the hall,
> *Red as a rose* is she."

Can you see her?

In these lines the poet is trying to make us *hear* something ("auditory" image):

> "A noise *like of a hidden brook*
> In the leafy month of June
> That to the *sleeping woods all night*
> *Singeth a quiet tune.*"

Do you hear the tune? Do you hear it as clearly as you can hear

> "*The tambourines*
> *Jing-jing-jingled in the hands of Queens*"?

In these lines the poet is trying to make us feel certain bodily sensations ("tactile" image):

"I closed my lids and kept them close,
  And the balls like pulses beat;
For the sky and the sea and the sea and the sky,
  Lay like a load on my weary eye,
And the dead were at my feet."

Do your eyes feel that pressure?

You are sitting quite motionless in your chair as you read these lines ("motor" image):

"I *sprang* to the stirrup, and Joris, and he;
  I *galloped*, Dirck *galloped*, we *galloped* all three!"

Are you instantly on horseback? If you are, the poet has put you there by conveying from his mind to yours, through the use of verbal imagery and rhythm, his "sense" of riding, which has now become *your* sense of riding.

If the reader can meet this test of realizing simple images through his own body-and-mind reaction to their stimulus, the door of poetry is open to him. He can enter into its limitless enjoyments. If he wishes to analyse more closely the nature of the pleasure which poetry affords, he may select any lines he happens to like, and ask himself how the various functions of the imagination are illustrated by them. Suppose the lines are Coleridge's description of the bridal procession, already quoted in part:

> "The bride hath paced into the hall,
>   Red as a rose is she;
>   Nodding their heads before her goes
>   The merry minstrelsy."

Here surely is imagination penetrative; the selection of some one characteristic trait of the object; that trait (the "redness" or the "nodding") re-presented to us, and emphasized by conferring, modifying or abstracting whatever elements the poet wishes to stress or to suppress. The result is a combination of imagery which forms an idealized picture, presenting the shows of things as the mind would like to see them and thus satisfying our sense of beauty. For there is no question that the mind takes a supreme satisfaction in such an idealization of reality as Coleridge's picture of the swift tropical sunset,

> "At one stride comes the dark,"

or Emerson's picture of the slow New England sunrise,

> "O tenderly the haughty day
> Fills his blue urn with fire."

Little has been said about beauty in this chapter, but no one doubts that a sense of beauty guides the "shaping spirit of imagination" in that dim region through which the poet feels his way before he comes to the conscious choice of expressive words and to the ordering of those words into beautiful rhythmical designs.

CHAPTER IV

THE POET'S WORDS

"Words are sensible signs necessary for communication."
JOHN LOCKE, *Human Understanding*, 3, 2, 1.

"As conceptions are the images of things to the mind within itself, so are words or names the marks of those conceptions to the minds of them we converse with." SOUTH, quoted in Johnson's *Dictionary*.

"Word: a sound, or combination of sounds, used in any language as the sign of a conception, or of a conception together with its grammatical relations. . . . A word is a spoken sign that has arrived at its value as used in any language by a series of historical changes, and that holds its value by virtue of usage, being exposed to such further changes, of form and of meaning, as usage may prescribe. . . . " *Century Dictionary*.

"A word is not a crystal — transparent and unchanged; it is the skin of a living thought, and may vary greatly in color and content according to the circumstances and the time in which it is used." Justice OLIVER WENDELL HOLMES, *Towne vs. Eisner*.

"I wish our clever young poets would remember my homely definitions of prose and poetry; that is, prose = words in their best order; — poetry = the *best* words in the best order." COLERIDGE, *Table Talk*.

1. The Eye and the Ear

"LITERARY" language is commonly distinguished from the language of ordinary life by certain heightenings or suppressions. The novelist or essayist, let us say, fashions his language more or less in accordance with his own mood, with his immediate aim in writing, with the capacity of his expected readers. He is discoursing with a certain real or imaginary audience. He may put himself on paper, as Montaigne said, as if he were talking to the first man he happens to meet; or he may choose to address himself to the few chosen spirits of his generation and of succeeding generations. He trusts the arbitrary written or printed symbols of word-sounds to carry his thoughts safely into the minds of other men. The "literary" user of language in modern times comes to depend upon the written or printed page; he tends to become more or less "eye-minded"; whereas the typical orator remains "ear-minded" — i.e. peculiarly sensitive to a series of sounds, and composing for the ear of listeners rather than for the eye of readers.

Now as compared with the typical novelist, the poet is surely, like the orator, "ear-minded." Tonal symbols of ideas and emotions, rather than visual symbols of ideas and emotions, are the primary stuff with which he is working, although as soon as the advancing civilization of his race brings an end to the primitive reciting of poetry and its transmission through oral repetition alone, it is obvious that he must depend, like other literary artists, or like the modern musicians, upon the written or printed signs for the sounds which he has composed.   But so stubborn are the habits of our eyes that we tend always to confuse the look of the poet's words upon the printed page with the sound of those words as they are perceived by the ear.   We are seldom guilty of this confusion in the case of the musician.   His "music" is not identified with the arbitrary black marks which make up his printed score.   For most of us there is no music until those marks are actually translated into terms of tone — although it is true that the trained reader of music can easily translate to his inner ear without any audible rendering of the indicated sounds.

This distinction is essential to the understanding of poetry. A poem is not primarily a series of printed word-signs addressed to the eye; it is a series of sounds addressed to the ear, and the arbitrary symbols for these sounds do not convey the poem unless they are audibly rendered — except to those readers who, like the skilled readers of printed music, can instantly hear the indicated sounds without any actual rendition of them into physical tone. Many professed lovers of poetry have no real ear for it. They are hopelessly "eye-minded." They try to decide questions of metre and stanza, of free verse and of emotionally patterned prose by the appearance of the printed page instead of by the nerves of hearing. Poets like Mr. Vachel Lindsay — who recites or chants his own verses after the manner of the primitive bard — have rendered a true service by leading us away from the confusions wrought by typography, and back to that sheer delight in rhythmic oral utterance in which poetry originates.

2. How Words convey Feeling

For it must never be forgotten that poetry begins in excitement, in some body-and-mind experience; that it is capable, through its rhythmic utterance of words which suggest this experience, of transmitting emotion to the hearer; and that the nature of language allows the emotion to be embodied in more or less permanent form. Let us look more closely at some of the questions involved in the origin, the transmission and embodiment of poetic feeling, remembering that we are now trying to trace these processes in so far as they are revealed by the poet's use of words. Rhythm will be discussed in the next chapter.

We have already noted that there are no mental images of feeling itself. The images recognized by the consciousness of poets are those of experiences and objects associated with feeling. The words employed to revive and transmit these images are usually described as "concrete" or "sensuous" in distinction from abstract or purely conceptual. They are "experiential" words, arising out of bodily or spiritual contact with objects or ideas that have been personalized, colored with individual feeling. Such words have a "fringe," as psychologists say. They are rich in overtones of meaning; not bare, like words addressed to the sheer intelligence, but covered with veils of association, with tokens of past experience. They are like ships laden with cargoes, although the cargo varies with the texture and the history of each mind. It is probable that this very word "ship," just now employed, calls up as many different mental images as there are readers of this page. Brander Matthews has recorded a curious divergence of imagery aroused by the familiar word "forest." Half a dozen well-known men of letters, chatting together in a London club, tried to tell one another what "forest" suggested to each:

"Until that evening I had never thought of forest as clothing itself in different colors and taking on different forms in the eyes of different men; but I then discovered that even the most innocent word may don strange disguises. To Hardy forest suggested the sturdy oaks to be assaulted by the woodlanders of Wessex; and to Du Maurier it evoked the trim and tidy avenues of the national domain of France. To Black the word naturally brought to mind the low scrub of the so-called deer-forests of Scotland; and to Gosse it summoned up a view of the green-clad mountains that towered up from the Scandinavian fiords. To Howells forest recalled the thick woods that in his youth fringed the rivers of Ohio; and to me there came back swiftly the memory of the wild growths, bristling unrestrained by man, in the Chippewa Reservation which I had crossed fourteen years before in my canoe trip from Lake Superior to the Mississippi. Simple as the word seemed, it was interpreted by each of us in accord with his previous personal experience. And these divergent experiences exchanged that evening brought home to me as never before the inherent and inevitable inadequacy of the vocabulary of every language, since there must always be two partners in any communication by means of words, and the verbal currency passing from one to the other has no fixed value necessarily the same to both of them."[1]

But one need not journey to London town in order to test this matter. Let half a dozen healthy young Americans stop before the window of a shop where sporting goods are exhibited. Here are fishing-rods, tennis racquets, riding-whips, golf-balls, running-shoes, baseball bats, footballs, oars, paddles, snow-shoes, goggles for motorists, Indian clubs and rifles. Each of these physical objects focuses the attention of the observer in more or less exact proportion to his interest in the particular sport suggested by the implement. If he is a passionate tennis-player, a thousand motor-tactile memories are stirred by the sight of the racquet. He is already balancing it in his fingers, playing his favorite strokes with it, winning tournaments with it — though he seems to be standing quietly in front of the window. The man next him is already snowshoeing over the frozen hills. But if a man has never played lacrosse, or been on horseback, or mastered a canoe, the lacrosse racquet or rid-

[1] Brander Matthews, *These Many Years*. Scribner's, New York, 1917.

ing-whip or paddle mean little to him emotionally, except that they may stir his imaginative curiosity about a sport whose pleasures he has never experienced. His eye is likely to pass them over as indifferently as if he were glancing at the window of a druggist or a grocer. These varying responses of the individual to the visual stimulus of this or that physical object in a heterogeneous collection may serve to illustrate his capacity for feeling. Our chance group before the shop window thus becomes a symbol of all human minds as they confront the actual visible universe. They hunger and thirst for this or that particular thing, while another object leaves them cold.

Now suppose that our half-dozen young men are sitting in the dark, talking — evoking body-and-mind memories by means of words alone. No two can possibly have the same memories, the same series of mental pictures. Not even the most vivid and picturesque word chosen by the best talker of the company has the same meaning for them all. They all understand the word, approximately, but each *feels* it in a way unexperienced by his friend. The freightage of significance carried by each concrete, sensuous, picture-making word is bound to vary according to the entire physical and mental history of the man who hears it. Even the commonest and most universal words for things and sensations — such as "hand," "foot," "dark," "fear," "fire," "warm," "home" — are suffused with personal emotions, faintly or clearly felt; they have been or are *my* hand, foot, fear, darkness, warmth, happiness. Now the poet is like a man talking or singing in the dark to a circle of friends. He cannot say to them "See this" or "Feel that" in the literal sense of "see" and "feel"; he can only call up by means of words and tunes what his friends have seen and felt already, and then under the excitement of such memories suggest new combinations, new weavings of the infinitely varied web of human experience, new voyages with fresh sails upon seas untried.

It is true that we may picture the poet as singing or talking to himself in solitude and darkness, obeying primarily the impulse of expression rather than of communication. Hence John Stuart Mill's distinction between the orator and the poet: "Eloquence is *heard;* poetry is *over*heard. Eloquence supposes an audience. The peculiarity of poetry appears to us to lie in the poet's utter unconsciousness of a listener. Poetry is feeling confessing itself to itself in moments of solitude, and embodying itself in symbols which are the nearest possible representations of the feeling in the exact shape in which it exists in the poet's mind."[1] But whether his primary aim be the relief of his own feelings (for a man swears even when he is alone!) or the communication of his feelings to other persons, it remains true that a poet's language betrays his bodily and mental history. "The poet," said Thoreau, "writes the history of his own body."

For example, a study of Browning's vocabulary made by Professor C. H. Herford [2] emphasizes that poet's acute tactual and muscular sensibilities, his quick and eager apprehension of space-relations:

"He gloried in the strong sensory-stimulus of glowing color, of dazzling light; in the more complex *motory*-stimulus of intricate, abrupt and plastic form. . . . He delighted in the angular,

[1] J. S. Mill, "Thoughts on Poetry," in *Dissertations*, vol. 1. See also F. N. Scott, "The Most Fundamental Differentia of Poetry and Prose." Published by Modern Language Association, 19, 2.

[2] *Robert Browning*, Modern English Writers, pp. 244–66. Blackwood & Sons, 1905.

indented, intertwining, labyrinthine varieties of
line and surface which call for the most delicate,
and at the same time most agile, adjustments of
the eye.   He caught at the edges of things. . . .
Spikes and *wedges* and *swords* run riot in his work.
. . . He loved the grinding, clashing and rending
sibilants and explosives as Tennyson the tender-
hefted liquids. . . . He is the poet of sudden surprises, unforseen transformations. . . . The simple
joy in abrupt changes of sensation which belonged
to his riotous energy of nerve lent support to
his peremptory way of imagining all change and
especially all vital and significant becoming."

The same truth is apparent as we pass from
the individual poet to the poetic literature of
his race.   Here too is the stamp of bodily history.   Hebrew poetry, as is well known, is
always expressing emotion in terms of bodily
sensation.

"*Anger*," says Renan,[1] "is expressed in Hebrew
in a throng of ways, each picturesque, and each
borrowed from physiological facts.   Now the metaphor is taken from the rapid and animated breathing which accompanies the passion, now from
heat or from boiling, now from the act of a noisy
breaking, now from shivering. *Discouragement* and
despair are expressed by the melting of the heart,
fear by the loosening of the reins. *Pride* is portrayed
by the holding high of the head, with the figure
straight and stiff. *Patience* is a long breathing,

[1] Quoted by J. H. Gardiner, *The Bible as Literature*, p. 114.

impatience short breathing, *desire* is thirst or pale-
ness. Pardon is expressed by a throng of metaphors borrowed from the idea of covering, of
hiding, of coating over the fault. In *Job* God sews
up sins in a sack, seals it, then throws it behind
him: all to signify that he forgets them. . . .

"My soul longeth, yea, even fainteth for the
courts of the Lord; my heart and my flesh crieth
out for the living God.

"Save me, O God; for the waters are come in
unto my soul.

"I sink in deep mire, where there is no standing: I am come into deep waters, where the floods
overflow me.

"I am weary of my crying: my throat is dried:
mine eyes fail while I wait for my God."

Greek poetry, likewise, is made out of
"warm, swift, vibrating" words, thrilling
with bodily sensation. Gilbert Murray [1] has
described the weaving of these beautiful single
words into patterns:

"The whole essence of lyric is rhythm. It is the
weaving of words into a song-pattern, so that the
mere arrangement of the syllables produces a kind
of dancing joy. . . . Greek lyric is derived directly
from the religious dance; that is, not merely the
pattering of the feet, *but the yearning movement of
the whole body*, the ultimate expression of emotion
that cannot be pressed into articulate speech,
compact of intense rhythm and intense feeling."

[1] "What English Poetry may Learn from Greek," *Atlantic
Monthly*, November, 1912.

Nor should it be forgotten that Milton, while praising "a graceful and ornate rhetoric," declares that poetry, compared with this, is "more simple, sensuous and passionate." [1] These words "sensuous" and "passionate," dulled as they have become by repetition, should be interpreted in their full literal sense. While language is unquestionably a social device for the exchange of ideas and feelings, it is also true that poetic diction is a revelation of individual experience, of body-and-mind contacts with reality. Every poet is still an Adam in the Garden, inventing new names as fast as the new wonderful Beasts — so terrible, so delightful!—come marching by.

3. Words as Current Coin

But the poet's words, stamped and colored as they are by unique individual experience, must also have a general *transmission value* which renders them current coin. If words were merely representations of private experience, merely our own nicknames for things, they would not pass the walls of the Garden inhabited by each man's imagination. "Expression" would be possible, but "communi-

[1] *Tract on Education.*

cation" would be impossible, and indeed there would be no recognizable terms of expression except the "bow-wow" or "pooh-pooh" or "ding-dong" of the individual Adam — and even these expressive syllables might not be the ones acceptable to Eve!

The truth is that though the impulse to expression is individual, and that in highly developed languages a single man can give his personal stamp to words, making them say what he wishes them to say, as Dante puts it, speech is nevertheless primarily a social function. A word is a social instrument. "It belongs," says Professor Whitney,[1] "not to the individual, but to the member of society. . . . What we may severally choose to say is not language until it be accepted and employed by our fellows. The whole development of speech, though initiated by the acts of individuals, is wrought out by the community. . . . A solitary man would never frame a language. Let a child grow up in utter seclusion, and, however rich and suggestive might be the nature around him, however full and appreciative his sense of that which lay without, and his consciousness of that which went on

[1] W. D. Whitney, *Language and the Study of Language*, p. 404.

within him, he would all his life remain a mute."

What is more, the individual's mastery of language is due solely to his social effort in employing it. Speech materials are not inherited; they are painfully acquired. It is well known that an English child brought up in China and hearing no word of English will speak Chinese without a trace of his English parentage in form or idiom.[1] His own body-and-mind experiences will be communicated in the medium already established by the body-and-mind experiences of the Chinese race. In that medium only can the thoughts of this English-born child have any transmission value. His father and mother spoke a tongue moulded by Chaucer and Shakspere, but to the boy whom we have imagined all that age-long labor of perfecting a social instrument of speech is lost without a trace. As far as language is concerned, he is a Chinaman and nothing else.

Now take the case of a Chinese boy who has come to an American school and college. Just before writing this paragraph I have

[1] See Baldwin's *Dictionary of Philosophy and Psychology,* article "Language."

read the blue-book of such a boy, written in a Harvard examination on Tennyson. It was an exceptionally well-expressed blue-book, in idiomatic English, and it revealed an unusual appreciation of Tennyson's delicate and sure felicities of speech. The Chinese boy, by dint of an intellectual effort of which most of his American classmates were incapable, had mastered many of the secrets of an alien tongue, and had taken possession of the rich treasures of English poetry. If he had been composing verse himself, instead of writing a college blue-book, it is likely that he would have preferred to use his own mother-tongue, as the more natural medium for the expression of his intimate thoughts and feelings. But that expression, no matter how artistic, would have "communicated" nothing whatever to an American professor ignorant of the Chinese language. It is clear that the power of any person to convey his ideas and emotions to others is conditioned upon the common possession of some medium of exchange.

4. Words an Imperfect Medium

And it is precisely here that we face one of the fundamental difficulties of the poet's task;

a difficulty that affects, indeed, all human intercourse. For words are notoriously an imperfect medium of communication. They "were not invented at first," says Professor Walter Raleigh in his book on Wordsworth, "and are very imperfectly adapted at best, for the severer purposes of truth. They bear upon them all the weaknesses of their origin, and all the maims inflicted by the prejudices and fanaticisms of generations of their employers. They perpetuate the memory or prolong the life of many noble forms of human extravagance, and they are the monuments of many splendid virtues. But with all their abilities and dignities they are seldom well fitted for the quiet and accurate statement of the thing that is. . . . Beasts fight with horns, and men, when the guns are silent, with words. The changes of meaning in words from good to bad and from bad to good senses, which are quite independent of their root meaning, is proof enough, without detailed illustration, of the incessant nature of the strife. The question is not what a word means, but what it imputes." [1]

Now if the quiet and accurate statement of

[1] Raleigh's *Wordsworth*. London, 1903.

things as they are is the ideal language of
prose, it is obvious that the characteristic diction of poetry is unquiet, inaccurate, incur-
ably emotional.   Herein lie its dangers and its
glories.   No poet can keep for very long to
the "neutral style," to the cool gray wall-
paper words, so to speak; he wants more color
— passionate words that will "stick fiery off"
against the neutral background of conventional diction.   In vain does Horace warn
him against "purple patches"; for he knows
that the tolerant Horace allowed himself to
use purple patches whenever he wished.   All
employers of language for emotional effect
— orators, novelists, essayists, writers of edi-
torials — utilize in certain passages these colored, heightened, figured words.   It is as if
they ordered their printers to set individual
words or whole groups of words in upper-case
type.

And yet these "upper-case words" of
heightened emotional value are not really
isolated from their context.   Their values
are relative and not absolute.   Like the high
lights of a picture, their effectiveness depends
upon the tone of the composition as a whole.
To insert a big or violent word for its own

potency is like sewing the purple patch upon a faded garment. The predominant thought and feeling of a passage give the richest individual words their penetrating power, just as the weight of the axe-head sinks the blade into the wood. "Futurist" poets like Marinetti have protested against the bonds of syntax, the necessity of logical subject and predicate, and have experimented with nouns alone. "Words delivered from the fetters of punctuation," says Marinetti, "will flash against one another, will interlace their various forms of magnetism, and follow the uninterrupted dynamics of force." [1] But do they? The reader may judge for himself in reading Marinetti's poem on the siege of a Turkish fort:

"Towers guns virility flights erection telemetre exstacy toumbtoumb 3 seconds toumbtoumb waves smiles laughs plaff poaff glouglouglouglou hide-and-seek crystals virgins flesh jewels pearls iodine salts bromide skirts gas liqueurs bubbles 3 seconds toumbtoumb officer whiteness telemetre cross fire megaphone sight-at-thousand-metres all-men-to-left enough every-man-to-his post incline-7-degrees splendour jet pierce immensity azure deflowering onslaught alleys cries

[1] There is an interesting discussion of Futurism in Sir Henry Newbolt's *New Study of English Poetry*. Dutton, 1919.

labyrinth mattress sobs ploughing desert bed precision telemetre monoplane cackling theatre applause monoplane equals balcony rose wheel drum trepan gad-fly rout arabs oxen blood-colour shambles wounds refuge oasis."

In these vivid nouns there is certainly some raw material for a poem, just as a heap of bits of colored glass might make material for a rose-window. But both poem and window must be built by somebody: the shining fragments will never fashion themselves into a whole.

5. Predominant Tone-Feeling

If each poem is composed in its own "key," as we say of music, with its own scale of "values," as we say of pictures, it is obvious that the separate words tend to take on tones and hues from the predominant tone-feeling of the poem. It is a sort of protective coloration, like Nature's devices for blending birds and insects into their background; or, to choose a more prosaic illustration, like dipping a lump of sugar into a cup of coffee. The white sugar and the yellowish cream and the black coffee blend into something unlike any of the separate ingredients, yet the presence of each is felt. It is true that some words refuse to be absorbed into the texture of the poem: they remain as it were foreign substances in the stream of imagery, something alien, stubborn, jarring, although expressive enough in themselves. All the pioneers in poetic diction assume this risk of using "unpoetic" words in their desire to employ expressive words. Classic examples are Wordsworth's homely "tubs" and "porringers," and Walt Whitman's catalogues of everyday implements used in various trades. *Othello* was hissed upon its first appearance on the Paris stage because of that "vulgar" word handkerchief. Thus "fork" and "spoon" have almost purely utilitarian associations and are consequently difficult terms for the service of poetry, but "knife" has a wider range of suggestion. Did not the peaceful Robert Louis Stevenson confess his romantic longing to "knife a man"?

But it is not necessary to multiply illustrations of this law of connotation. The true poetic value of a word lies partly in its history, in its past employments, and partly also in the new vitality which it receives from each brain which fills the word with its own life. It is like an old violin, with its subtle overtones, the

result of many vibrations of the past, but yet
each new player may coax a new tune from it.
When Wordsworth writes of

"The silence that is in the starry sky,
The sleep that is among the lonely hills,"

he is combining words that are immemorially
familiar into a total effect that is peculiarly
"Wordsworthian." Diction is obviously only
a part of a greater whole in which ideas and
emotions are also merged. A concordance of
all the words employed by a poet teaches us
much about him, and conversely a knowledge
of the poet's personality and of his governing
ideas helps us in the study of his diction.
Poets often have favorite words — like Marlowe's "black," Shelley's "light," Tennyson's
"wind," Swinburne's "fire." Each of these
words becomes suffused with the whole personality of the poet who employs it. It not
only cannot be taken out of its context in the
particular poem in which it appears, but it
cannot be adequately *felt* without some recognition of the particular sensational and emotional experience which prompted its use.
Many concordance-hunters thus miss the real
game, and fall into the Renaissance error of
word-grubbing for its own sake, as if mere

words had a value of their own independently
of the life breathed into them by living men.
I recall a conversation at Bormes with the
French poet Angellier. He was complaining
humorously of his friend L., a famous scholar
whose big book was "carrying all the treasures of French literature down to posterity
like a cold-storage transport ship." "But
he published a criticism of one of my poems,"
Angellier went on, "which proved that he did
not understand the poem at all. He had studied it too hard! The words of a poem are
stepping-stones across a brook. If you linger
on one of them too long, you will get your
feet wet! You must cross, *vite!*" If the poets
lead us from one mood to another over a
bridge of words, the words themselves are not
the goal of the journey. They are instruments used in the transmission of emotion.

6. Specific Tone-Color

It is obvious, then, that the full poetic
value of a word cannot be ascertained apart
from its context. The value is relative and
not absolute. And nevertheless, just as the bit
of colored glass may have a certain interest
and beauty of its own, independently of its

possible place in the rose-window, it is true
that separate words possess special qualities of
physical and emotional suggestiveness.   Dangerous as it is to characterize the qualities of
the sound of a word apart from the sense of
that word, there is undeniably such a thing
as "tone-color." A piano and a violin, striking
the same note, are easily differentiated by the
quality of the sound, and of two violins, playing the same series of notes, it is usually possible to declare which instrument has the
richer tone or timbre.   Words, likewise, differ
greatly in tone-quality.   A great deal of ingenuity has been devoted to the analysis of
"bright" and "dark" vowels, smooth and
harsh consonants, with the aim of showing that
each sound has its special expressive force, its
peculiar adaptability to transmit a certain kind
of feeling.   Says Professor A. H. Tolman: [1]

"Let us arrange the English vowel sounds in the
following scale:

ĭ (little)	ī (I)	ŏŏ (wood)
ĕ (met)	ū (due)	ow (cow)
ă (mat)	ăh (what)	ō (gold)
ē (mete)	āh (father)	ōō (gloom)
ai (fair)	oi (boil)	aw (awe)
ā (mate)	ŭ (but)	

[1] "The Symbolic Value of Sounds," in *Hamlet and Other
Essays*, by A. H. Tolman. Boston, 1904.

"The sounds at the beginning of this scale are especially fitted to express uncontrollable joy and delight, gayety, triviality, rapid movement, brightness, delicacy, and physical littleness; the sounds at the end are peculiarly adapted to express horror, solemnity, awe, deep grief, slowness of motion, darkness, and extreme or oppressive greatness of size. The scale runs, then, from the little to the large, from the bright to the dark, from ecstatic delight to horror, and from the trivial to the solemn and awful."

Robert Louis Stevenson in his *Some Technical Elements of Style in Literature*, and many other curious searchers into the secrets of words, have attempted to explain the physiological basis of these varying "tone-qualities." Some of them are obviously imitative of sounds in nature; some are merely suggestive of these sounds through more or less remote analogies; some are frankly imitative of muscular effort or of muscular relaxation. High-pitched vowels and low-pitched vowels, liquid consonants and harsh consonants, are unquestionably associated with muscular memories, that is to say, with individual body-and-mind experiences. Lines like Tennyson's famous

"The moan of doves in immemorial elms
And murmuring of innumerable bees"

thus represent, in their vowel and consonantal
expressiveness, the past history of countless
physical sensations, widely shared by innumerable individuals, and it is to this fact that
the "transmission value" of the lines is due.

Imitative effects are easily recognized, and
need no comment:

> "Brushed with the hiss of rustling wings"

> "The mellow ouzel fluting in the elm"

> "The wind that'll wail like a child
> and the sea that'll moan like a man."

Suggestive effects are more subtle. Sometimes they are due primarily to those rhythmical arrangements of words which we shall
discuss in the next chapter, but poetry often
employs the sound of single words to awaken
dim or bright associations. Robert Bridges's
catalogue of the Greek nymphs in "Eros and
Psyche" is an extreme example of risking the
total effect of a stanza upon the mere beautiful sounds of proper names.

"Swift to her wish came swimming on the waves
His lovely ocean nymphs, her guides to be,
The Nereids all, who live among the caves
And valleys of the deep, Cymodocè,
Agavè, blue-eyed Hallia and Nesæa,
Speio, and Thoë, Glaucè and Actæa,
Iaira, Melitè and Amphinomè,

"Apseudès and Nemertès, Callianassa,
  Cymothoë, Thaleia, Limnorrhea,
  Clymenè, Ianeira and Ianassa,
  Doris and Panopè and Galatea,
  Dynamenè, Dexamenè and Maira,
  Ferusa, Doto, Proto, Callianeira,
  Amphithoë, Oreithuia and Amathea."

Names of objects like "bobolink" and
"raven" may affect us emotionally by the
quality of their tone.   Through association
with the sounds of the human voice, heard
under stress of various emotions, we attribute joyous or foreboding qualities to the
bird's tone, and then transfer these associations to the bare name of the bird.

Names of places are notoriously rich in
their evocation of emotion.

"He caught a chill in the lagoons of Venice,
  And died in Padua."

Here the fact of illness and death may be
prosaic enough, but the very names of
"Venice" and "Padua" are poetry — like
"Rome," "Ireland," "Arabia," "California."

"Where the great Vision of the guarded mount
  Looks toward Namancos and Bayona's hold."

Who knows precisely where that "guarded
mount" is upon the map?   And who cares?

"The sailor's heart," confesses Lincoln Colcord,[1] "refutes the prose of knowledge, and still believes in delectable and sounding names. He dreams of capes and islands whose appellations are music and a song. . . . The first big land sighted on the outward passage is Java Head; beside it stands Cape Sangian Sira, with its name like a battle-cry. We are in the Straits of Sunda: name charged with the heady languor of the Orient, bringing to mind pictures of palm-fringed shores and native villages, of the dark-skinned men of Java clad in bright sarongs, clamoring from their black-painted dugouts, selling fruit and brilliant birds. These waters are rich in names that stir the blood, like Krakatoa, Gunong Delam, or Lambuan; or finer, more sounding than all the rest, Telok Betong and Rajah Bassa, a town and a mountain — Telok Betong at the head of Lampong Bay and Rajah Bassa, grand old bulwark on the Sumatra shore, the cradle of fierce and sudden squalls."

It may be urged, of course, that in lines of true poetry the sense carries the sound with it, and that nothing is gained by trying to

[1] *The New Republic*, September 16, 1916.

analyse the sounds apart from the sense. Professor C. M. Lewis [1] asserts bluntly: "When you say Titan you mean something big, and when you say tittle you mean something small; but it is not the sound of either word that means either bigness or littleness, it is the sense. If you put together a great many similar consonants in one sentence, they will attract special attention to the words in which they occur, and the significance of those words, whatever it may be, is thereby intensified; but whether the words are 'a team of little atomies' or 'a triumphant terrible Titan,' it is not the sound of the consonants that makes the significance. When Tennyson speaks of the shrill-edged shriek of a mother, his words suggest with peculiar vividness the idea of a shriek; but when you speak of stars that shyly shimmer, the same sounds only intensify the idea of shy shimmering." This is refreshing, and yet it is to be noted that "Titan" and "tittle" and "shrill-edged shriek" and "shyly shimmer" are by no means identical in sound: they have merely certain consonants in common. A fairer test of tone-color may be found if we

[1] *Principles of English Verse.* New York, 1906.

turn to frank nonsense-verse, where the
formal elements of poetry surely exist without any control of meaning or "sense":

> "The Jabberwock, with eyes of flame,
>   Came whiffling through the tulgey wood,
>   And burbled as it came!
>
> "'T was brillig, and the slithy toves
>   Did gyre and gimble in the wabe;
> All mimsy were the borogoves,
>   And the mome raths outgrabe."

"It seems rather pretty," commented the wise
Alice, "but it's rather hard to understand! Somehow it seems to fill my head with ideas — only I
don't exactly know what they are!"

This is precisely what one feels when one
listens to a poem recited in a language of
which one happens to be ignorant. The wonderful colored words are there, and they seem
somehow to fill our heads with ideas, only we
do not know what they are. Many readers
who know a little Italian or German will
confess that their enjoyment of a lyric in
those languages suffers only a slight, if any,
impairment through their ignorance of the
precise meaning of all the words in the poem:
if they know enough to feel the predominant
mood — as when we listen to a song sung in

a language of which we are wholly ignorant —
we can sacrifice the succession of exact ideas.
For words bare of meaning to the intellect
may be covered with veils of emotional association due to the sound alone.   Garrick
ridiculed — and doubtless at the same time
envied — George Whitefield's power to make
women weep by the rich overtones with
which he pronounced "that blessed word
Mesopotamia."

The capacities and the limitations of tone-
quality in itself may be seen no less clearly in
parodies.   Swinburne, a master technician
in words and rhythm, occasionally delighted,
as in "Nephelidia," [1] to make fun of himself
as well as of his poetic contemporaries:

"Surely no spirit or sense of a soul that was soft
    to the spirit and soul of our senses
Sweetens the stress of surprising suspicion that
    sobs in the semblance and sound of a sigh;
Only this oracle opens Olympian, in mystical
    moods and triangular tenses, —
'Life is the lust of a lamp for the light that is
    dark till the dawn of the day when we die.'"

Or, take Calverley's parody of Robert
Browning:

[1] Quoted in Carolyn Wells, *A Parody Anthology*.   New York,
1904.

"You see this pebble-stone? It's a thing I bought
Of a bit of a chit of a boy i' the mid o' the day.
I like to dock the smaller parts o' speech,
As we curtail the already cur-tail'd cur — "

The characteristic tone-quality of the vocabulary of each of these poets—whether it be

"A soul that was soft to the spirit and soul of our
        senses"

or

"A bit of a chit of a boy i' the mid o' the day" —

is as perfectly conveyed by the parodist as if
the lines had been written in dead earnest.
Poe's "Ulalume" is a masterly display of tone-
color technique, but exactly what it means,
or whether it means anything at all, is a
matter upon which critics have never been
able to agree.   It is certain, however, that a
poet's words possess a kind of physical suggestiveness, more or less closely related to
their mental significance.   In nonsense-verse
and parodies we have a glimpse, as it were, at
the *body* of poetry stripped of its soul.

7. "*Figures of Speech*"

To understand why poets habitually use
figurative language, we must recall what has
been said in Chapter III about verbal images.

Under the heat and pressure of emotion, things alter their shape and size and quality, ideas are transformed into concrete images, diction becomes impassioned, plain speech tends to become metaphorical. The language of any excited person, whether he is uttering himself in prose or verse, is marked by "tropes"; i.e. "turnings" — images which express one thing in the terms of another thing. The language of feeling is characteristically "tropical," and indeed every man who uses metaphors is for the moment talking like a poet — unless, as too often happens both in prose and verse, the metaphor has become conventionalized and therefore lifeless. The born poet thinks in "figures," in "pictured" language, or, as it has been called, in "re-presentative" language,[1] since he represents, both to his own mind and to those with whom he is communicating, the objects of poetic emotion under new forms. If he wishes to describe an eagle, he need not say: "A rapacious bird of the falcon family, remarkable for its strength, size, graceful figure, and extraordinary flight." He represents these facts by making a picture:

[1] G. L. Raymond, *Poetry as a Representative Art*, chap. 19.

"He clasps the crag with crooked hands;
  Close to the sun in lonely lands,
  Ring'd with the azure world, he stands.

"The wrinkled sea beneath him crawls;
  He watches from his mountain walls,
  And like a thunderbolt he falls." [1]

Or suppose the poet is a woman, meditating upon the coming of old age, and reflecting that age brings riches of its own. Observe how this thought is "troped"; i.e. turned into figures which re-present the fundamental idea:

"Come, Captain Age,
  With your great sea-chest full of treasure!
  Under the yellow and wrinkled tarpaulin
  Disclose the carved ivory
  And the sandalwood inlaid with pearl,
  Riches of wisdom and years.
  Unfold the India shawl,
  With the border of emerald and orange and
        crimson and blue,
  Weave of a lifetime.
  I shall be warm and splendid
  With the spoils of the Indies of age." [2]

It is true, of course, that a poet may sometimes prefer to use unornamented language, "not elevated," as Wordsworth said, "above

---

[1] Tennyson, "The Eagle."
[2] Sarah N. Cleghorn, "Come, Captain Age."

the level of prose." Such passages may nevertheless be marked by poetic beauty, due to the circumstances or atmosphere in which the plain words are spoken. The drama is full of such instances. "I loved you not," says Hamlet; to which Ophelia replies only: "I was the more deceived." No figure of speech could be more moving than that.

I once found in an old graveyard on Cape Cod, among the sunny, desolate sandhills, these lines graven on a headstone:

> "She died, and left to me
> This heath, this calm and quiet scene;
> This memory of what hath been,
> And nevermore will be."

I had read the lines often enough in books, but here I realized for the first time the perfection of their beauty.

But though a poet, for special reasons, may now and then renounce the use of figurative language, it remains true that this is the characteristic and habitual mode of utterance, not only of poetry but of all emotional prose. Here are a few sentences from an English sailor's account of the fight off Heligoland on August 28, 1915. He was on a destroyer:

"Scarcely had we started when from out the mist and across our front, in furious pursuit, came the first cruiser squadron — the town class, Birmingham, etc. — each unit a match for three Mainzes; and as we looked and reduced speed they opened fire, *and the clear ' bang-bang !' of their guns was just a cooling drink.* . . .

"The Mainz was immensely gallant. The last I saw of her, absolutely wrecked alow and aloft, her whole midships a fuming inferno, she had one gun forward and one aft still spitting forth fury and defiance *like a wildcat mad with wounds.*

"Our own four-funnel friend recommenced at this juncture with a couple of salvos, but rather half-heartedly, and we really did not care a d——, for there, straight ahead of us, in lordly procession, *like elephants walking through a pack of dogs,* came the Lion, Queen Mary, Invincible, and New Zealand, our battle cruisers, great and grim and *uncouth as some antediluvian monsters.* How solid they looked! How utterly *earthquaking!*"

The use and the effectiveness of figures depend primarily, then, upon the mood and intentions of the writer. Figures are figures, whether employed in prose or verse. Mr. Kipling does not lose his capacity for employing metaphors as he turns from writing verse to writing stories, and the rhetorician's analysis of similes, personifications, allegories, and all the other devices of "tropical" language is precisely the same, whether he is studying poetry or prose. Any good text-book in rhetoric gives adequate examples of these various classes of figures, and they need not be repeated here.

8. *Words as Permanent Embodiment of Poetic Feeling*

We have seen that the characteristic vocabulary of poetry originates in emotion and that it is capable of transmitting emotion to the hearer or reader. But how far are words capable of embodying emotion in permanent form? Poets themselves, in proud consciousness of the enduring character of their creations, have often boasted that they were building monuments more enduring than bronze or marble. When Shakspere asserts this in his sonnets, he is following not only an Elizabethan convention, but a universal instinct of the men of his craft. Is it a delusion? Here are words — mere vibrating sounds, light and winged and evanescent things, assuming a meaning value only through the common consent of those who interchange them, altering that meaning more or less from year to year, often passing wholly from the living speech of men, decaying when races decay and civilizations change. What transiency, what waste and oblivion like that which waits upon millions on millions of autumn leaves!

Yet nothing in human history is more indisputable than the fact that certain passages of poetry do survive, age after age, while empires pass, and philosophies change and science alters the mental attitude of men as well as the outward circumstances of life upon this planet.

Some thoughts and feelings, then, eternalize themselves in human speech; most thoughts and feelings do not. Wherein lies the difference? If most words are perishable stuff, what is it that keeps other words from perishing? Is it superior organization and arrangement of this fragile material, "fame's great antiseptic, style"? Or is it by virtue of some secret passionate quality imparted to words by the poet, so that the apparently familiar syllables take on a life and significance which is really not their own, but his? And is this intimate personalized quality of words "style," also, as well as that more external "style" revealed in clear and orderly and idiomatic arrangement? Or does the mystery of permanence reside in the poet's generalizing power, by which he is able to express universal, and hence permanently interesting human experience? And therefore, was not the late Professor Courthope right when he declared, "I take all great poetry to be not so much what Plato thought it, the utterance of individual genius, half inspired, half insane, as the enduring voice of the soul and conscience of man living in society"?

Answers to such questions as these depend somewhat upon the "romantic" or "classic" bias of the critics. Romantic criticism tends to stress the significance of the personality of the individual poet. The classic school of criticism tends to emphasize the more general and universal qualities revealed by the poet's work. But while the schools and fashions of criticism shift their ground and alter their verdicts as succeeding generations change in taste, the great poets continue as before to particularize and also to generalize, to be "romantic" and "classic" by turns, or even in the same poem. They defy critical augury, in their unending quest of beauty and truth. That they succeed, now and then, in giving a permanently lovely embodiment to their

vision is surely a more important fact than the
rightness or wrongness of whatever artistic
theory they may have invoked or followed.

For many a time, surely, their triumphs are
a contradiction of their theories. To take a
very familiar example, Wordsworth's theory
of poetic diction shifted like a weathercock.
In the Advertisement to the *Lyrical Ballads*
(1798) he asserted: "The following poems
are to be considered as experiments. They
were written chiefly with a view to ascertain
how far the language of conversation in the
middle and lower classes of society is adapted
to the purposes of poetic pleasure." In the
Preface of the second edition (1800) he announced that his purpose had been "to
ascertain how far, by fitting to metrical arrangement a selection of the real language of
men in a state of vivid sensation, that sort of
pleasure and that quantity of pleasure may
be imparted, which a poet may rationally
endeavour to impart." But in the famous
remarks on poetic diction which accompanied
the third edition (1802) he inserted after the
words "A selection of language really used
by men" this additional statement of his intention: "And at the same time to throw over

them a certain colouring of the imagination whereby ordinary things should be presented to the mind in an unusual aspect." In place of the original statement about the conversation of the middle and lower classes of society, we are now assured that the language of poetry "if selected truly and judiciously, must necessarily be dignified and variegated and alive with metaphors and figures. . . . This selection will form a distinction . . . and will entirely separate the composition from the vulgarity and meanness of ordinary life."

What an amazing change in theory in four years! Yet it is no more remarkable than Wordsworth's successive emendations in the text of his poems. In 1807 his blind Highland boy had gone voyaging in

> "A Household Tub, like one of those
> Which women use to wash their clothes;
> This carried the blind Boy."

In 1815 the wash-tub becomes

> "The shell of a green turtle, thin
> And hollow — you might sit therein,
> It was so wide and deep."

And in 1820 the worried and dissatisfied artist changes that unlucky vessel once more into the final banality of

> "A shell of ample size, and light
> As the pearly car of Amphitrite
> That sportive dolphins drew."

Sometimes, it is true, this adventurer in poetic diction had rather better fortune in his alterations. The much-ridiculed lines of 1798 about the child's grave —

> "I've measured it from side to side,
> 'T is three feet long and two feet wide" —

became in 1820:

> "Though but of compass small and bare
> To thirsty suns and parching air."

Like his friend Coleridge, Wordsworth forsook gradually his early experiments with matter-of-fact phrases, with quaintly grotesque figures. Revolt against conventional eighteenth-century diction had given him a blessed sense of freedom, but he found his real strength later in subduing that freedom to a sense of law. Archaisms, queernesses, flatly naturalistic turns of speech gave place to a vocabulary of simple dignity and austere beauty. Wordsworth attained his highest originality as an artist by disregarding singularity, by making familiar words reveal new potencies of expression.

For after all, we must come back to what

William James called the long "loop-line," to that reservoir of ideas and feelings which stores up the experience of individuals and of the race, and to the words which most effectively evoke that experience. Two classes at Columbia University, a few years ago, were asked to select fifty English words of basic importance in the expression of human life. In choosing these words, they were to aim at reality and strength rather than at beauty. When the two lists were combined, they presented these seventy-eight different words, which are here arranged alphabetically: age, ambition, beauty, bloom, country, courage, dawn, day, death, despair, destiny, devotion, dirge, disaster, divine, dream, earth, enchantment, eternity, fair, faith, fantasy, flower, fortune, freedom, friendship, glory, glow, god, grief, happiness, harmony, hate, heart, heaven, honor, hope, immortality, joy, justice, knell, life, longing, love, man, melancholy, melody, mercy, moon, mortal, nature, noble, night, paradise, parting, peace, pleasure, pride, regret, sea, sigh, sleep, solitude, song, sorrow, soul, spirit, spring, star, suffer, tears, tender, time, virtue, weep, whisper, wind and youth.[1]

[1] See *Nation*, February 23, 1911.

Surely these words, selected as they were for their significance, are not lacking in beauty of sound. On the contrary, any list of the most beautiful words in English would include many of them. But it is the meaning of these "long-loop" words, rather than their formal beauty alone, which fits them for the service of poetry. And they acquire in that service a "literary" value, which is subtly blended with their "sound" value and logical "meaning" value. They connote so much! They suggest more than they actually say. They unite the individual mood of the moment with the soul of mankind.

And there is still another mode of union between the individual and the race, which we must attempt in the next chapter to regard more closely, but which should be mentioned here in connection with the permanent embodiment of feeling in words, — namely, the mysterious fact of rhythm. Single words are born and die, we learn them and forget them, they alter their meanings, they always say less than we really intend, they are imperfect instruments for signaling from one brain to another. Yet these crumbling particles of speech may be miraculously held together and built into a tune, and with the tune comes another element of law, order, permanence. The instinct for the drum-beat lies deep down in our bodies; it affects our mental life, the organization of our emotions, and our response to the rhythmical arrangement of words. For mere ideas and words are not poetry, but only part of the material for poetry. A poem does not come into full being until the words begin to dance.

CHAPTER V

RHYTHM AND METRE

"Rhythm is the recurrence of stress at intervals; metre is the regular, or measured, recurrence of stress."

M. H. SHACKFORD, *A First Book of Poetics*

"Metres being manifestly sections of rhythm."

ARISTOTLE, *Poetics*, 4. (Butcher's translation)

"Thoughts that voluntary move
Harmonious numbers."

MILTON

1. The Nature of Rhythm

AND why must the words begin to dance? The answer is to be perceived in the very nature of Rhythm, that old name for the ceaseless pulsing or "flowing" of all living things. So deep indeed lies the instinct for rhythm in our consciousness that we impute it even to inanimate objects. We hear the ticking of the clock as tíck-tock, tíck-tock, or else tick-tóck, tick-tóck, although psychologists assure us that the clock's wheels are moving with indifferent, mechanical precision, and that it is simply our own focusing of attention upon alternate beats which creates the impression of rhythm. We hear a rhythm in the wheels of the train, and in the purring of the motor-engine, knowing all the while that it is we who impose or make-up the rhythm, in our human instinct for organizing the units of attention. We cannot help it, as long as our own pulses beat. No two persons catch quite the same rhythm in the sounds of the animate and inanimate world, because no two persons have absolutely identical pulse-beats, identical powers of attention, an identical psycho-physical organism. We all perceive that there is a rhythm in a racing crew, in a perfectly timed stroke of golf, in a fisherman's fly-casting, in a violinist's bow, in a close-hauled sailboat fighting with the wind. But we appropriate and organize these objective impressions in subtly different ways.

When, for instance, we listen to poetry read aloud, or when we read it aloud ourselves, some of us are instinctive "timers," [1] paying primary attention to the spaced or measured intervals of time, although in so doing we are not wholly regardless of those points of "stress" which help to make the

[1] See W. M. Patterson, *The Rhythm of Prose.* Columbia University Press, 1916.

time-intervals plainer.   Others of us are
natural "stressers," in that we pay primary
attention to the "weight" of words, — the
relative loudness or pitch, by which their
meaning or importance is indicated, — and
it is only secondarily that we think of these
weighted or "stressed" words as separated
from one another by approximately equal
intervals of time. Standing on the rocks
at Gloucester after an easterly storm, a
typical "timer" might be chiefly conscious
of the steady sequence of the waves, the
measured intervals between their summits;
while the typical stresser, although subconsciously aware of the steady iteration of
the giant rollers, might watch primarily their
foaming crests, and listen chiefly to their
crashing thunder. The point to be remembered is this: that neither the "timing" instinct nor the "stressing" instinct excludes
the other, although in most individuals one
or the other predominates. Musicians, for
instance, are apt to be noticeable "timers,"
while many scholars who deal habitually with
words in their varied shifts of meaning, are
professionally inclined to be "stressers."

2. *The Measurement of Rhythm*

Let us apply these facts to some of the
more simple of the vexed questions of prosody.
No one disputes the universality of the
rhythmizing impulse; the quarrel begins as
soon as any prosodist attempts to dogmatize
about the nature and measurement of those
flowing time-intervals whose arrangement we
call rhythm. No one disputes, again, that
the only arbiter in matters of prosody is the
trained ear, and not the eye. Infinitely deceptive is the printed page of verse when
regarded by the eye. Verse may be made to
look like prose and prose to look like verse.
Capital letters, lines, rhymes, phrases and
paragraphs may be so cunningly or conven-
tionally arranged by the printer as to disguise
the real nature of the rhythmical and metrical
pattern. When in doubt, close your eyes!

We agree, then, that in all spoken language
— and this is as true of prose as it is of verse
— there are time-intervals more or less clearly
marked, and that the ear is the final judge as
to the nature of these intervals. But can
the ear really measure the intervals with any
approximation to certainty, so that proso-

dists, for instance, can agree that a given
poem is written in a definite metre? In one
sense "yes." No one doubts that the
Odyssey is written in "dactylic hexameters,"
i.e., in lines made up of six "feet," each one
of which is normally composed of a long syllable plus two short syllables, or of an acceptable equivalent for that particular combination. But when we are taught in school
that Longfellow's *Evangeline* is also written
in "dactylic hexameters," trouble begins for
the few inquisitive, since it is certain that if
you close your eyes and listen carefully to a
dozen lines of Homer's Greek, and then to
a dozen lines of Longfellow's English, each
written in so-called "hexameters," you are
listening to two very different arrangements
of time-intervals, so different, in fact, that the
two poems are really not in the same "measure" or "metre" at all. For the Greek poet
was, as a metrist, thinking primarily of
quantity, of the relative "timing" of his
syllables, and the American of the relative
"stress" of his syllables.[1]

[1] "Musically speaking — because the musical terms are
exact and not ambiguous — true dactyls are in 2-4 time and
the verse of *Evangeline* is in 3-8 time." T. D. Goodell, *Nation,*
October 12, 1911.

That illustration is drearily hackneyed, no
doubt, but it has a double value. It is perfectly clear; and furthermore, it serves to
remind us of the instinctive differences between different persons and different races as
regards the ways of arranging time-intervals
so as to create the rhythms of verse.   The
individual's standard of measurement — his
poetic foot-rule, so to speak — is very elastic,
— "made of rubber" indeed, as the experiments of many psychological laboratories
have demonstrated beyond a question.   Furthermore, the composers of poetry build it
out of very elastic units.   They are simply
putting syllables of words together into a
rhythmical design, and these "airy syllables,"
in themselves mere symbols of ideas and feelings, cannot be weighed by any absolutely
correct sound-scales.   They cannot be measured in time by any absolutely accurate
watch-dial, or exactly estimated in their
meaning, whether that be literal or figurative,
by any dictionary of words and phrases.   But
this is only saying that the syllables which
make up the units of verse, whether the units
be called "foot" or "line" or "phrase," are
not dead, mechanical things, but live things,

moving rhythmically, entering thereby into
the pulsing, chiming life of the real world,
and taking on more fullness of life and beauty
in elastic movement, in ordered but infinitely
flexible design, than they ever could possess
as independent particles.

3. Conflict and Compromise

And everywhere in the arrangement of
syllables into the patterns of rhythm and
metre we find conflict and compromise, the
surrender of some values of sound or sense
for the sake of a greater unity. To revert to
considerations dealt with in an earlier chapter, we touch here upon the old antinomy —
or it may be, harmony — between "form"
and "significance," between the "outside"
and the "inside" of the work of art. For
words, surely, have one kind of value as *pure
sound*, as "cadences" made up of stresses,
slides, pauses, and even of silences when the
expected syllable is artfully withheld. It is
this sound-value, for instance, which you
perceive as you listen to a beautifully recited
poem in Russian, a language of which you
know not a single word; and you may experience a modification of the same pleasure

in closing your mind wholly to the "sense" of a richly musical passage in Swinburne, and delighting your ear by its mere beauty of tone. But words have also that other value as *meaning*, and we are aware how these meaning values shift with the stress and turns of thought, so that a given word has a greater or less weight in different sentences or even in different clauses of the same sentence. "Meaning" values, like sound values, are never precisely fixed in a mechanical and universally agreed-upon scale, they are relative, not absolute. Sometimes meaning and sound conflict with one another, and one must be sacrificed in part, as when the normal accent of a word refuses to coincide with the verse-accent demanded by a certain measure, so that we "wrench" the accent a trifle, or make it "hover" over two syllables without really alighting upon either. And it is significant that lovers of poetry have always found pleasure in such compromises.[1] They enjoy minor departures from and returns to the normal, the expected measure of both sound and sense, just as a man likes to sail a

[1] Compare the passage about Chopin's piano-playing, quoted from Alden in the Notes and Illustrations for this chapter.

boat as closely into the wind as he conveniently can, making his actual course a compromise between the line as laid by the compass, and the actual facts of wind and tide and the behavior of his particular boat. It is thus that the sailor "makes it," triumphantly! And the poet "makes it" likewise, out of deep, strong-running tides of rhythmic impulse, out of arbitrary words and rebellious moods, out of

"Thoughts hardly to be packed
Into a narrow act,
Fancies that broke through language and escaped,"

until he compels rhythm and syllables to move concordantly, and blend into that larger living whole — the dancing, singing crowd of sounds and meanings which make up a poem.

4. The Rhythms of Prose

Just here it may be of help to us to turn away for a moment from verse rhythm, and to consider what Dryden called "the other harmony" of prose. For no one doubts that prose has rhythm, as well as verse. Vast and learned treatises have been written on the prose rhythms of the Greeks and Romans, and Saintsbury's *History of English Prose*

Rhythm is a monumental collection of wonderful prose passages in English, with the scansion of "long" and "short" syllables and of "feet" marked after a fashion that seems to please no one but the author. But in truth the task of inventing an adequate system for notating the rhythm of prose, and securing a working agreement among prosodists as to a proper terminology, is almost insuperable. Those of us who sat in our youth at the feet of German masters were taught that the distinction between verse and prose was simple: verse was, as the Greeks had called it, "bound speech" and prose was "loosened speech." But a large proportion of the poetry published in the last ten years is "free verse," which is assuredly of a "loosened" rather than a "bound" pattern. Apparently the old fence between prose and verse has been broken down. Or, if one conceives of indubitable prose and indubitable verse as forming two intersecting circles, there is a neutral zone, which some would call "prose poetry" and some "free verse," and which, according to the experiments of Dr. Patterson [1] may be appropriated as "prose experience" or "verse experience" according to the rhythmic instinct of each individual. Indeed Mr. T. S. Omond has admitted that "the very same words, with the very same natural stresses, may be prose or verse according as we treat them. The difference is in ourselves, in the mental rhythm to which we unconsciously adjust the words." [2] Many familiar sentences from the English Bible or Prayer-Book, such as the words from the *Te Deum*, "We, therefore, pray thee, help thy servants, whom thou hast redeemed with thy precious blood," have a rhythm which may be felt as prose or verse, according to the mental habit or mood or rhythmizing impulse of the hearer.

Nevertheless it remains true in general that the rhythms of prose are more constantly varied, broken and intricate than the rhythms of verse. They are characterized, according to the interesting experiments of Dr. Patter-

---

[1] *The Rhythm of Prose*, already cited.
[2] Quoted in R. M. Alden, "The Mental Side of Metrical Form," *Modern Language Review*, July, 1914.

son, by syncopated time,[1] whereas in normal verse there is a fairly clean-cut coincidence between the pulses of the hearer and the strokes of the rhythm. Every one seems to agree that there is a certain danger in mixing these infinitely subtle and "syncopated" tunes of prose with the easily recognized tunes of verse. There is, unquestionably, a natural "iambic" roll in English prose, due to the predominant alternation of stressed and unstressed syllables in our native tongue, but when Dickens — to cite what John Wesley would call "an eminent sinner" in this respect — inserts in his emotional prose line after line of five-stress "iambic" verse, we feel instinctively that the presence of the blank verse impairs the true harmony of the prose.[2] Delicate writers of English prose usually avoid this coincidence of pattern with the more familiar patterns of verse, but it is impossible to avoid it wholly, and some of the most beautiful cadences of English prose

[1] "For a 'timer' the definition of prose as distinguished from verse experience depends upon a predominance of syncopation over coincidence in the coördination of the accented syllables of the text with the measuring pulses." *Rhythm of Prose*, p. 22.

[2] Observe, in the "Notes and Illustrations" for this chapter, the frequency of the blank-verse lines in Robert G. Ingersoll's "Address over a Little Boy's Grave."

might, if detached from their context, be scanned for a few syllables as perfect verse. The free verse of Whitman, Henley and Matthew Arnold is full of these embedded fragments of recognized "tunes of verse," mingled with the unidentifiable tunes of prose. There has seldom been a more curious example of accidental coincidence than in this sentence from a prosaic textbook on "The Parallelogram of Forces": "And hence no force, however great, can draw a cord, however fine, into a horizontal line which shall be absolutely straight." This is precisely the "four-stressed iambic" metre of *In Memoriam*, and it even preserves the peculiar rhyme order of the *In Memoriam* stanza:

> "And hence no force, however great,
> Can draw a cord, however fine,
> Into a horizontal line
> Which shall be absolutely straight."

We shall consider more closely, in the section on Free Verse in the following chapter, this question of the coincidence and variation of pattern as certain types of loosened verse pass in and out of the zone which is commonly recognized as pure prose. But it is highly important here to remember another fact, which professional psychologists in their laboratory experiments with the notation of verse and prose have frequently forgotten, namely, the existence of a type of ornamented prose, which has had a marked historical influence upon the development of English style. This ornamented prose, elaborated by Greek and Roman rhetoricians, and constantly apparent in the pages of Cicero, heightened its rhythm by various devices of alliteration, assonance, tone-color, cadence, phrase and period. Greek oratory even employed rhyme in highly colored passages, precisely as Miss Amy Lowell uses rhyme in her polyphonic or "many-voiced" prose. Medieval Latin took over all of these devices from Classical Latin, and in its varied oratorical, liturgical and epistolary forms it strove to imitate the various modes of *cursus* ("running") and *clausula* ("cadence") which had characterized the rhythms of Isocrates and Cicero.[1] From the Medieval Latin Missal and

[1] A. C. Clark, *Prose Rhythm in English.* Oxford, 1913.

Morris W. Croll, "The Cadence of English Oratorical Prose," *Studies in Philology.* January, 1919.

Oliver W. Elton, "English Prose Numbers," in *Essays and Studies* by members of the English Association, 4th Series. Oxford, 1913.

Breviary these devices of prose rhythm, particularly those affecting the end of sentences, were taken over into the Collects and other parts of the liturgy of the English Prayer-Book. They had a constant influence upon the rhythms employed by the translators of the English Bible, and through the Bible the cadences of this ancient ornamented prose have passed over into the familiar but intricate harmonies of our "heightened" modern prose.

While this whole matter is too technical to be dealt with adequately here, it may serve at least to remind the reader that an appreciation of English prose rhythms, as they have been actually employed for many centuries, requires a sensitiveness to the rhetorical position of phrases and clauses, and to "the use of sonorous words in the places of rhetorical emphasis, which cannot be indicated by the bare symbols of prosody." [1] For that sonority and cadence and balance which constitute a harmonious prose sentence cannot be adequately felt by a possibly illiterate scientist in his laboratory for acoustics; the "literary" value of words, in all strongly

[1] New York *Nation*, February 27, 1913.

emotional prose, is inextricably mingled with the bare sound values: it is thought-units that must be delicately "balanced" as well as stresses and slides and final clauses; it is the elevation of ideas, the nobility and beauty of feeling, as discerned by the trained literary sense, which makes the final difference between enduring prose harmonies and the mere tinkling of the "musical glasses." [1] The student of verse may very profitably continue to exercise himself with the rhythms of prose. He should learn to share the unwearied enthusiasm of Professor Saintsbury for the splendid cadences of our sixteenth-century English, for the florid decorative period of Thomas Browne and Jeremy Taylor, for the eloquent "prose poetry" of De Quincey and Ruskin and Charles Kingsley, and for the strangely subtle effects wrought by Pater and Stevenson. But he must not imagine that any laboratory system of tapping syncopated time, or any painstaking marking of macrons (–) breves (‿) and cæsuras (‖) will give him full initiation into the mysteries of prose cadences which have been

[1] This point is suggestively discussed by C. E. Andrews, *The Writing and Reading of Verse*, chap. 5. New York, 1918.

built, not merely out of stressed and unstressed syllables, but out of the passionate
intellectual life of many generations of men.
He may learn to feel that life as it pulsates in
words, but no one has thus far devised an
adequate scheme for its notation.

5. *Quantity, Stress and Syllable*

The notation of verse, however, while certainly not a wholly simple matter, is far
easier. It is practicable to indicate by conventional printer's devices the general rhythmical and metrical scheme of a poem, and to
indicate the more obvious, at least, of its
incidental variations from the expected pattern. It remains as true of verse as it is of
prose that the "literary" values of words —
their connotations or emotional overtones —
are too subtle to be indicated by any marks
invented by a printer; but the alternation
or succession of long or short syllables, of
stressed or unstressed syllables, the nature of
particular feet and lines and stanzas, the
order and interlacing of rhymes, and even the
devices of tone-color, are sufficiently external
elements of verse to allow easy methods of
indication.

When you and I first began to study Virgil
and Horace, for instance, we were taught that
the Roman poets, imitating the Greeks, built
their verses upon the principle of *Quantity*.
The metrical unit was the foot, made up of
long and short syllables in various combinations, two short syllables being equivalent to
one long one.   The feet most commonly used
were the Iambus (⌣–), the Anapest (⌣⌣–), the
Trochee (–⌣), the Dactyl (–⌣⌣), and the Spondee (– –).   Then we were instructed that a
"verse" or line consisting of one foot was
called a monometer, of two feet, a dimeter,
of three, a trimeter, of four, a tetrameter, of
five, a pentameter, of six, a hexameter.   This
looked like a fairly easy game, and before
long we were marking the quantities in the
first line of the Æneid, as other school-
children had done ever since the time of
St. Augustine:

Ārmă vĭ|rŭmquĕ că|nō̄ || Trō|jāē quī | prīmŭs ăb|ōrĭs.

Or perhaps it was Horace's

Mā̄ecē|nā̄s, ătăvīs || ēdĭtĕ rēg|ĭbŭs.

We were told, of course, that it was not all
quite as simple as this: that there were frequent metrical variations, such as trochees

changing places with dactyls, and anapests with iambi; that feet could be inverted, so that a trochaic line might begin with an iambus, an anapestic line with a dactyl, or *vice versa;* that syllables might be omitted at the beginning or the end or even in the middle of a line, and that this "cutting-off" was called *catalexis;* that syllables might even be added at the beginning or end of certain lines and that these syllables were called *hyper-metric;* and that we must be very watchful about pauses, particularly about a somewhat mysterious chief pause, liable to occur about the middle of a line, called a *cæsura.* But the magic password to admit us to this unknown world of Greek and Roman prosody was after all the word *Quantity.*

If a few of us were bold enough to ask the main difference between this Roman system of versification and the system which governed modern English poetry — even such rude playground verse as

> "Eeny, meeny, miny, mo,
> Catch a nigger by the toe" —

we were promptly told by the teacher that the difference was a very plain one, namely, that English, like all the Germanic languages, obeyed in its verse the principles of *Stress*. Instead of looking for "long" and "short" syllables, we had merely to look for "stressed" and "unstressed" syllables. It was a matter, not of quantity, but of accent; and if we remembered this fact, there was no harm, but rather a great convenience, in retaining the technical names of classical versification. Only we must be careful that by "iambus," in English poetry, we *meant* an unstressed syllable, rather than a short syllable followed by a long one. And so with "trochee," "dactyl," "anapest" and the rest; if we knew that accent and not quantity was what we really had in mind, it was proper enough to speak of *Paradise Lost* as written in "iambic pentameter," and *Evangeline* in "dactylic hexameter," etc. The trick was to count stresses and not syllables, for was not Coleridge's *Christabel* written in a metre which varied its syllables anywhere from four to twelve for the line, yet maintained its music by regularity of stress?

Nothing could be plainer than all this. Yet some of us discovered when we went to college and listened to instructors who grew strangely excited over prosody, that it was

not all as easy as this distinction between
Quantity and *Stress* would seem to indicate.
For we were now told that the Greek and
Roman habits of daily speech in prose had
something to do with their instinctive choice
of verse-rhythms: that at the very time when
the Greek heroic hexameters were being
composed, there was a natural dactylic roll
in spoken prose; that Roman daily speech
had a stronger stress than Greek, so that
Horace, in imitating Greek lyric measures,
had stubborn natural word-accents to recon-
cile with his quantitative measures; that the
Roman poets, who had originally allowed
normal word-accent and verse-pulse to coincide for the most part, came gradually to
enjoy a certain clash between them, keeping all the while the quantitative principle
dominant; so that when Virgil and Horace
read their verses aloud, and word-accent
and verse-pulse fell upon different syllables,
the verse-pulse yielded slightly to the word-
accent, thus adding something of the charm
of conversational prose to the normal time-
values of the rhythm.   In a word, we were
now taught — if I may quote from a personal
letter of a distinguished American Latinist

— that "the almost universal belief that Latin verse is a matter of quantity only is a mistake. Word-accent was not lost in Latin verse."

And then, as if this undermining of our schoolboy faith in pure Quantity were not enough, came the surprising information that the Romans had kept, perhaps from the beginning of their poetizing, a popular type of accented verse, as seen in the rude chant of the Roman legionaries,

Mílle Fráncos mílle sémel Sármatás occídimús.[1]

Certainly those sun-burnt "doughboys" were not bothering themselves about trochees and iambi and such toys of cultivated "literary" persons; they were amusing themselves on the march by inventing words to fit the "goose-step." Their

Unus homo mille mille mille decollavimus

which Professor Courthope scans as trochaic verse,[2] seems to me nothing but "stress" verse, like

"*Háy-foot, straw-foot, belly full of bean-soup —*
Hép — Hép!"

[1] See C. M. Lewis, *Foreign Sources of Modern English Versification.* Halle, 1898.

[2] *History of English Poetry,* vol. 1, p. 73.

Popular accentual verse persisted, then, while
the more cultivated Roman public acquired
and then gradually lost, in the course of centuries, its ear for the quantitative rhythms
which originally had been copied from the
Greeks.

Furthermore, according to our ingenious
college teachers, there was still a third principle of versification to be reckoned with, not
depending on Quantity or Stress, but merely
Syllabic, or syllable-counting. This was immemorially old, it seemed, and it had reap-
peared mysteriously in Europe in the Dark
Ages.

Dr. Lewis cites from a Latin manuscript
poem of the ninth century: [1]

*"Beatissimus namque Dionysius |Athenis quondam
episcopus,
Quem Sanctus Clemens direxit in Galliam |propter
prædicandi gratiam,* etc.

Each verse contains 21 syllables, with a
cæsura after the 12th. No further regularity,
either metrical or rhythmical, can be perceived. Such a verse could probably not have
been written except for music." Church-
music, apparently, was also a factor in the

[1] *Foreign Sources,* etc., p. 3.

development of versification, — particularly
that "Gregorian" style which demanded
neither quantitative nor accentual rhythm,
but simply a fair count of syllables in the
libretto, note matching syllable exactly. But
when the great medieval Latin hymns, like
Dies iræ, were written, the Syllabic principle
of versification, like the Quantitative principle, dropped out of sight, and we witness
once more the emergence of the Stress or
accentual system, heavily ornamented with
rhymes.[1] Yet the Syllabic method reappears
once more, we were told, in French prosody,
and thus affects the verse of Chaucer and of
subsequent English poetry, and it still may
be studied, isolated as far as may be from
considerations of quantity and stress, in
certain English songs written for music,
where syllable carefully matches note. The
"long metre" (8 syllables), "short metre"
(6 syllables) and "common metre" (7 syllables, 6 syllables) of the hymn books is a convenient illustration of thinking of metre in
terms of syllables alone.

[1] See the quotation from Taylor's *Classical Heritage of the
Middle Ages* printed in the "Notes and Illustrations" for this
chapter.

6. *The Appeal to the Ear*

At this point, perhaps, having set forth the three theories of *Quantity*, *Stress* and *Syllable*, our instructors were sensible enough to make an appeal to the ear. Reminding us that stress was the controlling principle in Germanic poetry, — although not denying that considerations of quantity and number of syllables might have something to do with the effect, — they read aloud to us some Old English verse. Perhaps it was that *Song of the Battle of Brunanburh* which Tennyson has so skilfully rendered into modern English words while preserving the Old English metre. And here, though the Anglo-Saxon words were certainly uncouth, we caught the chief stresses without difficulty, usually four beats to the line. If the instructor, while these rude strokes of rhythm were still pounding in our ears, followed the Old English with a dozen lines of Chaucer, we could all perceive the presence of a newer, smoother, more highly elaborated verse-music, where the number of syllables had been cunningly reckoned, and the verse-accent seemed always to fall upon a syllable long and strong enough to bear the weight easily, and the rhymes rippled like a brook. Whether we called the metre of the *Prologue* rhymed couplets of iambic pentameter, or rhymed couplets of ten-syllabled, five-stressed verse, the music, at least, was clear enough. And so was the music of the "blank" or unrhymed five-stress lines of Marlowe and Shakspere and Milton, and as we listened it was easy to believe that "stress" and "quantity" and "syllable," all playing together like a chime of bells, are concordant and not quarrelsome elements in the harmony of modern English verse. Only, to be richly concordant, each must be prepared to yield a little if need be, to the other!

I have taken too many pages, perhaps, in thus sketching the rudimentary education of a college student in the elements of rhythm and metre, and in showing how the theoretical difficulties of the subject — which are ad-mittedly great — often disappear as soon as one resolves to let the ear decide. A satisfied ear may soothe a dissatisfied mind. I have quoted from a letter of an American scholar about quantity being the "controlling" ele-ment of cultivated Roman verse, and I now quote from a personal letter of an American poet, emphasizing the necessity of "reading poetry as it was meant to be read": "My point is *not* that English verse has no quantity, but that the controlling element is not quantity but accent. The lack of fixed *syllabic* quantity is just what I emphasize. This lack makes definite *beat* impossible: or at least it makes it absurd to attempt to scan English verse by feet. The proportion of 'irregularities' and 'exceptions' becomes painful to the student and embarrassing to the professor. He is put to fearful straits to explain his prosody and make it fit the verse. And when he has done all this, the student, if he has a good ear, forthwith forgets it all, and reads the verse as it was meant to be read, as a succession of musical bars (without pitch, of course), in which the accent marks the rhythm, and pauses and *rests* often take the place of missing syllables. To this ingenuous student I hold out my hand and cast in my lot with him. He is the man for whom English poetry is written."

It may be objected, of course, that the phrase "reading poetry as it was meant to be read" really begs the question. For English poets have often amused themselves by composing purely quantitative verse, which they wish us to read as quantitative. The result may be as artificial as the painfully composed Latin quantitative verse of English schoolboys, but the thing can be done. Tennyson's experiments in quantity are well known, and should be carefully studied. He was proud of his hexameter:

"High winds roaring above me, dark leaves falling
    about me,"

and of his pentameter:

"All men alike hate slops, particularly gruel."

Here the English long and short syllables — as far as "long" and "short" can be definitely distinguished in English — correspond precisely to the rules of Roman prosody. The present Laureate, Robert Bridges, whose investigations in English and Roman prosody have been incessant, has recently published a book of experiments in writing English quantitative hexameters.[1] Here are half a dozen lines:

"Midway of all this tract, with secular arms an
    immense elm
Reareth a crowd of branches, aneath whose lofty
    protection

[1] *Ibant Obscuri.*   New York, Oxford University Press, 1917.

Vain dreams thickly nestle, clinging unto the foli-
    age on high:
And many strange creatures of monstrous form
    and features
Stable about th' entrance, Centaur and Scylla's
    abortion,
And hundred-handed Briareus, and Lerna's wild
    beast. . . . "

These are lines interesting to the scholar, but
they are somehow "non-English" in their
rhythm — not in accordance with "the
genius of the language," as we vaguely but
very sensibly say. Neither did the stressed
"dactylic" hexameters of Longfellow, written
though they were by a skilful versifier, quite
conform to "the nature of the language."

7. The Analogy with Music

One other attempt to explain the difficulties of English rhythm and metre must at
least be mentioned here, namely the "musical" theory of the American poet and musician, Sidney Lanier. In his *Science of English
Verse*, an acute and very suggestive book, he
threw over the whole theory of stress — or at
least, retained it as a mere element of assist-
ance, as in music, to the marking of time,
maintaining that the only necessary element

in rhythm is equal time-intervals, corresponding to bars of music. According to
Lanier, the structure of English blank verse,
for instance, is not an alternation of unstressed with stressed syllables, but a series of
bars of 3/8 time, thus:

$$\frac{3}{8} \; c \; \hat{r} \; \Big| \; c \; \hat{r} \; \Big| \; c \; \hat{r} \; \Big| \; c \; \hat{r} \; \Big| \; c \; \hat{r} \; \Big|$$

Thomson, Dabney and other prosodists
have followed Lanier's general theory, without
always agreeing with him as to whether blank
verse is written in 3/8 or 2/4 time. Alden,
in a competent summary of these various
musical theories as to the basis of English
verse,[1] quotes with approval Mr. T. S.
Omond's words: "Musical notes are almost
pure symbols. In theory at least, and no
doubt substantially in practice, they can be
divided with mathematical accuracy — into
fractions of 1/2, 1/4, 1/8, 1/16, etc. — and
the ideal of music is absolute accordance with
time. Verse has other methods and another
ideal. Its words are concrete things, not
readily carved to such exact pattern. . . . The

[1] *Introduction to Poetry*, pp. 190–93. See also Alden's *English Verse*, Part 3, "The Time-Element in English Verse."

perfection of music lies in absolute accordance
with time, that of verse is continual slight
departures from time. This is why no musical representations of verse ever seem satisfactory. They assume regularity where none
exists."

8. *Prosody and Enjoyment*

It must be expected then, that there will be
different preferences in choosing a nomenclature for modern English metres, based upon
the differences in the individual physical organism of various metrists, and upon the
strictness of their adherence to the significance of stress, quantity and number of syllables in the actual forms of verse. Adherents
of musical theories in the interpretation of
verse may prefer to speak of "duple time"
instead of iambic-trochaic metres, and of
"triple" time for anapests and dactyls. Natural "stressers" may prefer to call iambic and
anapestic units "rising" feet, to indicate the
ascent of stress as one passes from the weaker
to the stronger syllables; and similarly, to
call trochaic and dactylic units "falling" feet,
to indicate the descent or decline of stress as
the weaker syllable or syllables succeed the

stronger. Or, combining these two modes of nomenclature, one may legitimately speak of iambic feet as "duple rising,"

"And never lifted up a single stone";

trochaic as "duple falling,"

"Here they are, my fifty perfect poems";

anapestic as "triple rising,"

"But he lived with a lot of wild mates, and they
never would let him be good";

and dactylic as "triple falling";

"Cannon to right of them, cannon to left of them."

If a line is felt as "metrical," i.e. divided into approximately equal time-intervals, the particular label employed to indicate the nature of the metre is unimportant. It may be left to the choice of each student of metre, provided he uses his terms consistently. The use of the traditional terminology "iambic," "trochaic," etc., is convenient, and is open to no objection if one is careful to make clear the sense in which he employs such ambiguous terms.

It should also be added, as a means of reconciling the apparently warring claims of stress and quantity in English poetry, that recent investigations in recording through delicate instruments the actual time-intervals used by different persons in reading aloud the same lines of poetry, prove what has long been suspected, namely, the close affiliation of quantity with stress.[1]   Miss Snell's experiments show that the foot in English verse is made up of syllables 90 per cent of which are, in the stressed position, longer than those in the unstressed.   The average relation of short to long syllables, is, in spite of a good deal of variation among the individual readers, almost precisely as 2 to 4 — which has always been the accepted ratio for the relation of short to long syllables in Greek and Roman verse.   If one examines English words in a dictionary, the quantities of the syllables are certainly not "fixed" as they are in Greek and Latin, but the moment one begins to read a passage of English poetry aloud, and becomes conscious of its underlying type of rhythm, he fits elastic units of "feet" into the steadily flowing or pulsing intervals of time. The "foot" becomes, as it were, a rubber link in a moving bicycle chain.   The revolutions

[1] "Syllabic Quantity in English Verse," by Ada F. Snell, *Pub. of Mod. Lang. Ass.*, September, 1918.

of the chain mark the rhythm; and the stressed or unstressed or lightly stressed syllables in each "link" or foot, accommodate themselves, by almost unperceived expansion and contraction, to the rhythmic beat of the passage as a whole.

Nor should it be forgotten that the "sense" of words, their meaning-weight, their rhetorical value in certain phrases, constantly affects the theoretical number of stresses belonging to a given line. In blank verse, for instance, the theoretical five chief stresses are often but three or four in actual practice, lighter stresses taking their place in order to avoid a pounding monotony, and conversely, as in Milton's famous line,

"Rocks, caves, lakes, dens, bogs, fens, and shades
    of death,"

the rhetorical significance of the monosyllables compels an overloading of stresses which heightens the desired poetic effect. Corson's *Primer of English Verse* and Mayor's *English Metres* give numerous examples from the blank verse of Milton and Tennyson to illustrate the constant substitution and shifting of stresses in order to secure variety of music and suggestive adaptations of sound to sense.

It is well known that Shakspere's blank
verse, as he developed in command of his
artistic resources, shows fewer "end-stopped"
lines and more "run-on" lines, with an in-
creasing proportion of light and weak endings.
But the same principle applies to every type
of English rhythm. As soon as the dominant
beat — which is commonly, but not always,
apparent in the opening measures of the poem
— once asserts itself, the poet's mastery of
technique is revealed through his skill in satisfying the ear with a verbal music which is
never absolutely identical in its time-intervals,
its stresses or its pitch, with the fixed, wooden
pattern of the rhythm he is using.

For the human voice utters syllables which
vary their duration, stress and pitch with
each reader. Photographs of voice-waves, as
printed by Verrier, Scripture, and many other
laboratory workers, show how great is the
difference between individuals in the intervals covered by the upward and downward
slides or "inflections" which indicate doubt
or affirmation. And these "rising" and "falling" and "circumflex" and "suspended" inflections, which make up what is called
"pitch-accent," are constantly varied, like

the duration and stress of syllables, by the emotions evoked in reading. Words, phrases, lines and stanzas become colored with emotional overtones due to the feeling of the instant. Poetry read aloud as something sensuous and passionate cannot possibly conform exactly to a set mechanical pattern of rhythm and metre. Yet the hand-woven Oriental rug, though lacking the geometrical accuracy of a rug made by machinery, reveals a more vital and intimate beauty of design and execution. Many well-known poets — Tennyson being perhaps the most familiar example — have read aloud their own verses with a peculiar chanting sing-song which seemed to over-emphasize the fundamental rhythm. But who shall correct them? And who is entitled to say that a line like Swinburne's

"Full-sailed, wide-winged, poised softly forever asway"

is irregular according to the foot-rule of traditional prosody, when it is probable, as Mr. C. E. Russell maintains, that Swinburne was here composing in purely musical and not prosodical rhythm? [1]

[1] "Swinburne and Music," by Charles E. Russell, *North American Review,* November, 1907. See the quotation in the "Notes and Illustrations" for this chapter.

Is it not true, furthermore, as some metrical sceptics like to remind us, that if we once admit the principle of substitution and equivalence, of hypermetrical and truncated syllables, of pauses taking the place of syllables, that you can often make one metre seem very much like another? The question of calling a given group of lines "iambic" or "trochaic," for instance, can be made quite arbitrary, depending upon where you begin to count syllables. "Iambic" with initial truncation or " trochaic " with final truncation? Tweedle-dum or tweedle-dee? Do you count waves from crest to crest or from hollow to hollow? When you count the links in a bicycle chain, do you begin with the slender middle of each link or with one of the swelling ends? So is it with this "iambic" and "trochaic" matter. Professor Alden, in a suggestive pamphlet,[1] confesses that these contrasting concepts of rising and falling metre are nothing more than concepts, alterable at will.

But while the experts in prosody continue to differ and to dogmatize, the lover of poetry should remember that versification is far

[1] "The Mental Side of Metrical Form," already cited.

older than the science of prosody, and that the enjoyment of verse is, for millions of human beings, as unaffected by theories of metrics as the stars are unaffected by the theories of astronomers. It is a satisfaction to the mind to know that the stars in their courses are amenable to law, even though one be so poor a mathematician as to be incapable of grasping and stating the law. The mathematics of music and of poetry, while heightening the intellectual pleasure of those capable of comprehending it, is admittedly too difficult for the mass of men. But no lover of poetry should refuse to go as far in theorizing as his ear will carry him. He will find that his susceptibility to the pulsations of various types of rhythm, and his delight in the intricacies of metrical device, will be heightened by the mental effort of attention and analysis. The danger is that the lover of poetry, wearied by the quarrels of prosodists, and forgetting the necessity of patience, compromise and freedom from dogmatism, will lose his curiosity about the infinite variety of metrical effects. But it is this very curiosity which makes his ear finer, even if his theories may be wrong. Hundreds of metricists admire and envy Pro-

fessor Saintsbury's ear for prose and verse
rhythms while disagreeing wholly with his
dogmatic theories of the "foot," and his system of notation. There are sure to be some
days and hours when the reader of poetry will
find himself bored and tired with the effort of
attention to the technique of verse. Then he
can stop analysing, close his eyes, and drift
out to sea upon the uncomprehended music.

"The stars of midnight shall be dear
To her; and she shall lean her ear
In many a secret place
Where rivulets dance their wayward round,
And beauty born of murmuring sound
Shall pass into her face."

CHAPTER VI

RHYME, STANZA AND FREE VERSE

"Subtle rhymes, with ruin rife,
Murmur in the house of life."

EMERSON

"When this verse was first dictated to me I consider'd a Monotonous Cadence like that used by Milton & Shakspeare, & all writers of English Blank Verse, derived from the modern bondage of Rhyming, to be a necessary and indispensible part of the verse. But I soon found that in the mouth of a true Orator, such monotony was not only awkward, but as much a bondage as rhyme itself. I therefore have produced a variety in every line, both of cadences & number of syllables. Every word and every letter is studied and put into its fit place: the terrific numbers are reserved for the terrific parts, the mild & gentle for the mild & gentle parts, and the prosaic for inferior parts: all are necessary to each other. Poetry Fetter'd Fetters the Human Race!"

WILLIAM BLAKE

1. Battles Long Ago

As we pass from the general consideration of Rhythm and Metre to some of the special questions involved in Rhyme, Stanza and Free Verse, it may be well to revert to the old distinction between what we called for convenience the "outside" and the "inside" of a work of art. In the field of music we saw that this distinction is almost, if not quite, meaningless, and in poetry it ought not to be

pushed too far.   Yet it is useful in explaining
the differences among men as they regard, now
the external form of verse, and now its inner
spirit, and as they ask themselves how these
two elements are related.   Professor Butcher,
in his *Aristotle's Theory of Poetry and Fine Art*,[1]
describes the natural tendencies of two sorts
of men, who are quite as persistent to-day as
ever they were in Greece in looking at one
side only of the question:

"We need not agree with a certain modern
school who would empty all poetry of poetical
thought and etherealize it till it melts into a
strain of music; who sing to us we hardly know
of what, but in such a way that the echoes of the
real world, its men and women, its actual stir and
conflict, are faint and hardly to be discerned.   The
poetry, we are told, resides not in the ideas conveyed, not in the blending of soul and sense, but
in the sound itself, in the cadence of the verse.
Yet, false as this view may be, it is not perhaps
more false than that other which wholly ignores
the effect of musical sound and looks only to the
thought that is conveyed.   Aristotle comes peril-
ously near this doctrine."

But it is not Aristotle only who permits
himself at times to undervalue the formal
element in verse.   It is also Sir Philip Sidney,

[1] Page 147.

with his famous "verse being but an ornament
and no cause to poetry" and "it is not riming
and versing that maketh a poet."   It is Shelley with his "The distinction between poets
and prose writers in a vulgar error. . . . Plato
was essentially a poet — the truth and splendor of his imagery, and the melody of his
language, are the most intense that it is possible to conceive. . . . Lord Bacon was a poet."
It is Coleridge with his "The writings of
Plato, and Bishop Taylor, and the *Theoria
Sacra* of Burnet, furnish undeniable proofs
that poetry of the highest kind may be written
without metre."

In such passages as these, how generous are
Sidney, Shelley, and Coleridge to the prose-
men!   And yet these same poet-critics, in
dozens of other passages, have explained the
fundamental justification of metre, rhyme
and stanza as elements in the harmony of
verse.   Harmony may be attained, it is true,
by rhythms too complicated to be easily
scanned in metrical feet, and by measures
which disregard rhyme and stanza; and poets,
as well as critics, by giving exclusive attention
to a single element in harmony, are able to
persuade themselves for the moment that all

other elements are relatively negligible. Milton, in his zeal for blank verse, attacked rhyme, in which he had already proved himself a master, quite as fiercely as any of our contemporary champions of free verse. Campion, a trained musician, argued for a quantitative system of English prosody during the very period when he was composing, in the accentual system, some of the most exquisite songs in the language. Daniel, whose *Defense of Rhyme* (1603) was a triumphant reply to Campion's theory, gave courteous praise to his opponent's practice. Dryden, most flexible-minded of critics, argues now for, and now against the use of rhymed heroic couplets in the drama, fitting his theories to the changing currents of contemporary taste as well as to the varying, self-determined technique of his own plays. "Never wholly out of the way, nor in it," was Dryden's happy phrase to describe the artist's freedom, a freedom always conscious of underlying law.

2. *Rhyme as a Form of Rhythm*

However theory and practice may happen to coincide or to drift apart, the fundamental law which justifies rhyme and stanza seems to be this: if rhythm is a primary fact in poetry, and metre is, as Aristotle called it, sections of rhythm, any device of repeating identical or nearly identical sounds at measured intervals is an aid to rhythmical effect. Rhyme is thus a form, an "externalizing" of rhythm. It is structural as well as decorative, or rather, it is *one way* of securing structure, of building verse. There are other devices, of course, for attaining symmetrical patterns, for conveying an impression of unity in variety. The "parallel" structure of Hebrew poetry, where one idea and phrase is balanced against another,

> "I have slain a man to my wounding —
> And a young man to my hurt — "

or the "envelope" structure of many of the Psalms, where the initial phrase or idea is repeated at the close, after the insertion of illustrative matter, thus securing a pattern by the "return" of the main idea — the closing of the "curve" — may serve to illustrate the universality of the principle of balance and contrast and repetition in the architecture of verse. For Hebrew poetry, like the poetry of many primitive peoples, utilized the natural pleasure which the ear takes in listen-

ing for and perceiving again an already
uttered sound. Rhyme is a gratification of
expectation, like the repetition of a chord in
music [1] or of colors in a rug. It assists the
mind in grasping the sense-rhythm, — the
design of the piece as a whole. It assists the
emotions through the stimulus to the attention, through the reinforcement which it gives
to the pulsations of the psycho-physical organism.

> "And *sweep* through the *deep*
>   While the stormy tempests blow,
>   While the battle rages long and loud
>   And the stormy tempests blow."

The pulses cannot help quickening as the
rhymes quicken.

But in order to perform this structural,
rhythmical purpose it is not necessary that
rhyme be of any single recognized type. As
long as the ear receives the pleasure afforded
by accordant sound, any of the various historical forms of rhyme may serve. It may be

[1] "Most musical compositions are written in quite obvious
rhymes; and the array of familiar and classical works that have
not only rhymes but distinct stanzaic arrangements exactly like
those of poetry is worth remembering. Mendelssohn's 'Spring
Song' and Rubinstein's 'Romance in E Flat' will occur at
once as examples in which the stanzas are unmistakable."
C. E. Russell, "Swinburne and Music," *North American Review,* November, 1907.

Alliteration, the letter-rhyme or "beginning-rhyme" of Old English poetry:

> "*H*im be *h*ealfe stod   *h*yse unweaxen,
> *C*niht on gecampe,   se full *c*aflice."

Tennyson imitates it in his "Battle of Brunanburh":

> "Mighty the Mercian,
> Hard was his hand-play,
> Sparing not any of
> Those that with Anlaf,
> Warriors over the
> Weltering waters
> Borne in the bark's-bosom,
> Drew to this island —
> Doomed to the death."

This repetition of initial letters survives in phrases of prose like "dead and done with," "to have and to hold," and it is utilized in modern verse to give further emphasis to accentual syllables. But masters of alliterative effects, like Keats, Tennyson and Verlaine, constantly employ alliteration in unaccented syllables so as to color the tone-quality of a line without a too obvious assault upon the ear. The unrhymed songs of *The Princess* are full of these delicate modulations of sound.

In Common rhyme, or "end-rhyme"(found

— abound), the accented vowel and all succeeding sounds are repeated, while the consonants preceding the accented vowel vary.
Assonance, in its stricter sense, means the
repetition of an accented vowel (blackness —
dances), while the succeeding sounds vary, but
the terms "assonance" and "consonance"
are often employed loosely to signify harmonious effects of tone-color within a line
or group of lines. Complete or "identical"
rhymes (fair — affair), which were legitimate
in Chaucer's time, are not now considered
admissible in English. "Masculine" rhymes
are end-rhymes of one syllable; "feminine"
rhymes are end-rhymes of two syllables (un-
certain — curtain); internal or "middle-
rhymes" are produced by the repetition at
the end of a line of a rhyme-sound already
employed within the line.

> "We were the *first* that ever *burst*
> Into that silent sea."

In general, the more frequent the repetitions
of rhyme, the quicker is the rhythmic movement of the poem, and conversely. Thus,
the *In Memoriam* stanza attains its peculiar
effect of retardation by rhyming the first line
with the fourth, so that the ear is compelled to

wait for the expected recurrence of the first rhyme sound.

> "Beside the river's wooded reach,
>   The fortress and the mountain ridge,
>   The cataract flashing from the bridge,
>   The breaker breaking on the beach."

This gives a movement markedly different from that secured by rearranging the same lines in alternate rhymes:

> "Beside the river's wooded reach,
>   The fortress and the mountain ridge,
>   The breaker breaking on the beach,
>   The cataract flashing from the bridge."

If all the various forms of rhyme are only different ways of emphasizing rhythm through the repetition of accordant sounds, it follows that the varying rhythmical impulses of poets and of readers will demand now a greater and now a less dependence upon this particular mode of rhythmical satisfaction. Chaucer complained of the scarcity of rhymes in English as compared with their affluence in Old French, and it is true that rhyming is harder in our tongue than in the Romance languages. We have had magicians of rhyme, like Swinburne, whose very profusion of rhyme-sounds ends by cloying the taste of many a reader, and sending him back to blank verse or on to free verse. The Spenserian stanza, which calls for one fourfold set of rhymes, one threefold, and one double, all cunningly interlaced, is as complicated a piece of rhyme-harmony as the ear of the average lover of poetry can carry. It is needless to say that there are born rhymers, who think in rhyme and whose fecundity of imagery is multiplied by the excitement of matching sound with sound. They are often careless in their prodigality, inexact in their swift catching at any rhyme-word that will serve. At the other extreme are the self-conscious artists in verse who abhor imperfect concordances, and polish their rhymes until the life and freshness disappear. For sheer improvising cleverness of rhyme Byron is still unmatched, but he often contents himself with approximate rhymes that are nearly as bad as some of Mrs. Browning's and Whittier's. Very different is the deliberate artifice of the following lines, where the monotony of the rhyme-sound fits the "solemn ennui" of the trailing peacocks:

I

"From out the temple's pillared portico,
  Thence to the gardens where blue poppies blow

The gold and emerald peacocks saunter slow,
Trailing their solemn ennui as they go,
Trailing their melancholy and their woe.

II

"Trailing their melancholy and their woe,
Trailing their solemn ennui as they go
The gold and emerald peacocks saunter slow
From out the gardens where blue poppies blow
Thence to the temple's pillared portico." [1]

Rhyme, then, is not merely a "jingle," it is rather, as Samuel Johnson said of all versification, a "joining music with reason." Its blending of decorative with structural purpose is in truth "a dictate of nature," or, to quote E. C. Stedman, "In real, that is, spontaneous minstrelsy, the fittest assonance, consonance, time, even rime, . . . *come of themselves with imaginative thought.*"

3. Stanza

There are some lovers of poetry, however, who will grant this theoretical justification of rhyme as an element in the harmony of verse, without admitting that the actual rhyming stanzas of English verse show "spon-

[1] Frederic Adrian Lopere, "World Wisdom," *The International,* September, 1915.

taneous minstrelsy." The word "stanza" or "strophe" means literally "a resting-place," a halt or turn, that is to say, after a uniform group of rhymed lines. Alden defines it in his *English Verse* as "the largest unit of verse-measure ordinarily recognized. It is based not so much on rhythmical divisions as on periods either rhetorical or melodic; that is, a short stanza will roughly correspond to the period of a sentence, and a long one to that of a paragraph, while in lyrical verse the original idea was to conform the stanza to the melody for which it was written." "Normally, then," Alden adds in his *Introduction to Poetry*, "all the stanzas of a poem are identical in the number, the length, the metre, and the rime-scheme of the corresponding verses." The question arises, therefore, whether those units which we call "stanzas" are arbitrary or vital. Have the lines been fused into their rhymed grouping by passionate feeling, or is their unity a mere mechanical conformation to a pattern? In Theodore Watts-Dunton's well-known article on "Poetry" in the *Encyclopædia Brittanica* [1]

---

[1] Now reprinted, with many expansions, in his *Poetry and the Renascence of Wonder*. E. P. Dutton, New York.

the phrases "stanzaic law" and "emotional law" are used to represent the two principles at issue:

"In modern prosody the arrangement of the rhymes and the length of the lines in any rhymed metrical passage may be determined either by a fixed stanzaic law, or by a law infinitely deeper — by the law which impels the soul, in a state of poetic exultation, to seize hold of every kind of metrical aid, such as rhyme, cæsura, etc., for the purpose of accentuating and marking off each shade of emotion as it arises, regardless of any demands of stanza. . . . If a metrical passage does not gain immensely by being written independently of stanzaic law, it loses immensely; and for this reason, perhaps, that the great charm of the music of all verse, as distinguished from the music of prose, is inevitableness of cadence. In regular metres we enjoy the pleasure of feeling that the rhymes will inevitably fall under a recognized law of couplet or stanza. But if the passage flows independently of these, it must still flow inevitably — it must, in short, show that it is governed by another and a yet deeper force, the inevitableness of emotional expression."

This distinction between "stanzaic law" and "emotional law" is highly suggestive and not merely in its application to the metres of the famous regular and irregular odes of English verse. It applies also to the infinite variety of stanza-patterns which English

poetry has taken over from Latin and French
sources and developed through centuries of
experimentation, and it affords a key, as we
shall see in a moment, to some of the vexed
questions involved in free verse.

Take first the more familiar of the stanza
forms of English verse. They are conveniently indicated by using letters of the al-
phabet to correspond with each rhyme-sound,
whenever repeated.

Thus the rhymed couplet

> "Around their prows the ocean roars,
>   And chafes beneath their thousand oars"

may be marked as "four-stress iambic,"
rhyming *aa;* the heroic couplet

> "The zeal of fools offends at any time,
>   But most of all the zeal of fools in rhyme "

as five-stress iambic, rhyming *aa*. The familiar measure of English ballad poetry,

> "The King has written a braid letter,
>   And signed it wi' his hand,
>   And sent it to Sir Patrick Spence,
>   Was walking on the sand"

is alternating four-stress and three-stress
iambic, rhyming *ab cb*. The *In Memoriam*
stanza,

> "Now rings the woodland loud and long,
>   The distance takes a lovelier hue,
>   And drown'd in yonder living blue
> The lark becomes a sightless song"

is four-stress iambic, rhyming *ab ba.*

The Chaucerian stanza rhymes *a b a b b c c:*

> "'Loke up, I seye, and telle me what she is
> Anon, that I may gone aboute thi nede:
> Know iche hire ought? for my love telle me this;
> Thanne wolde I hopen the rather for to spede.'
> Tho gan the veyne of Troilus to blede,
> For he was hit, and wex alle rede for schame;
> 'Aha!' quod Pandare, 'here bygynneth game.'"

Byron's "ottava rima" rhymes *a b a b a b c c:*

> "A mighty mass of brick, and smoke, and ship-
>   ping,
>   Dirty and dusky, but as wide as eye
> Could reach, with here and there a sail just skip-
>   ping
>   In sight, then lost amidst the forestry
> Of masts; a wilderness of steeples peeping
>   On tiptoe through their sea-coal canopy;
> A huge, dun cupola, like a foolscap crown
> On a fool's head — and there is London Town!"

The Spenserian stanza rhymes *a b a b b c b c c,*
with an extra foot in the final line:

> "Hee had a faire companion of his way,
>   A goodly lady clad in scarlot red,
>   Purfled with gold and pearle of rich assay;
>   And like a Persian mitre on her hed

Shee wore, with crowns and owches garnished,
The which her lavish lovers to her gave:
Her wanton palfrey all was overspred
With tinsell trappings, woven like a wave,
Whose bridle rung with golden bels and bosses
    brave."

In considering these various groups of lines which we call stanzas it is clear that we have to do with thought-units as well as feeling-units, and that both thought-units and feeling-units should be harmonized, if possible, with the demands of beauty and variety of sound as represented by the rhymes. It is not absurd to speak of the natural "size" of poetic thoughts. Pope, for instance, often works with ideas of couplet size, just as Martial sometimes amused himself with ideas of a still smaller epigram size, or Omar Khayyám with thoughts and fancies that came in quatrain sizes. Many sonnets fail of effectiveness because the contained thought is too scanty or too full to receive adequate expression in the fourteen lines demanded by the traditional sonnet form. They are sometimes only quatrain ideas, blown up big with words to fill out the fourteen lines, or, on the contrary, as often with the Elizabethans, they are whole odes or elegies, remorselessly packed into the fashionable fourteen-line limit. No one who has given attention to the normal length of phrases and sentences doubts that there are natural "breathfuls" of words corresponding to the units of ideas; and when ideas are organized by emotion, there are waves, gusts, or ripples of words, matching the waves of feeling. In the ideal poetic "pattern," these waves of idea, feeling and rhythmic speech would coincide more or less completely; we should have a union of "emotional law" with "stanzaic law," the soul of poetry would find its perfect embodiment.

But if we turn the pages of any collection of English poetry, say the *Golden Treasury* or the *Oxford Book of English Verse*, we find something very different from this ideal embodiment of each poetic emotion in a form delicately moulded to the particular species of emotion revealed. We discover that precisely similar stanzaic patterns — like similar metrical patterns — are often used to express diametrically opposite feelings, — let us say, joy and sorrow, doubt and exultation, victory and defeat. The "common metre" of English hymnology is thus seen to be a rough

mould into which almost any kind of religious emotion may be poured. If "trochaic"
measures do not always trip it on a light
fantastic toe, neither do "iambic" measures
always pace sedately. Doubtless there is a
certain general fitness, in various stanza
forms, for this or that poetic purpose: the
stanzas employed by English or Scotch balladry are admittedly excellent for story-telling; Spenser's favorite stanza is unrivalled
for painting dream-pictures and rendering
dream-music, but less available for pure narration; Chaucer's seven-line stanza, so delicately balanced upon that fourth, pivotal
line, can paint a picture and tell a story too;
Byron's *ottava rima* has a devil-may-care
jauntiness, borrowed, it is true, from his
Italian models, but perfectly fitted to Byron's
own mood; the rhymed couplets of Pope
sting and glitter like his antitheses, and the
couplets of Dryden have their "resonance
like a great bronze coin thrown down on
marble"; each great artist in English verse,
in short, chooses by instinct the general
stanza form best suited to his particular
purpose, and then moulds its details with
whatever cunning he may possess.

But the significant point is this: "stanzaic law" makes for uniformity, for the endless repetition of the chosen pattern, which must still be recognized as a pattern, however subtly the artist modulates his details; and in adjusting the infinitely varied material of thought and feeling, phrase and image, picture and story to the fixed stanzaic design, there are bound to be gaps and patches, stretchings and foldings of the thought-stuff, — for even as in humble tailorcraft, this many-colored coat of poetry must be cut according to the cloth as well as according to the pattern. How many pages of even the *Oxford Book of English Verse* are free from some touch of feebleness, of redundancy, of constraint due to the remorseless requirements of the stanza? The line must be filled out, whether or not the thought is quite full enough for it; rhyme must match rhyme, even if the thought becomes as far-fetched as the rhyming word; the stanza, in short, demands one kind of perfection as a constantly repeated musical design, as beauty of form; and another kind of perfection as the expression of human emotion. Sometimes these two perfections

of "form" and "significance" are miraculously wedded, stanza after stanza, and we
have our "Ode to a Nightingale," or "Ode
to Autumn" as the result. (And perhaps
the best, even in this kind, are but shadows,
when compared with the absolute union of
truth and beauty as the poetic idea first took
rhythmic form in the brain of the poet.)

Yet more often lovers of poetry must content themselves, not with such "dictates of
nature" as these poems, but with approxi-
mations. Each stanzaic form has its con-
veniences, its "fatal facility," its natural fitness for singing a song or telling a story or
turning a thought over and over into music.
Intellectual readers will always like the epigrammatic "snap" of the couplet, and Spenser
will remain, largely because of his choice of
stanza, the "poet's poet." Perhaps the very
necessity of fitting rhymes together stimulates as much poetic activity as it discourages;
for many poets have testified that the delight
of rhyming adds energy to the imagination.
If, as Shelley said, "the mind in creation is
as a fading coal, which some invisible influence, like an inconstant wind, awakens to
transitory brightness," why may it not be

the breath of rhyme, as well as any other form of rhythmic energy, which quickens its drooping flame? And few poets, furthermore, will admit that they are really in bondage to their stanzas. They love to dance in these fetters, and even when wearing the same fetters as another poet, they nevertheless invent movements of their own, so that Mr. Masefield's "Chaucerian" stanzas are really not so much Chaucer's as Masefield's.

Each Ulysses makes and bends his own bow, after all; it is only the unsuccessful suitors for the honors of poetic craftsmanship who complain of its difficulties. Something of our contemporary impatience with fixed stanzaic forms is due perhaps to the failure to recognize that the greater poets succeed in making over every kind of poetic pattern in the act of employing it, just as a Chopin minuet differs from a Liszt minuet, although both composers are using the same fundamental form of dance-music. We must allow for the infinite variety of creative intention, technique and result. The true defence of rhyme and stanza against the arguments of extreme advocates of free verse is to

point out that rhyme and stanza are natural
structural devices for securing certain effects.
There are various types of bridges for crossing different kinds of streams; no one type of
bridge is always and everywhere the best. To
do away with rhyme and stanza is to renounce
some modes of poetic beauty; it is to resolve
that there shall be one less way of crossing the
stream. An advocate of freedom in the arts
may well admit that the artist may bridge his
particular stream in any way he can, — or he
may ford it or swim it or go over in an air-
plane if he chooses. But some method must
be found of getting his ideas and emotions "across" into the mind and feelings of
the readers of his poetry. If this can adequately be accomplished without recourse to
rhyme and stanza, very well; there is *Paradise Lost*, for instance, and *Hamlet*. But
here we are driven back again upon the countless varieties of artistic intention and craftsmanship and effect. Each method — and
there are as many methods as there are poets
and far more, for craftsmen like Milton and
Tennyson try hundreds of methods in their
time — is only a medium through which the
artist is endeavoring to attain a special re-

sult.   It is one way — only one, and perhaps
not the best way — of trying to cross the
stream.

4. Free Verse

Recalling now the discussion of the rhythms
of prose in the previous chapter, and remembering that rhyme and stanza are special
forms of reinforcing the impulse of rhythm,
what shall be said of free verse?   It belongs,
unquestionably, in that "neutral zone" which
some readers, in Dr. Patterson's phrase, instinctively appropriate as "prose experience,"
and others as "verse experience."   It re-
nounces metre — or rather endeavors to renounce it, for it does not always succeed.   It
professes to do away with rhyme and stanza,
although it may play cunningly upon the
sounds of like and unlike words, and it may
arrange phrases into poetic paragraphs, which,
aided by the art of typography, secure a kind
of stanzaic effect.   It cannot, however, do
away with the element of rhythm, with ordered time.   The moment free verse ceases to
be felt as rhythmical, it ceases to be felt as
poetry.   This is admitted by its advocates
and its opponents alike.   The real question at

issue then, is the manner in which free verse
may secure the effects of rhythmic unity and
variety, without, on the one hand, resorting
to the obvious rhythms of prose, or on the
other hand, without repeating the recognized
patterns of verse. There are many competent critics who maintain with Edith Wyatt
that "on an earth where there is nothing to
wear but clothes, nothing to eat but food,
there is also nothing to read but prose and
poetry." "According to the results of our
experiments," testifies Dr. Patterson, "there
is no psychological meaning to claims for a
third *genre* between regular verse and prose,
except in the sense of a jumping back and
forth from one side of the fence to the other."[1]
And in the preface to his second edition, after
having listened to Miss Amy Lowell's read-
ings of free verse, Dr. Patterson remarks:
"What is achieved, as a rule, in Miss Lowell's
case, is emotional prose, emphatically phrased,
excellent and moving. *Spaced prose*, we may
call it."

Now "spaced prose" is a useful expression,
inasmuch as it calls attention to the careful
emphasis and balance of phrases which make

[1] *The Rhythm of Prose*, p. 77.

up so much of the rhetorical structure of free
verse, and it also serves to remind us of the
part which typography plays in "spacing"
these phrases, and stressing for the eye their
curves and "returns." But we are all agreed
that typographical appeals to the eye are infinitely deceptive in blurring the distinction
between verse and prose, and that the trained
ear must be the only arbiter as to poetical and
pseudo-poetical effects. Ask a lover of Walt
Whitman whether "spaced prose" is the
right label for " Out of the Cradle Endlessly
Rocking," and he will scoff at you. He will
maintain that following the example of the
rich broken rhythms of the English Bible, the
example of Ossian, Blake, and many another
European experimenter during the Romantic
epoch, Whitman really succeeded in elaborat-
ing a mode of poetical expression, nearer for
the most part to recitative than to aria, yet
neither pure declamation nor pure song: a
unique embodiment of passionate feeling, a
veritable "neutral zone," which refuses to let
itself be annexed to either "prose" or "verse"
as those terms are ordinarily understood, but
for which "free verse" is precisely the right
expression. *Leaves of Grass* (1855) remains

the most interesting of all experiments with free verse, written as it was by an artist whose natural rhythmical endowment was extraordinary, and whose technical curiosity and patience in modulating his tonal effects was unwearied by failures and undiscouraged by popular neglect. But the case for free verse does not, after all, stand or fall with Walt Whitman. His was merely the most powerful poetic personality among the countless artificers who have endeavored to produce rhythmic and tonal beauty through new structural devices.

Readers who are familiar with the experiments of contemporary poets will easily recognize four prevalent types of "free verse":

(a) Sometimes what is printed as "free verse" is nothing but prose disguised by the art of typography, i.e. judged by the ear, it is made up wholly of the rhythms of prose.

(b) Sometimes the prose rhythms predominate, without excluding a mixture of the recognized rhythms of verse.

(c) Sometimes verse rhythms predominate, and even fixed metrical feet are allowed to appear here and there.

(d) Sometimes verse rhythms and metres

are used exclusively, although in new combinations which disguise or break up the metrical pattern.

A parody by F. P. A. in *The Conning Tower* affords a convenient illustration of the "a" type:

ADD SPOON RIVER ANTHOLOGY

Peoria, Ill., Jan. 24. — The Spoon River levee, which protected thousands of acres of farm land below Havana, Ill., fifty-five miles south of here, broke this morning.

A score or more of families fled to higher ground. The towns of Havana, Lewiston and Duncan Mills are isolated. Two dozen head of cattle are reported drowned on the farm of John Himpshell, near Havana. — Associated Press dispatch.

Edgar Lee Masters wrote a lot of things
About me and the people who
Inhabited my banks.
All of them, all are sleeping on the hill.
Herbert Marshall, Amelia Garrick, Enoch Dunlap,
Ida Frickey, Alfred Moir, Archibald Highbie and
    the rest.
Me he gave no thought to —
Unless, perhaps, to think that I, too, was asleep.
Those people on the hill, I thought,
Have grown famous;
But nobody writes about me.
I was only a river, you know,
But I had my pride,
So one January day I overflowed my banks;

It was n't much of a flood, Mr. Masters,
But it put me on the front page
And in the late dispatches
Of the Associated Press.

It is clear that the quoted words of the Associated Press dispatch from Peoria are pure prose, devoid of rhythmical pattern, devoted to a plain statement of fact. So it is with the imaginary speech of the River. Not until the borrowed fourth line:

"All of them, all are sleeping on the hill,"

do we catch the rhythm (and even the metre) of verse, and F. P. A. is here imitating Mr. Masters's way of introducing a strongly rhythmical and even metrical line into a passage otherwise flatly "prosaic" in its time-intervals. But "free verse" adopts many other cadences of English prose besides this "formless" structure which goes with matter-of-fact statement. It also reproduces the neat, polished, perhaps epigrammatic sentence which crystallizes a fact or a generalization; the more emotional and "moving" period resulting from heightened feeling, and finally the frankly imitative and ornamented cadences of descriptive and highly impassioned prose. Let us take some illustrations from

Sidney Lanier's *Poem Outlines*, a posthumously published collection of some of his sketches for poems, "jotted in pencil on the backs of envelopes, on the margins of musical programmes, or little torn scraps of paper."

"The United States in two hundred years has made Emerson out of a witch-burner."

This is polished, graphic prose. Here is an equally graphic, but more impassioned sentence, with the staccato rhythm and the alliterative emphasis of good angry speech:

To the Politicians

"You are servants. Your thoughts are the thoughts of cooks curious to skim perquisites from every pan, your quarrels are the quarrels of scullions who fight for the privilege of cleaning the pot with most leavings in it, your committees sit upon the landings of back-stairs, and your quarrels are the quarrels of kitchens."

But in the following passage, apparently a first draft for some lines in *Hymns of the Marshes*, Lanier takes a strongly rhythmical, heavily punctuated type of prose, as if he were writing a Collect:

"The courses of the wind, and the shifts thereof, as also what way the clouds go; and that which is happening a long way off; and the full face of the sun; and the bow of the Milky Way from end to

end; as also the small, the life of the fiddler-crab,
and the household of the marsh-hen; and more,
the translation of black ooze into green blade of
marsh-grass, which is as if filth bred heaven: This
a man seeth upon the marsh."

In that rhapsody of the marsh there is no
recognizable metrical scheme, in spite of the
plainly marked rhythm, but in the following
symbolic sketch the imitation of the horse's
ambling introduces an element of regular
metre:

"Ambling, ambling round the ring,
  Round the ring of daily duty,
Leap, Circus-rider, man, through the paper hoop
    of death,
— Ah, lightest thou, beyond death, on this same
    slow-ambling, padded horse of life."

And finally, in such fragments as the following, Lanier uses a regular metre of "English
verse" — it is true with a highly irregular
third line —

"And then
  A gentle violin mated with the flute,
  And both flew off into a wood of harmony,
  Two doves of tone."

It is clear that an artist in words, in jotting
down thoughts and images as they first emerge,
may instinctively use language which is subtly

blended of verse and prose, like many rhapsodical passages in the private journals of Thoreau and Emerson. When duly elaborated, these passages usually become, in the hands of the greater artists, either one thing or the other, i.e. unmistakable prose or unmistakable verse. But it remains true, I think, that there is another artistic instinct which impels certain poets to blend the types in the endeavor to reach a new and hybrid beauty.[1]

Take these illustrations of the "b" type — i.e. prose rhythms predominant, with some admixture of the rhythms of verse:

"I hear footsteps over my head all night.
They come and go. Again they come and again
they go all night.
They come one eternity in four paces and they go
one eternity in four paces, and between the
coming and the going there is Silence and
Night and the Infinite.
For infinite are the nine feet of a prison cell, and
endless is the march of him who walks between the yellow brick wall and the red
iron gate, thinking things that cannot be
chained and cannot be locked, but that
wander far away in the sunlit world, in their
wild pilgrimage after destined goals.

[1] Some examples of recent verse are printed in the "Notes and Illustrations" for this chapter.

Throughout the restless night I hear the footsteps
over my head.
Who walks? I do not know. It is the phantom
of the jail, the sleepless brain, a man, the
man, the Walker.
One — two — three — four; four paces and the
wall." [1]

Or take this:

"Jerusalem a handful of ashes blown by the wind,
extinct,
The Crusaders' streams of shadowy midnight
troops sped with the sunrise,
Amadis, Tancred, utterly gone, Charlemagne,
Roland, Oliver gone,
Palmerin, ogre, departed, vanish'd the turrets that
Usk from its waters reflected,
Arthur vanish'd with all his knights, Merlin and
Lancelot and Galahad, all gone, dissolv'd
utterly like an exhalation;
Pass'd! Pass'd! for us, forever pass'd, that once so
mighty world, now void, inanimate, phan-
tom world,
Embroider'd, dazzling, foreign world, with all its
gorgeous legends, myths,
Its kings and castles proud, its priests and warlike
lords and courtly dames,
Pass'd to its charnel vault, coffin'd with crown and
armor on,
Blazon'd with Shakspere's purple page,
And dirged by Tennyson's sweet sad rhyme." [2]

[1] From Giovanitti's "The Walker."
[2] Whitman, "Song of the Exposition."

Here are examples of the "c" type — i.e.
predominant verse rhythms, with occasional
emphasis upon metrical feet:

"Would you hear of an old-time sea-fight?
Would you learn who won by the light of the moon
      and stars?
List to the yarn, as my grandmother's father the
      sailor told it to me.

"Our foe was no skulk in his ship I tell you,
      (said he,)
His was the surly English pluck, and there is no
      tougher or truer, and never was, and never
      will be;
Along the lower'd eve he came horribly raking us.

  .   .   .   .

"Our frigate takes fire,
The other asks if we demand quarter?
If our colors are struck and the fighting done?

"Now I laugh content, for I hear the voice of
      my little captain,
We have not struck, he composedly cries, *we have
      just begun our part of the fighting.*

  .   .   .   .

"One of the pumps has been shot away, it is
      generally thought we are sinking.

" Serene stands the little captain,
He is not hurried, his voice is neither high nor low,
His eyes give more light to us than our battle-
      lanterns.

"Toward twelve there in the beams of the moon
    they surrender to us."[1]

Read William Blake's description of the
Bastille, in his recently printed poem on "The
French Revolution":

"'Seest thou yonder dark castle, that moated
    around, keeps this city of Paris in awe?
Go, command yonder tower, saying: "Bastille,
    depart! and take thy shadowy course;
Overstep the dark river, thou terrible tower, and
    get thee up into the country ten miles.
And thou black southern prison, move along the
    dusky road to Versailles; there
Frown on the gardens — and, if it obey and de-
    part, then the King will disband
This war-breathing army; but, if it refuse, let the
    Nation's Assembly thence learn
That this army of terrors, that prison of horrors,
    are the bands of the murmuring kingdom."'

"Like the morning star arising above the black
    waves, when a shipwrecked soul sighs for
    morning,
Thro' the ranks, silent, walk'd the Ambassador
    back to the Nation's Assembly, and told
The unwelcome message. Silent they heard; then
    a thunder roll'd round loud and louder;
Like pillars of ancient halls and ruins of times re-
    mote, they sat.
Like a voice from the dim pillars Mirabeau rose;
    the thunders subsided away;

[1] Whitman, "Song of Myself."

A rushing of wings around him was heard as he
    brighten'd, and cried out aloud:
'Where is the General of the Nation?' The walls
    re-echo'd: 'Where is the General of the
    Nation?'"

And here are passages made up exclusively of
the rhythms and metres of verse, in broken
or disguised patterns ("d" type):

"Under a stagnant sky,
Gloom out of gloom uncoiling into gloom,
The River, jaded and forlorn,
Welters and wanders wearily — wretchedly — on;
Yet in and out among the ribs
Of the old skeleton bridge, as in the piles
Of some dead lake-built city, full of skulls,
Worm-worn, rat-riddled, mouldy with memories,
Lingers to babble, to a broken tune
(Once, O the unvoiced music of my heart!)
So melancholy a soliloquy
It sounds as it might tell
The secret of the unending grief-in-grain,
The terror of Time and Change and Death,
That wastes this floating, transitory world." [1]

Or take this:

"They see the ferry
On the broad, clay-laden
Lone Chorasmian stream; — thereon,
With snort and strain,
Two horses, strongly swimming, tow
The ferry-boat, with woven ropes

[1] W. E. Henley, "To James McNeill Whistler."

To either bow
Firm-harness'd by the mane; a chief,
With shout and shaken spear,
Stands at the prow, and guides them; but astern
The cowering merchants in long robes
Sit pale beside their wealth
Of silk-bales and of balsam-drops,
Of gold and ivory,
Of turquoise-earth and amethyst,
Jasper and chalcedony,
And milk-barr'd onyx-stones.
The loaded boat swings groaning
In the yellow eddies;
The Gods behold them." [1]

5. *Discovery and Rediscovery*

It is not pretended that the four types of free verse which have been illustrated are marked by clear-cut generic differences. They shade into one another. But they are all based upon a common sensitiveness to the effects of rhythmic prose, a common restlessness under what is felt to be the restraint of metre and rhyme, and a common endeavor to break down the conventional barrier which separates the characteristic beauty of prose speech from the characteristic beauty of verse. In this endeavor to obliterate boundary lines, to secure in one art the effects

[1] Arnold, "The Strayed Reveller."

hitherto supposed to be the peculiar property of another, free verse is only one more evidence of the widespread "confusion of the genres" which marks contemporary artistic effort. It is possible, with the classicists, to condemn outright this blurring of values.[1] One may legitimately maintain, with Edith Wyatt, that the traditional methods of English verse are to the true artist not oppressions but liberations. She calls it "a fallacious idea that all individual and all realistic expression in poetry is annulled by the presence of distinctive musical discernment, by the movement of rhyme with its keen heightening of the impulse of rhythm, by the word-shadows of assonance, by harmonies, overtones and the still beat of ordered time, subconsciously perceived but precise as the sense of the symphony leader's flying baton. To readers, to writers for whom the tonal quality of every language is an intrinsic value these faculties of poetry serve not at all as cramping oppressions, but as great liberations for the communication of truth."[2] But many practitioners of free verse would reply that this is not a matter

[1] See, for instance, Irving Babbitt, *The New Laokoon.* Houghton Mifflin Company, 1910.

[2] *New Republic*, August 24, 1918.

for theorizing, but of individual preference, and that in their endeavor to communicate new modes of feeling, new aspects of beauty, they have a right to the use of new forms, even if those new forms be compounded out of the wreck of old ones. This argument for freedom of experiment is unanswerable; the true test of its validity lies in the results secured. That free verse has now and then succeeded in creating lovely flowering hybrids seems to me as indubitable as the magical tricks which Mr. Burbank has played with flowers and fruits. But the smiling Dame Nature sets her inexorable limits to "Burbanking"; she allows it to go about so far, and no farther. Freakish free verse, like freakish plants and animals, gets punished by sterility. Some of the "imagist" verse patterns are uniquely and intricately beautiful. Wrought in a medium which is neither wholly verse nor wholly prose, but which borrows some of the beauty peculiar to each art, they are their own excuse for being. And nevertheless they may not prove fertile. It may be that they have been produced by "pushing a medium farther than it will go."

It must be admitted, furthermore, that a

great deal of contemporary free verse has been
written by persons with an obviously incom-
plete command over the resources of expression. Max Eastman has called it "Lazy
Verse," the product of "aboriginal indolence";
and he adds this significant distinction, "In
all arts it is the tendency of those who are
ungrown to confuse the expression of intense
feeling with the intense expression of feeling
— which last is all the world will long listen
to." Shakspere, Milton, Keats are masters
of concentrated, intensest expression: their
verse, at its best, is structural as an oak.
Those of us who have read with keen momen-
tary enjoyment thousands of pages of the
"New Verse," are frequently surprised to
find how little of it stamps itself upon the
memory. Intense feeling has gone into these
formless forms, very certainly, but the medium soaks up the feeling like blotting-paper.
In order to live, poetry must be plastic, a
stark embodiment of emotion, and not a solution of emotion.

That fragile, transient fashions of expression have their own evanescent type of beauty
no one who knows the history of Euphuism
will deny. And much of the New Verse is

Euphuistic, not merely in its self-conscious cleverness, its delightful toying with words and phrases for their own sake, its search of novel cadences and curves, but also in its naïve pleasure in rediscovering and parodying what the ancients had discovered long before. "Polyphonic prose," for instance, as announced and illustrated by Mr. Paul Fort and Miss Amy Lowell, is prose that makes use of all the "voices" of poetry, — viz. metre, *vers libre*, assonances, alliteration, rhyme and return. "Metrical verse," says Miss Lowell in the Preface to *Can Grande's Castle*, "has one set of laws, cadenced verse another; 'polyphonic prose' can go from one to the other in the same poem with no sense of incongruity. . . . I finally decided to base my form upon the long, flowing cadence of oratorical prose. The variations permitted to this cadence enable the poet to change the more readily into those of *vers libre*, or even to take the regular beat of metre, should such a marked time seem advisable. . . . Rhyme is employed to give a richness of effect, to heighten the musical feeling of a passage, but . . . the rhymes should seldom come at the ends of the cadences. . . . Return in 'polyphonic prose' is

usually achieved by the recurrence of a
dominant thought or image, coming in irreg-
ularly and in varying words, but still giving
the spherical effect which I have frequently
spoken of as imperative in all poetry."

Now every one of these devices is at least
as old as Isocrates. It was in this very fashion
that Euphues and his Friends delighted to
serve and return their choicest tennis balls of
Elizabethan phrase. But little De Quincey
could pull out the various stops of polyphonic prose even more cleverly than John
Lyly; and if one will read the admirable description of St. Mark's in *Can Grande's Castle*,
and then re-read Ruskin's description of St.
Mark's, he will find that the Victorian's
orchestration of many-voiced prose does not
suffer by comparison.

Yet though it is true enough of the arts, as
Chaucer wrote suavely long ago, that "There
nys no newe thing that is not olde," we must
remember that the arts are always profiting
by their naïve rediscoveries. It is more
important that the thing should seem new
than that it should really be new, and the
fresh sense of untried possibilities, the feeling
that much land remains to be possessed, has

given our contemporaries the spirits and the satisfactions of the pioneer. What matters it that a few antiquaries can trace on old maps the very rivers and harbors which the New Verse believed itself to be exploring for the first time? Poetry does not live by anti-quarianism, but by the passionate conviction that all things are made new through the creative imagination.

> "Have the elder races halted?
> Do they droop and end their lesson, wearied over
>   there beyond the seas?
> We take up the task eternal, and the burden and
>   the lesson,
>   Pioneers! O pioneers!"

PART II

THE LYRIC IN PARTICULAR

"O hearken, love, the battle-horn!
The triumph clear, the silver scorn!
O hearken where the echoes bring,
Down the grey disastrous morn,
Laughter and rallying!"

WILLIAM VAUGHN MOODY

CHAPTER VII

THE FIELD OF LYRIC POETRY

"'Lyrical,' it may be said, implies a form of musical utterance in words governed by overmastering emotion and set free by a powerfully concordant rhythm."

ERNEST RHYS, *Lyric Poetry*

THAT "confusion of the genres" which characterizes so much of contemporary art has not obliterated the ancient division of poetry into three chief types, namely, lyric, epic and dramatic. We still mean by these words very much what the Greeks meant: a "lyric" is something sung, an "epic" tells a story, a "drama" sets characters in action. Corresponding to these general purposes of the three kinds of poetry, is the difference which Watts-Dunton has discussed so suggestively: namely, that in the lyric the author reveals himself fully, while in the "epic" or narrative poem the author himself is but partly revealed, and in the drama the author is hidden behind his characters. Or, putting this difference in another way, the same critic points out that the true dramatists possess "absolute" vision, i.e. unconditioned by the personal impulses of

the poet himself, whereas the vision of the
lyrist is "relative," conditioned by his own
situation and mood. The pure lyrist, says
Watts-Dunton, has one voice and sings one
tune; the epic poets and quasi-dramatists
have one voice but can sing several tunes,
while the true dramatists, with their objective, "absolute" vision of the world, have
many tongues and can sing in all tunes.

1. A Rough Classification

Passing over the question of the historical
origins of those various species of poetry, such
as the relation of early hymnic songs and
hero-songs to the epic, and the relation of
narrative material and method to the drama,
let us try to arrange in some sort of order the
kinds of poetry with which we are familiar.
Suppose we follow Watts-Dunton's hint, and
start, as if it were from a central point, with
the Pure Lyric, the expression of the Ego in
song. Shelley's " Stanzas Written in Dejection near Naples," Coleridge's "Ode to Dejection," Wordsworth's "She dwelt among
the untrodden ways," Tennyson's "Break —
Break" will serve for illustrations. These
are subjective, personal poems. Their vision

is "relative" to the poet's actual circumstances. Yet in a "dramatic lyric" like Byron's "Isles of Greece" or Tennyson's "Sir Galahad" it is clear that the poet's vision is not occupied primarily with himself, but with another person. In a dramatic monologue like Tennyson's "Simeon Stylites" or Browning's "The Bishop orders his Tomb in St. Praxed's Church" it is not Tennyson and Browning themselves who are talking, but imaginary persons viewed objectively, as far as Tennyson and Browning were capable of such objectivity. The next step would be the Drama, preoccupied with characters in action — the "world of men," in short, and not the personal subjective world of the highly sensitized lyric poet.

Let us now move away from that pure lyric centre in another direction. In a traditional ballad like "Sir Patrick Spens," a modern ballad like Tennyson's "The Revenge," or Coleridge's "Ancient Mariner," is not the poet's vision becoming objectified, directed upon events or things outside of the circle of his own subjective emotion? In modern epic verse, like Tennyson's "Morte d'Arthur," Arnold's "Sohrab and Rustum," Morris's

"Sigurd the Volsung," and certainly in the
"Æneid" and the "Song of Roland," the
poet sinks his own personality, as far as possible, in the objective narration of events.   And
in like manner, the poet may turn from the
world of action to the world of repose, and
portray Nature as enfolding and subduing the
human element in his picture.   In Keats's
"Ode to Autumn," Shelley's "Autumn," in
Wordsworth's "Solitary Reaper," Browning's "Where the Mayne Glideth," we find
poets absorbed in the external scene or object
and striving to paint it.   It is true that the
born lyrists betray themselves constantly,
that they suffuse both the world of repose and
the world of action with the coloring of their
own unquiet spirits.   They cannot keep themselves wholly out of the story they are telling
or the picture they are painting; and it is for
this reason that we speak of "lyrical" passages even in the great objective dramas,
passages colored with the passionate personal
feelings of the poet.   For he cannot be wholly
"absolute" even if he tries: he will invent
favorite characters and make them the mouth-
piece of his own fancies: he will devise favorite
situations, and use them to reveal his moral

judgment of men and women, and his general
theory of human life.

2. Definitions

While we must recognize, then, that the
meaning of the word "lyrical" has been
broadened so as to imply, frequently, a quality
of poetry rather than a mere form of poetry,
let us go back for a moment to the original
significance of the word. Derived from
"lyre," it meant first a song written for musical accompaniment, say an ode of Pindar;
then a poem whose form suggests this original
musical accompaniment; then, more loosely,
a poem which has the quality of music, and
finally, purely personal poetry.[1] "All songs,
all poems following classical lyric forms; all
short poems expressing the writer's moods
and feelings in rhythm that suggests music,
are to be considered lyrics," says Professor
Reed.   "The lyric is concerned with the
poet, his thoughts, his emotions, his moods,
and his passions. . . . With the lyric subjective poetry begins," says Professor Schelling.

---

[1] See the definitions in John Erskine's *Elizabethan Lyric*, E. B.
Reed's *English Lyrical Poetry*, Ernest Rhys's *Lyric Poetry*, F. E.
Schelling's *The English Lyric*, John Drinkwater's *The Lyric*,
C. E. Whitmore in *Pub. Mod. Lang. Ass.*, December, 1918.

"The characteristic of the lyric is that it is the product of 'the pure poetic energy unassociated with other energies," says Mr. Drinkwater. These are typical recent definitions. Francis T. Palgrave, in the Preface to the *Golden Treasury of English Songs and Lyrics*, while omitting to stress the elements of musical quality and of personal emotion, gives a working rule for anthologists which has proved highly useful. He held the term "lyrical" "to imply that each poem shall turn on a single thought, feeling or situation." The critic Scherer also gave an admirable practical definition when he remarked that the lyric "*reflects* a situation or a desire." Keats's sonnet "On first looking into Chapman's Homer," Charles Kingsley's "Airlie Beacon" and Whitman's "O Captain! My Captain!" (*Oxford Book of Verse*, Nos. 634, 739 and 743) are suggestive illustrations of Scherer's dictum.

3. General Characteristics

But the lyric, however it may be defined, has certain general characteristics which are indubitable. The lyric "vision," that is to say, the experience, thought, emotion which gives its peculiar quality to lyric verse, making it "simple, sensuous, passionate" beyond other species of poetry, is always marked by freshness, by egoism, and by genuineness.

To the lyric poet all must seem new; each sunrise "*herrlich wie am ersten Tag.*" "Thou know'st 't is common," says Hamlet's mother, speaking of his father's death, "Why seems it so particular with thee?" But to men of the lyrical temperament everything is "particular." Age does not alter their exquisite sense of the novelty of experience. Tennyson's lines on "Early Spring," written at seventy-four, Browning's "Never the Time and the Place" written at seventy-two, Goethe's love-lyrics written when he was eighty, have all the delicate bloom of adolescence. Sometimes this freshness seems due in part to the poet's early place in the development of his national literature: he has had, as it were, the first chance at his particular subject. There were countless springs, of course, before a nameless poet, about 1250, wrote one of the first English lyrics for which we have a contemporary musical score:

> "Sumer is icumen in,
> Lhude sing cuccu."

But the words thrill the reader, even now, as
he hears in fancy that cuckoo's song,

> "Breaking the silence of the seas
> Beyond the farthest Hebrides."

Or, the lyric poet may have the luck to write
at a period when settled, stilted forms of
poetical expression are suddenly done away
with.   Perhaps he may have helped in the
emancipation, like Wordsworth and Coleridge in the English Romantic Revival, or
Victor Hugo in the France of 1830.   The new
sense of the poetic possibilities of language
reacts upon the imaginative vision itself.
Free verse, in our own time, has profited by
this rejuvenation of the poetic vocabulary,
by new phrases and cadences to match new
moods.   Sometimes an unwonted philosophical insight makes all things new to the poet
who possesses it.   Thus Emerson's vision of
the "Eternal Unity," or Browning's conception of Immortality, afford the very stuff out
of which poetry may be wrought.   Every new
experience, in short, like falling in love, like
having a child, like getting "converted,"[1]
gives the lyric poet this rapturous sense of
living in a world hitherto unrealized.   The

[1] See William James, *The Varieties of Religious Experience.*

old truisms of the race become suddenly
"particular" to him.   "As for man, his days
are as grass.   As a flower of the field, so he
flourisheth."   That was first a "lyric cry"
out of the depths of some fresh individual
experience.   It has become stale through
repetition, but many a man, listening to those
words read at the burial of a friend, has
seemed, in his passionate sense of loss, to
hear them for the first time.

Egoism is another mark of the lyric poet.
"Of every poet of this class," remarks Watts-
Dunton, "it may be said that his mind to
him ' a kingdom is,' and that the smaller the
poet the bigger to him is that kingdom."
He celebrates himself.   Contemporary lyrists
have left no variety of physical sensation un-
noted: they tell us precisely how they feel and
look when they take their morning tub.   Far
from avoiding that "pathetic fallacy" which
Ruskin analysed in a famous chapter,[1] and
which attributes to the external world qualities which belong only to the mind itself, they
revel in it.   "Day, like our souls, is *fiercely
dark*," sang Elliott, the Corn-Law Rhymer.
Hamlet, it will be remembered, could be

[1] *Modern Painters*, vol. 3, chap. 12.

lyrical enough upon occasion, but he retained
the power of distinguishing between things as
they actually were and things as they appeared
to him in his weakness and his melancholy.
"This goodly frame, the earth, seems *to me* a
sterile promontory; this most excellent can-
opy, the air, look you, this brave o'erhanging
firmament, this majestical roof fretted with
golden fire, why, it appears no other thing *to
me* than a foul and pestilent congregation of
vapors.   What a piece of work is a man! how
noble in reason! how infinite in faculty! . . .
And yet, *to me*, what is this quintessence of
dust?"

Nevertheless this lyric egoism has certain
moods in which the individual identifies himself with his family or tribe:

> "O Keith of Ravelstone,
> The sorrows of thy line!"

School and college songs are often, in reality,
tribal lyrics.   The choruses of Greek tragedies
dealing with the guilt and punishment of a
family, the Hebrew lyrics chanting, like "The
Song of Deborah," the fortunes of a great
fight, often broaden their sympathies so as to
include, as in "The Persians" of Æschylus,
the glory or the downfall of a race.   And this

sense of identification with a nation or race
implies no loss, but often an amplification
of the lyric impulse. Alfred Noyes's songs
about the English, D'Annunzio's and Hugo's
splendid chants of the Latin races, Kipling's
glorification of the White Man, lose nothing
of their lyric quality because of their nationalistic or racial inspiration. Read Wilfrid
Blunt's sonnet on "Gibraltar" (*Oxford Book
of Verse*, No. 821):

"Ay, this is the famed rock which Hercules
And Goth and Moor bequeath'd us. At this door
England stands sentry. God! to hear the shrill
Sweet treble of her fifes upon the breeze,
And at the summons of the rock gun's roar
To see her red coats marching from the hill!"

Are patriotic lyrics of this militant type
destined to disappear, as Tolstoy believed
they ought to disappear, with the breaking-
down of the barriers of nationality, or rather
with the coming of

"One common wave of thought and joy,
   Lifting mankind again"

over the barriers of nationality? Certainly
there is already a type of purely humanita-
rian, altruistic lyric, where the poet instinctively thinks in terms of "us men" rather

than of "I myself." It appeared long ago in that rebellious "Titanic" verse which took the side of oppressed mortals as against the unjust gods. Tennyson's "Lotos-Eaters" is a modern echo of this defiant or despairing cry of the "ill-used race of men." The songs of Burns reveal ever-widening circles of sympathy, — pure personal egoism, then songs of the family and of clan and of country-side, then passion for Scotland, and finally this fierce peasant affection for his own passes into the glorious

> "It 's comin' yet for a' that,
> That man to man the world o'er
> Shall brithers be for a' that."

One other general characteristic of the lyric mood needs to be emphasized, namely, its *genuineness.* It is impossible to feign

> "the lyric gush,
> And the wing-power, and the rush
> Of the air."

Second-rate, imitative singers may indeed assume the rôle of genuine lyric poets, but they cannot play it without detection. It is literally true that natural lyrists like Sappho, Burns, Goethe, Heine, "sing as the bird sings." Once endowed with the lyric tem-

perament and the command of technique,
their cry of love or longing, of grief or patriotism, is the inevitable resultant from a real
situation or desire.   Sometimes, like children, they do not tell us very clearly what
they are crying about, but it is easy to discover whether they are, like children, "making believe."

4. The Objects of the Lyric Vision

Let us look more closely at some of the
objects of the lyric vision; the sources or
material, that is to say, for the lyric emotion.
Goethe's often-quoted classification is as
convenient as any: the poet's vision, he says,
may be directed upon Nature, Man or God.

And first, then, upon Nature.   One characteristic of lyric poetry is the clearness with
which single details or isolated objects in
Nature may be visualized and reproduced.
The modern reflective lyric, it is true, often
depends for its power upon some philosophical generalization from a single instance,
like Emerson's "Rhodora" or Wordsworth's
"Small Celandine."   It may even attempt
a sort of logical or pseudo-logical deduction
from given premises, like Browning's famous

> "Morning's at seven;
>   The hillside's dew-pearled;
>   The lark's on the wing:
>   The snail's on the thorn;
>   God's in his Heaven —
>   *All's right with the world!*"

The imagination cannot be denied this right to synthesize and to interpret, and nevertheless Nature offers even to the most unphilosophical her endless profusion of objects that awaken delight.   She does not insist that the lyric poet should generalize unless he pleases. Moth and snail and skylark, daisy and field-mouse and water-fowl, seized by an eye that is quick to their poetic values, their interest to men, furnish material enough for lyric feeling.   The fondness of Romantic poets for isolating a single object has been matched in our day by the success of the Imagists in painting a single aspect of some phenomenon —

> 'Light as the shadow of the fish
>   That falls through the pale green water —"

any aspect, in short, provided it affords the "romantic quiver," the quick, keen sense of the beauty in things.   What an art-critic said of the painter W. M. Chase applies equally well to many contemporary Imagists who use the forms of lyric verse: "He saw the world as a display of beautiful surfaces which challenged his skill. It was enough to set him painting to note the nacreous skin of a fish, or the satiny bloom of fruit, or the wind-smoothed dunes about Shinnecock, or the fine specific olive of a woman's face. . . . He took objects quite at their face value, and rarely invested them with the tenderness, mystery and understanding that comes from meditation and remembered feelings. . . . We get in him a fine, bare vision, and must not expect therewith much contributary enrichment from mind and mood." [1] Our point is that this "fine, bare vision" is often enough for a lyric. It has no time for epic breadth of detail, for the rich accumulation of harmonious images which marks Arnold's "Sohrab and Rustum" or Keats's "Eve of St. Agnes."

The English Romantic poets were troubled about the incursion of scientific fact into the poet's view of nature. The awful rainbow in heaven might be turned, they thought, through the curse of scientific knowledge, into the "dull catalogue of common things."

[1] *The Nation*, November 2, 1916.

But Wordsworth was wiser than this.   He
saw that if the scientific fact were emotionalized, it could still serve as the stuff of
poetry.   Facts could be transformed into
truths.   No aspect of Tennyson's lyricism is
more interesting than his constant employ-
ment of the newest scientific knowledge of
his day, for instance, in geology, chemistry
and astronomy.   He set his facts to music.
Eugene Lee-Hamilton's poignant sonnet about
immortality is an illustration of the ease with
which a lyric poet may find material in scientific fact, if appropriated and made rich by
feeling.[1]

If lyric poetry shows everywhere this tendency to humanize its "bare vision" of Nature, it is also clear that the lyric, as the
most highly personalized species of poetry,
exhibits an infinite variety of visions of
human life.   Any anthology will illustrate
the range of observation, the complexity of
situations and desires, the constant changes
in key, as the lyric attempts to interpret this
or that aspect of human emotion.   Take for
example, the Elizabethan love-lyric.   Here
is a single human passion, expressing itself in

[1] Quoted in chap. VIII, section 7.

the moods and lyric forms of one brief generation of our literature. Yet what variety of personal accent, what kaleidoscopic shiftings of mind and imagination, what range of lyric beauty! Or take the passion for the wider interests of Humanity, expressed in the lyrics of Schiller and Burns, running deep and turbid through Revolutionary and Romantic verse, and still coloring — perhaps now more strongly than ever — the stream of twentieth-century poetry. Here is a type of lyric emotion where self-consciousness is lost, absorbed in the wider consciousness of kinship, in the dawning recognition of the oneness of the blood and fate of all nations of the earth.

The purest type of lyric vision is indicated in the third word of Goethe's triad. It is the vision of God. Here no physical fact intrudes or mars. Here thought, if it be complete thought, is wholly emotionalized. Such transcendent vision, as in the Hebrew lyrists and in Dante, is itself worship, and the lyric cry of the most consummate artist among English poets of the last generation is simply an echo of the ancient voices:

"Hallowed be Thy Name — Hallelujah!"

If Tennyson could not phrase anew the ineffable, it is no wonder that most hymn-writers fail. They are trying to express in conventionalized religious terminology and in "long and short metre" what can with difficulty be expressed at all, and if at all, by the unconscious art of the Psalms or by a sustained metaphor, like "Crossing the Bar" or the "Recessional." The medieval Latin hymns clothed their transcendent themes, their passionate emotions, in the language of imperial Rome. The modern sectaries succeed best in their hymnology when they choose simple ideas, not too definite in content, and clothe them, as Whittier did, in words of tender human association, in parables of longing and of consolation.

5. *The Lyric Imagination*

The material thus furnished by the lyric poet's experience, thought and emotion is re-shaped by an imagination working simply and spontaneously. The lyrist is born and not made, and he cannot help transforming the actual world into his own world, like Don Quixote with the windmills and the serving-women. Sometimes his imagination fastens upon a single trait or aspect of reality, and the resultant metaphor seems truer than any logic.

"Death lays his *icy hand* on Kings."

"I wandered *lonely as a cloud*."

Sometimes his imagination fuses various aspects of an object into a composite effect:

"A lily of a day
    Is fairer far in May,
    Although it fall and die that night;
    It was the *plant and flower of light*."

The lyric emotion, it is true, does not always catch at imagery. It may deal directly with the fact, as in Burns's immortal

"If we ne'er had met sae kindly,
    If we ne'er had loved sae blindly,
    Never loved, and never parted,
    We had ne'er been broken-hearted."

The lyric atmosphere, heavy and clouded with passionate feeling, idealizes objects as if they were seen through the light of dawn or sunset. It is never the dry clear light of noon.

"She was *a phantom* of delight."

"Thy soul was *like a star*, and dwelt apart,
    Thou hadst a voice whose sound was *like the sea*,
    Pure as the naked heavens . . . "

This idealization is often not so much a magnification of the object as a simplification of it. Confusing details are stripped away. Contradictory facts are eliminated, until heart answers to heart across the welter of immaterialities.

Although the psychologists, as has been already noted, are now little inclined to distinguish between the imagination and the fancy, it remains true that the old distinction between superficial or "fanciful" resemblances, and deeper or "imaginative" likenesses, is a convenient one in lyric poetry. E. C. Stedman, in his old age, was wont to say that our younger lyrists, while tuneful and fanciful enough, had no imagination or passion, and that what was needed in America was some adult male verse. The verbal felicity and richness of fancy that characterized the Elizabethan lyric were matched by its sudden gleams of penetrative imagination, which may be, after all, only the "fancy" taking a deeper plunge. In the familiar song from *The Tempest*, for example, we have in the second and third lines examples of those fanciful conceits in which the age delighted, but that does not impair

the purely imaginative beauty of the last
three lines of the stanza, — the lines that are
graven upon Shelley's tombstone in Rome:

> "Full fathom five thy father lies;
> Of his bones are coral made;
> Those are pearls that were his eyes:
> Nothing of him that doth fade
> But doth suffer a sea-change
> Into something rich and strange."

So it was that Hawthorne's "fancy" first
won a public for his stories, while it is by his
imagination that he holds his place as an
artist.   For the deeply imaginative line of
lyric verse, like the imaginative conception of
novelist or dramatist, often puzzles or repels
a poet's contemporaries.   Jeffrey could find
no sense in Wordsworth's superb couplet in
the "Ode to Duty":

"Thou dost preserve the stars from wrong;
And the most ancient heavens, through Thee, are
    fresh and strong."

And oddly enough, Emerson, the one man
upon this side of the Atlantic from whom an
instinctive understanding of those lines was
to be expected, was as much perplexed by
them as Jeffrey.

6. *Lyric Expression*

Is it possible to formulate the laws of lyric expression? "I do not mean by expression," said Gray, "the mere choice of words, but the whole dress, fashion, and arrangement of a thought." [1] Taking expression, in this larger sense, as the final element in that three-fold process by which poetry comes into being, and which has been discussed in an earlier chapter, we may assert that there are certain general laws of lyric form.

One of them is the law of brevity. It is impossible to keep the lyric pitch for very long. The rapture turns to pain. "I need scarcely observe," writes Poe in his essay on "The Poetic Principle," "that a poem deserves its title only inasmuch as it excites, by elevating the soul. The value of the poem is in the ratio of this elevating excitement. But all excitements are, through a psychical necessity, transient. That degree of excitement which would entitle a poem to be so called at all, cannot be sustained throughout a composition of any great length. After the lapse of half an hour, at the very utmost,

[1] Gray's *Letters*, vol. 2, p. 333. (Gosse ed.)

it flags — fails — a revulsion ensues — and then the poem is, in effect, and in fact, no longer such."

In another passage, from the essay on "Hawthorne's 'Twice-Told Tales,'" Poe emphasizes this law of brevity in connection with the law of unity of impression. It is one of the classic passages of American literary criticism:

"Were we bidden to say how the highest genius could be most advantageously employed for the best display of its own powers, we should answer, without hesitation — in the composition of a rhymed poem, not to exceed in length what might be perused in an hour. Within this limit alone can the highest order of true poetry exist. We need only here say, upon this topic, that, in almost all classes of composition, the unity of effect or impression is a point of the greatest importance. It is clear, moreover, that this unity cannot be thoroughly preserved in productions whose perusal cannot be completed at one sitting. We may continue the reading of a prose composition, from the very nature of prose itself, much lönger than we can preserve, to any good purpose, in the perusal of a poem. This latter, if truly fulfilling the demands of the poetic sentiment, induces an exaltation of the soul which cannot be long sustained. All high excitements are necessarily transient. Thus a long poem is a paradox. And, without unity of impression, the deepest effects cannot be brought about. Epics were the off-spring of an imperfect sense of Art, and their reign is no more. A poem *too* brief may produce a vivid, but never an intense or enduring impression. Without a certain continuity of effort — without a certain duration or repetition of purpose — the soul is never deeply moved."

Gray's analysis of the law of lyric brevity is picturesque, and too little known:

"The true lyric style, with all its flights of fancy, ornaments, and heightening of expression, and harmony of sound, is in its nature superior to every other style; which is just the cause why it could not be borne in a work of great length, no more than the eye could bear to see all this scene that we constantly gaze upon, — the verdure of the fields and woods, the azure of the sea-skies, turned into one dazzling expanse of gems. The epic, therefore, assumed a style of graver colors, and only stuck on a diamond (borrowed from her sister) here and there, where it best became her. . . . To pass on a sudden from the lyric glare to the epic solemnity (if I may be allowed to talk nonsense). . ." [1]

It is evident that the laws of brevity and unity cannot be disassociated. The unity of emotion which characterizes the successful lyric corresponds to the unity of action in the drama, and to the unity of effect in the short

[1] Gray's *Letters*, vol. 2, p. 304. (Gosse ed.)

story. It is this fact which Palgrave stressed in his emphasis upon "some single thought, feeling, or situation." The sonnets, for instance, that most nearly approach perfection are those dominated by one thought. This thought may be turned over, indeed, as the octave passes into the sextet, and may be viewed from another angle, or applied in an unexpected way. And yet the content of a sonnet, considered as a whole, must be as integral as the sonnet's form. So must it be with any song. The various devices of rhyme, stanza and refrain help to bind into oneness of form a single emotional reflection of some situation or desire.

Watts-Dunton points out that there is also a law of simplicity of grammatical structure which the lyric disregards at its peril. Browning and Shelley, to mention no lesser names, often marred the effectiveness of their lyrics by a lack of perspicuity. If the lyric cry is not easily intelligible, the sympathy of the listener is not won. Riddle-poems have been loved by the English ever since Anglo-Saxon times, but the intellectual satisfaction of solving a puzzle may be purchased at the cost of true poetic pleasure. Let us quote Gray

once more, for he had an unerring sense of the
difficulty of moulding ideas into "pure, perspicuous and musical form."

"Extreme conciseness of expression, yet pure,
perspicuous, and musical, is one of the grand
beauties of lyric poetry. This I have always
aimed at, and never could attain; the necessity of
rhyming is one great obstacle to it: another and
perhaps a stronger is, that way you have chosen
of casting down your first ideas carelessly and at
large, and then clipping them here and there, and
forming them at leisure; this method, after all
possible pains, will leave behind it in some places a
laxity, a diffuseness; the frame of a thought (otherwise well invented, well turned, and well placed) is
often weakened by it. Do I talk nonsense, or do
you understand me?" [1]

Poe, whose theory of poetry comprehends
only the lyric, and indeed chiefly that re-
stricted type of lyric verse in which he himself was a master, insisted that there was a
further lyric law, — the law of vagueness or
indefiniteness. "I know," he writes in his
"Marginalia," "that indefiniteness is an element of the true music — I mean of the true
musical expression. Give to it any undue
decision — imbue it with any very determi-
nate tone — and you deprive it, at once, of its

[1] Gray's *Letters,* vol. 2, p. 352. (Gosse ed.)

ethereal, its ideal, its intrinsic and essential
character. You dispel its luxury of dream.
You dissolve the atmosphere of the mystic
upon which it floats. You exhaust it of its
breath of faëry. It now becomes a tangible
and easily appreciable idea — a thing of the
earth, earthy."

This reads like a defence of Poe's own private practice, and yet many poets and critics
are inclined to side with him. Edmond
Holmes, for instance, goes quite as far as Poe.
"The truth is that poetry, which is the expression of large, obscure and indefinable
feelings, finds its appropriate material in
vague words — words of large import and with
many meanings and shades of meaning. Here
we have an almost unfailing test for determining the poetic fitness of words, a test which
every true poet unconsciously, but withal
unerringly, applies. Precision, whether in
the direction of what is commonplace or of
what is technical, is always unpoetical."[1]
This doctrine, it will be observed, is in direct
opposition to the Imagist theory of "hardness and economy of speech; the exact word,"
and it also would rule out the highly technical

[1] *What is Poetry,* p. 77. London and New York, 1900.

vocabulary of camp and trail, steamship and jungle, with which Mr. Kipling has greatly delighted our generation. No one who admires the splendid vitality of "McAndrew's Hymn" is really troubled by the slang and lingo of the engine-room.

One of the most charming passages in Stedman's *Nature and Elements of Poetry* (pp. 181–85) deals with the law of Evanescence. The "flowers that fade," the "airs that die," "the snows of yester-year," have in their very frailty and mortality a haunting lyric value. Don Marquis has written a poem about this exquisite appeal of the transient, calling it "The Paradox":

"'T is evanescence that endures;
The loveliness that dies the soonest has the longest
    life."

But we touch here a source of lyric beauty too delicate to be analysed in prose. It is better to read "Rose Aylmer," or to remember what Duke Orsino says in *Twelfth Night:*

"Enough; no more:
'T is not so sweet now as it was before."

7. *Expression and Impulse*

A word must be added, nevertheless, about lyric expression as related to the lyric impulse. No one pretends that there is such a thing as a set lyric pattern.

"There are nine-and-sixty ways of constructing
    tribal lays,
And every single one of them is right."

No two professional golfers, for instance, take precisely the same stance. Each man's stance is the expression, the result, of his peculiar physical organization and his muscular habits. There are as many "styles" as there are players, and yet each player strives for "style," i.e. economy and precision and grace of muscular effort, and each will assert that the chief thing is to "keep your eye on the ball" and "follow through." "And every single one of them is right."

Apply this analogy to the organization of a lyric poem. Its material, as we have seen, is infinitely varied. It expresses all conceivable "states of soul." Is it possible, therefore, to lay down any general formula for it, something corresponding to the golfer's "keep your eye on the ball" and "follow through"?

John Erskine, in his book on *The Elizabethan Lyric*, ventures upon this precept: "Lyric emotion, in order to express itself intelligibly, must first reproduce the cause of its existence. If the poet will go into ecstasies over a Grecian urn, to justify himself he must first show us the urn." Admitted. Can one go farther? Mr. Erskine attempts it, in a highly suggestive analysis: "Speaking broadly, all successful lyrics have three parts. In the first the emotional stimulus is given — the object, the situation, or the thought from which the song arises. In the second part the emotion is developed to its utmost capacity, until as it begins to flag the intellectual element reasserts itself. In the third part the emotion is finally resolved into a thought, a mental resolution, or an attribute." [1] Let the reader choose at random a dozen lyrics from the *Golden Treasury*, and see how far this orderly arrangement of the thought-stuff of the lyric is approximated in practice. My own impression is that the critic postulates more of an "intellectual element" than the average English song will supply. But at least here is a clear-cut statement of what one

[1] *The Elizabethan Lyric,* p. 17.

may look for in a lyric. It shows how the lyric impulse tends to mould lyric expression into certain lines of order.

Most of the narrower precepts governing lyric form follow from the general principles already discussed. The lyric vocabulary, every one admits, should not seem studied or consciously ornate, for that breaks the law of spontaneity. It may indeed be highly finished, the more highly in proportion to its brevity, but the clever word-juggling of such prestidigitators as Poe and Verlaine is perilous. Figurative language must spring only from living, figurative thought, otherwise the lyric falls into verbal conceits, frigidity, conventionality. Stanzaic law must follow emotional law, just as Kreisler's accompanist must keep time with Kreisler. All the rich devices of rhyme and tone-color must heighten and not cloy the singing quality. But why lengthen this list of truisms? The combination of genuine lyric emotion with expertness of technical expression is in reality very rare. Goethe's "Ueber allen Gipfeln ist Ruh" and Coleridge's "Kubla Khan" are miracles of art, yet one was scribbled in a moment, and the other dreamed in an opium slumber. The lyric is the commonest, and yet, in its perfection, the rarest type of poetry; the earliest, and yet the most modern; the simplest, and yet in its laws of emotional association, perhaps the most complex; and it is all these because it expresses, more intimately than other types of verse, the personality of the poet.

CHAPTER VIII

RELATIONSHIPS AND TYPES OF THE LYRIC

"*Milk-Woman.* What song was it, I pray? Was it 'Come, shepherds, deck your heads'? or, 'As at noon Dulcina rested'? or, 'Phillida flouts me'? or, 'Chevy Chase'? or, 'Johnny Armstrong'? or, 'Troy Town'?"

ISAAC WALTON, *The Complete Angler*

WE have already considered, at the beginning of the previous chapter, the general relationship of the three chief types of poetry. Lyric, epic and drama, i.e. song, story and play, have obviously different functions to perform. They may indeed deal with a common fund of material. A given event, say the settlement of Virginia, or the episode of Pocahontas, provides situations and emotions which may take either lyric or narrative or dramatic shape. The mental habits and technical experience of the poet, or the prevalent literary fashions of his day, may determine which general type of poetry he will employ. There were born lyrists, like Greene in the Elizabethan period, who wrote plays because the public demanded drama, and there have been natural dramatists who were compelled, in a period when the theatre fell into disrepute, to give their material a narrative form. But we must also take into account the dominant mood or quality of certain poetic minds. Many passages in narrative and dramatic verse, for instance, while fulfilling their primary function of telling a story or throwing characters into action, are colored by what we have called the lyric quality, by that passionate, personal feeling whose natural mode of expression is in song. In Marlowe's *Tamburlaine*, for instance, or Victor Hugo's *Hernani*, there are superb pieces of lyric declamation, in which we feel that Marlowe and Hugo themselves — not the imaginary Tamburlaine and Hernani — are chanting the desires of their own hearts. Arnold's "Sohrab and Rustum," after finishing its tragic story of the son slain by the unwitting father, closes with a lyric description of the majestic Oxus stream flowing on to the Aral sea. Objective as it all seems, this close is intensely personal, permeated with the same tender stoicism which colors Arnold's "Dover Beach" and "A Summer Night." The device of using a Nature picture at the end of a narrative, to heighten, by harmony or contrast, the mood induced by the story itself, was freely utilized by Tennyson in his *English Idylls*, such as "Audley Court," "Edwin Morris," "Love and Duty," and "The Golden Year." It adds the last touch of poignancy to Robert Frost's "Death of the Hired Man." These descriptive passages, though lacking the song form, are as purely lyrical in their function as the songs in *The Princess* or the songs in *The Winter's Tale*.

1. The Blending of Types

While the scope of the present volume, as explained in the Preface, precludes any specific study of drama and epic, the reader must bear in mind that the three main types of poetry are not separated, in actual practice, by immovably hard and fast lines. Pigeonhole classifications of drama, epic and lyric types are highly convenient to the student for purposes of analysis. But the moment one reads a ballad like "Edward, Edward" (*Oxford*, No. 373) or "Helen of Kirconnell" (*Oxford*, No. 387) the pigeon-hole distinctions must be subordinated to the actual fact that these ballads are a blend of drama, story and song. The "form" is lyrical, the stuff is narrative, the mode of presentation is often that of purely dramatic dialogue.

Take a contemporary illustration of this blending of types. Mr. Vachel Lindsay has told us the origins of his striking poem "The Congo." He was already in a "national-theme mood," he says, when he listened to a sermon about missionaries on the Congo River. The word "Congo" began to haunt him. "It echoed with the war-drums and cannibal yells of Africa." Then, for a list of colors for his palette, he had boyish memories of Stanley's *Darkest Africa*, and of the dances of the Dahomey Amazons at the World's Fair in Chicago. He had seen the anti-negro riots in Springfield, Illinois. He had gone through a score of negro-saloons — "barrel-houses" — on Eleventh Avenue, New York, and had "accumulated a jungle impression that remains with me yet." Above all, there was Conrad's *Heart of Darkness*. "I wanted to reiterate the word Congo — and the several refrains in a way that would echo stories like that. I wanted to suggest the terror, the reeking swamp-fever, the forest splendor, the black-lacquered loveliness, and above all the eternal fatality of Africa, that Conrad has

written down with so sure a hand. I do not
mean to say, now that I have done, that I
recorded all these things in rhyme. But
every time I rewrote 'The Congo' I reached
toward them. I suppose I rewrote it fifty
times in these two months, sometimes three
times in one day."

It is not often that we get so veracious an
account of the making of a poem, so clear
a conception of the blending of sound-mo-
tives, color-motives, story-stuff, drama-stuff,
personal emotion, into a single whole.

Nor is there any clear separation of types
when we strive to look back to the primitive
origins of these various forms of poetry. In
the opinion of many scholars, the origins are
to be traced to a common source in the
dance. "Dances, as overwhelming evidence,
ethnological and sociological, can prove, were
the original stuff upon which dramatic, lyric
and epic impulses wove a pattern that is
traced in later narrative ballads mainly as
incremental repetition. Separation of its elements, and evolution to higher forms, made
the dance an independent art, with song,
and then music, ancillary to the figures
and the steps; song itself passed to lyric

triumphs quite apart from choral voice and choral act; epic went its artistic way with nothing but rhythm as memorial of the dance, and the story instead of dramatic situation; drama retained the situation, the action, even the chorus and the dance, but submitted them to the shaping and informing power of individual genius." [1] In another striking passage, Professor Gummere asks us to visualize "a throng of people without skill to read or write, without ability to project themselves into the future, or to compare themselves with the past, or even to range their experience with the experience of other communities, gathered in festal mood, and by loud song, perfect rhythm and energetic dance, expressing their feelings over an event of quite local origin, present appeal and common interest. Here, in point of evolution, is the human basis of poetry, the foundation courses of the pyramid."

2. Lyrical Element in Drama

We cannot here attempt to trace, even in outline, the course of this historic evolution of *genres*. But in contemporary types of

[1] Gummere, *The Popular Ballad*, p. 106.

both dramatic and narrative poetry, there may still be discovered the influence of lyric form and mood. We have already noted how the dramatist, for all of his supposed objectivity, cannot refrain from coloring certain persons and situations with the hues of his own fancy. Ibsen, for instance, injects his irony, his love for symbolism, his theories for the reconstruction of society, into the very blood and bone of his characters and into the structure of his plots. So it is with Shaw, with Synge, with Hauptmann, with Brieux. Even if their plays are written in prose, these men are still "makers," and the prose play may be as highly subjective in mood, as definitely individual in phrasing, as full of atmosphere, as if it were composed in verse.

But the lyric possibilities of the drama are more easily realized if we turn from the prose play to the play in verse, and particularly to those Elizabethan dramas which are not only poetical in essence, but which utilize actual songs for their dramatic value. No less than thirty-six of Shakspere's plays contain stage-directions for music, and his marvelous command of song-words is universally recognized.

The English stage had made use of songs, in fact, ever since the liturgical drama of the Middle Ages. But Shakspere's unrivalled knowledge of stage-craft, as well as his own instinct for harmonizing lyrical with theatrical effects, enabled him to surpass all of his contemporaries in the art of using songs to bring actors on and off the stage, to anticipate following action, to characterize personages, to heighten climaxes, and to express emotions beyond the reach of spoken words.[1] The popularity of such song-forms as the "madrigal," which was sung without musical accompaniment, made it easy for the public stage to cater to the prevalent taste. The "children of the Chapel" or "of Paul's," who served as actors in the early Elizabethan dramas, were trained choristers, and songs were a part of their stock in trade. Songs for sheer entertainment, common enough upon the stage when Shakspere began to write, turned in his hands into exquisite instruments of character revelation and of dramatic passion, until they became, on the lips of an Ophelia or a Desdemona, the most

[1] These points are fully discussed in J. Robert Moore's Harvard dissertation (unpublished) on *The Songs in the English Drama*.

touching and poignant moments of the drama. "Music within" is a frequent stage direction in the later Elizabethan plays, and if one remembers the dramatic effectiveness of the Easter music, off-stage, in Goethe's *Faust*, or the horn in *Hernani*, one can understand how Wagner came to believe that a blending of music with poetry and action, as exhibited in his "music-dramas," was demanded by the ideal requirements of dramatic art. Wagner's theory and practice need not be rehearsed here. It is sufficient for our purpose to recall the indisputable fact that in some of the greatest plays ever written, lyric forms have contributed richly and directly to the total dramatic effect.

3. The Dramatic Monologue

There is still another *genre* of poetry, however, where the inter-relations of drama, of narrative, and of lyric mood are peculiarly interesting. It is the dramatic monologue. The range of expressiveness allowed by this type of poetry was adequately shown by Browning and Tennyson, and recent poets like Edwin Arlington Robinson, Robert Frost and Amy Lowell have employed it with

consummate skill. The dramatic monologue
is a dynamic revelation of a soul in action,
not a mere static bit of character study. It
chooses some representative and specific occasion, — let us say a man's death-bed view
of his career, as in "The Bishop orders his
Tomb" or the first "Northern Farmer." It
is something more than a soliloquy over-
heard. There is a listener, who, though
without a speaking part, plays a very real
rôle in the dialogue. For the dramatic
monologue is in essence a dialogue of which
we hear only the chief speaker's part, as in
"My Last Duchess," or in E. A. Robinson's
"Ben Jonson Entertains a Man from Strat-
ford." It is as if we were watching and
listening to a man telephoning. Though we
see and hear but one person, we are aware
that the talk is shaped to a certain extent by
the personality at the other end of the line.
In Tennyson's "Rizpah," for example, the
characteristics of the well-meaning, Bible-
quoting parish visitor determine some of the
finest lines in the old mother's response. In
Browning's "Andrea del Sarto" the painter's
wife, Lucrezia, says never a word, but she
has a more intense physical presence in that

poem than many of the *dramatis personæ* of
famous plays. Tennyson's "Ulysses" and
"Sir Galahad" and "The Voyage of Mael-
dune" are splendid soliloquies and nothing
more. The first "Locksley Hall" is likewise
a soliloquy, but in the second "Locksley
Hall" and "To-Morrow," where scraps of
talk from the unseen interlocutor are caught
up and repeated by the speaker in passionate
rebuttal, we have true drama of the "con-
frontation" type. We see a whole soul in
action.

Now this intense, dynamic fashion of re-
vealing character through narrative talk —
and it is commonly a whole life-story which
is condensed within the few lines of a dramatic
monologue — touches lyricism at two points.
The first is the fact that many dramatic
monologues use distinctively lyric measures.
The six-stress anapestic line which Tennyson
preferred for his later dramatic monologues
like "Rizpah" is really a ballad measure, and
is seen as such to its best advantage in "The
Revenge." But in his monologues of the
pure soliloquy type, like "St. Agnes" and
"Sir Galahad," the metre is brilliantly lyrical,
and the lyric associations of the verse are

carried over into the mood of the poem. And
the other fact to be remembered is that the
poignant self-analysis and self-betrayal of
the dramatic monologue, its "egoism" and
its ultimate and appalling sincerities, are a
part of the very nature of the lyric impulse.
These revealers of their souls may use the
speaking, rather than the singing voice, but
their tones have the deep, rich lyric intimacy.

4. Lyric and Narrative

In narrative poetry, no less than in drama,
we must note the intrusion of the lyric mood,
as well as the influence of lyric forms. Theoretically, narrative or "epic" poetry is
based upon an objective experience. Something has happened, and the poet tells us
about it. He has heard or read, or possibly
taken part in, an event, and the event, rather
than the poet's thought or feeling about it,
is the core of the poem. But as soon as he
begins to tell his tale, we find that he is apt
to "set it out" with vivid description. He is
obliged to paint a picture as well as to spin
a yarn, and not even Homer and Virgil —
"objective" as they are supposed to be —
can draw a picture without betraying some-

thing of their attitude and feeling towards their material. Like the messenger in Greek drama, their voices are shaken by what they have seen or heard. In the popular epic like the Nibelungen story, there is more objectivity than in the epic of art like *Jerusalem Delivered* or *Paradise Lost*. We do not know who put together in their present form such traditional tales as the *Lay of the Nibelungs* and *Beowulf*, and the personal element in the narrative is only obscurely felt, whereas *Jerusalem Delivered* is a constant revelation of Tasso, and the personality of Milton colors every line in *Paradise Lost*. When Matthew Arnold tells us that Homer is rapid, plain, simple and noble, he is depicting the characteristics of a poet as well as the impression made by the *Iliad* and the *Odyssey*. Those general traits of epic poetry which have been discussed ever since the Renaissance, like "breadth," and "unity" and the sustained "grand" style, turn ultimately upon the natural qualities of great story-tellers. They are not mere rhetorical abstractions.

The narrative poet sees man as accomplishing a deed, as a factor in an event. His primary business is to report action, not to philosophize or to dissect character or to paint landscape. Yet so sensitive is he to the environing circumstances of action, and so bent upon displaying the varieties of human motive and conduct, that he cannot help reflecting in his verse his own mental attitude toward the situations which he depicts. He may surround these situations, as we have seen, with all the beauties and pomps and terrors of the visible world. In relating "God's ways to man" he instinctively justifies or condemns. He cannot even tell a story exactly as it was told to him: he must alter it, be it ever so slightly, to make it fit his general conceptions of human nature and human fate. He gives credence to one witness and not to another. His imagination plays around the noble and base elements in his story until their original proportions are altered to suit his mind and purpose. Study the Tristram story, as told by Gottfried of Strassburg, by Malory, Tennyson, Arnold, Swinburne and Wagner, and you will see how each teller betrays his own personality through these instinctive processes of transformation of his material. It is like the Roman murder story told so many times over in

Browning's *Ring and the Book :* the main facts
are conceded by each witness, and yet the in-
ferences from the facts range from Heaven
to Hell.

Browning is of course an extreme instance
of this irruption of the poet's personality upon
the stuff of his story. He cannot help lyri-
cising and dramatizing his narrative material,
any more than he can help making all his
characters talk "Browningese." But Byron's tales in verse show the same subjective
tendency. He was so little of a dramatist
that all of his heroes, like Poe's, are images of
himself. No matter what the raw material
of his narrative poems may be, they become
uniformly "Byronic" as he writes them down.
And all this is "lyricism," however disguised.
William Morris, almost alone among modern
English poets, seemed to stand gravely aloof
from the tales he told, as his master Chaucer stood smilingly aloof. Yet the "tone" of
Chaucer is perceived somehow upon every
page, in spite of his objectivity.

The whole history of medieval verse Romances, indeed, illustrates this lyrical tendency to rehandle inherited material. Tales
of love, of enchantment, of adventure, could

not be held down to prosaic fact. Whether
they dealt with "matter of France," or "matter of Brittany," whether a brief "lai" or a
complicated cycle of stories like those about
Charlemagne or King Arthur, whether a
merry "fabliau" or a beast-tale like "Rey-
nard the Fox," all the Romances allow to the
author a margin of mystery, an opportunity
to weave his own web of brightly colored
fancies. A specific event or legend was there,
of course, as a nucleus for the story, but the
sense of wonder, of strangeness in things, of
individual delight in brocading new patterns
upon old material, dominated over the sense
of fact. "Time," said Shelley, "which de-
stroys the beauty and the use of the story of
particular facts, stripped of the poetry which
should invest them, augments that of poetry,
and forever develops new and wonderful ap-
plications of the eternal truth which it contains. . . . A story of particular facts is as a
mirror which obscures and distorts that which
should be beautiful: poetry is a mirror which
makes beautiful that which is distorted."

And in modern narrative verse, surely, the
line between "epic" quality and "lyric"
quality is difficult to draw. Choose almost at

random a half-dozen story-telling poems from the *Oxford Book of English Verse*, say "The Ancient Mariner," "The Burial of Sir John Moore," "La Belle Dame sans Merci," "Porphyria's Lover," "The Forsaken Merman," "He Fell among Thieves." Each of these poems narrates an event, but what purely lyric quality is there which cannot be found in "La Belle Dame sans Merci" and "The Ancient Mariner"? And does not each of the other poems release and excite the lyric mood?

We must admit, furthermore, that narrative measures and lyric measures are frequently identical, and help to carry over into a story a singing quality. Ballad measures are an obvious example. Walter Scott's facile couplets were equally effective for story and for song. Many minor species of narrative poetry, like verse satire and allegory, are often composed in traditional lyric patterns. Even blank verse, admirably suited as it is for story-telling purposes, yields in its varieties of cadence many a bar of music long associated with lyric emotion. Certainly the blank verse of Wordsworth's "Michael" is far different in its musical values from the blank verse, say, of Tennyson's *Princess* —

perhaps truly as different as the metre of *Sigurd the Volsung* is from that of *The Rape of the Lock*. The perfect matching of metrical form to the nature of the narrative material, whether that material be traditional or first-hand, simple or complex, rude or delicate, demands the finest artistic instinct. Yet it appears certain that many narrative measures affect us fully as much through their intimate association with the moods of song as through their specific adaptiveness to the purposes of narrative.

5. *The Ballad*

The supreme illustration of this blending of story and song is the ballad. The word "ballad," like "ode" and "sonnet," is very ancient and has been used in various senses. We think of it to-day as a song that tells a story, usually of popular origin. Derived etymologically from *ballare*, to dance, it means first of all, a "dance-song," and is the same word as "ballet." Solomon's "Song of Songs" is called in the Bishops' Bible of 1568 "The Ballet of Ballets of King Solomon." But in Chaucer's time a "ballad" meant primarily a French form of lyric verse, — not a

narrative lyric specifically. In the Elizabethan period the word was used loosely for
"song." Only after the revival of interest in
English and Scottish popular ballads in the
eighteenth century has the word come gradually to imply a special type of story-telling
song, with no traces of individual authorship, and handed down by oral tradition.
Scholars differ as to the precise part taken by
the singing, dancing crowd in the composition
and perpetuation of these traditional ballads.
Professor Child, the greatest authority upon
English and Scottish balladry, and Professors
Gummere, Kittredge and W. M. Hart have
emphasized the element of "communal" composition, and illustrated it by many types of
song-improvisation among savage races, by
sailors' "chanties," and negro "work-songs."
It is easy to understand how a singing, dancing crowd carries a refrain, and improvises,
through some quick-tongued individual, a
new phrase, line or stanza of immediate popular effect; and it is also easy to perceive, by a
study of extant versions of various ballads,
such as Child printed in glorious abundance,
to see how phrases, lines and stanzas get
altered as they are passed from lip to lip of

unlettered people during the course of centuries. But the actual historical relationship
of communal dance-songs to such narrative
lyrics as were collected by Bishop Percy,
Ritson and Child is still under debate.[1]

"All poetry," said Professor Gummere in
reply to a critic of his theory of communal
composition of ballads, "springs from the
same poetic impulse, and is due to individuals;
but the conditions under which it is made,
whether originally composed in a singing,
dancing throng and submitted to oral tradition, or set down on paper by the solitary and
deliberate poet, have given birth to that distinction of 'popular' and 'artistic,' or whatever the terms may be, which has obtained in
some form with nearly all writers on poetry
since Aristotle." Avoiding questions that
are still in controversy, let us look at some of
the indubitable characteristics of the "popular" ballads as they are shown in Child's collection.[2] They are impersonal. There is

[1] See Louise Pound, "The Ballad and the Dance," *Pub.
Mod. Lang. Ass.*, vol. 34, No. 3 (September, 1919), and An-
drew Lang's article on "Ballads" in Chambers' *Cyclopedia of
Eng. Lit.*, ed. of 1902.

[2] Now reprinted in a single volume of the "Cambridge
Poets" (Houghton Mifflin Company), edited with an introduction by G. L. Kittredge.

no trace whatever of individual authorship. "This song was made by Billy Gashade," asserts the author of the immensely popular American ballad of "Jesse James." But we do not know what "Billy Gashade" it was who first made rhymes about Robin Hood or Johnny Armstrong, or just how much help he had from the crowd in composing them. In any case, the method of such ballads is purely objective. They do not moralize or sentimentalize. There is little description, aside from the use of set, conventional phrases. They do not "motivate" the story carefully, or move logically from event to event. Rather do they "flash the story at you" by fragments, and then leave you in the dark. They leap over apparently essential points of exposition and plot structure; they omit to assign dialogue to a specific person, leaving you to guess who is talking. Over certain bits of action or situation they linger as if they hated to leave that part of the story. They make shameless use of "commonplaces," that is, stock phrases, lines or stanzas which are conveniently held by the memory and which may appear in dozens of different ballads. They are not afraid of repetition, — indeed the theory of choral collaboration implies a constant use of repetition and refrain, as in a sailor's "chanty." One of their chief ways of building a situation or advancing a narrative is through "incremental repetition," as Gummere termed it, i.e. the successive additions of some new bits of fact as the bits already familiar are repeated.

"'Christine, Christine, tread a measure for me!
A silken sark I will give to thee.'

"'A silken sark I can get me here,
But I'll not dance with the Prince this year.'

"'Christine, Christine, tread a measure for me,
Silver-clasped shoes I will give to thee!'

"'Silver-clasped shoes,'" etc.

American cowboy ballads show the same device:

"I started up the trail October twenty-third,
I started up the trail *with the 2-U herd*."

Strikingly as the ballads differ from consciously "artistic" narrative in their broken movement and allusive method, the contrast is even more different if we consider the naïve quality of their refrains. Sometimes the refrain is only a sort of musical accompaniment:

"There was an old farmer in Sussex did dwell,
   (*Chorus of Whistlers*)
There was an old farmer in Sussex did dwell
And he had a bad wife, as many knew well.
   (*Chorus of Whistlers*)"

Or,

"The auld Deil cam to the man at the pleugh,
   Rumchy ae de aidie."

Sometimes the words of the choral refrain
have a vaguely suggestive meaning:

"There were three ladies lived in a bower,
   Eh vow bonnie
And they went out to pull a flower,
   On the bonnie banks of Fordie."

Sometimes the place-name, illustrated in the
last line quoted, is definite:

"There was twa sisters in a bower,
   Edinburgh, Edinburgh,
There was twa sisters in a bower,
   Stirling for aye
There was twa sisters in a bower,
There came a knight to be their wooer,
   Bonny Saint Johnston stands upon Tay."

But often it is sheer faëry-land magic:

"He's ta'en three locks o' her yellow hair,
   Binnorie, O Binnorie!
And wi' them strung his harp sae rare
   By the bonnie milldams o' Binnorie."
                    (*Oxford*, No. 376.)

It is through the choral refrains, in fact, that the student of lyric poetry is chiefly fascinated as he reads the ballads. Students of epic and drama find them peculiarly suggestive in their handling of narrative and dramatic material, while to students of folklore and of primitive society they are inexhaustible treasures. The mingling of dance-motives and song-motives with the pure story-element may long remain obscure, but the popular ballad reinforces, perhaps more persuasively than any type of poetry, the conviction that the lyrical impulse is universal and inevitable. As Andrew Lang, scholar and lover of balladry, wrote long ago: "Ballads sprang from the very heart of the people and flit from age to age, from lip to lip of shepherds, peasants, nurses, of all the class that continues nearest to the state of natural man. The whole soul of the peasant class breathes in their burdens, as the great sea resounds in the shells cast up on the shores. Ballads are a voice from secret places, from silent peoples and old times long dead; and as such they stir us in a strangely intimate fashion to which artistic verse can never attain." [1]

[1] *Encyclopædia Brittanica*, article "Ballads."

6. *The Ode*

If the ballad is thus an example of "popular" lyricism, with a narrative intention, an example of "artistic" lyricism is found in the Ode. Here there is no question of communal origins or of communal influence upon structure. The ode is a product of a single artist, working not naïvely, but consciously, and employing a highly developed technique. Derived from the Greek verb meaning "to sing," the word "ode" has not changed its meaning since the days of Pindar, except that, as in the case of the word "lyric" itself, we have gradually come to grow unmindful of the original musical accompaniment of the song. Edmund Gosse, in his collection of *English Odes*, defines the ode as "any strain of enthusiastic and exalted lyrical verse directed to a fixed purpose and dealing progressively with one dignified theme." Spenser's "Epithalamium" or marriage ode, Wordsworth's "Ode on the Intimations of Immortality," Tennyson's elegiac and encomiastic "Ode on the Death of the Duke of Wellington," Lowell's "Harvard Commemoration Ode," are among the most familiar examples of the general type.

English poetry has constantly employed, however, both of the two metrical species of odes recognized by the ancients. The first, made up of uniform stanzas, was called "Æolian" or "Horatian," — since Horace imitated the simple, regular strophes of his Greek models. The other species of ode, the "Dorian," is more complex, and is associated with the triumphal odes of Pindar. It utilizes groups of voices, and its divisions into so-called "strophe," "antistrophe" and "epode" (sometimes called fancifully "wave," "answering wave" and "echo") were determined by the movements of the groups of singers upon the Greek stage, the "singers moving to one side during the strophe, retracing their steps during the antistrophe (which was for that reason metrically identical with the strophe), and standing still during the epode." [1]

It must be observed, however, that the English odes written in strictly uniform stanzas differ greatly in the simplicity of the stanzaic pattern. Andrew Marvell's "Horatian Ode upon Cromwell's Return from Ire-

[1] See Bronson's edition of the poems of Collins. Athenæum Press.

land," Collins's "Ode to Evening," Shelley's "To a Skylark," and Wordsworth's "Ode to Duty" are all in very simple stanza forms. But Collins's "Ode on the Superstitions of the Highlands," Shelley's "Ode to Liberty" and Coleridge's "Ode to France" follow very complicated patterns, though all the stanzas are alike. The English "Horatian" ode, then, while exhibiting the greatest differences in complexity of stanzaic forms, is "homostrophic."

To understand the "Pindaric" English ode, we must remember that a few scholars, like Ben Jonson, Congreve and Gray, took peculiar pleasure in reproducing the general effect of the Greek strophic arrangement of "turn," "counterturn" and "pause." Ben Jonson's "Ode to Sir Lucius Cary and Sir H. Morison" (*Oxford*, No. 194) has been thought to be the first strictly Pindaric ode in English, and Gray's "Bard" and "Progress of Poesy" (*Oxford*, Nos. 454, 455) are still more familiar examples of this type. But the great popularity of the so-called "Pindaric" ode in English in the seventeenth century was due to Cowley, and to one of those periodic loyalties to lawlessness which are characteristic of the

English. For Cowley, failing to perceive that
Pindar's apparent lawlessness was due to the
corruption of the Greek text and to the modern ignorance of the rules of Greek choral
music, made his English "Pindaric" odes an
outlet for rebellion against all stanzaic law.
The finer the poetic frenzy, the freer the lyric
pattern! But, alas, rhetoric soon triumphed
over imagination, and in the absence of metrical restraint the ode grew declamatory,
bombastic, and lowest stage of all, "official,"
the last refuge of laureates who felt obliged to
produce something sonorous in honor of a
royal birthday or wedding. This official ode
persisted long after the pseudo-Pindaric flag
was lowered and Cowley had become neg-
lected.

With the revival of Romantic imagination,
however, came a new interest in the "irregular" ode, whose strophic arrangement ebbs and
flows without apparent restraint, subject only
to what Watts-Dunton termed "emotional
law." Wordsworth's "Ode on the Intimations of Immortality" moves in obedience to
its own rhythmic impulses only, like Coleridge's "Kubla Khan" and Emerson's "Bac-
chus." Metrical variety can nowhere be

shown more freely and gloriously than in the
irregular ode: there may be any number of
lines in each strophe, and often the strophe
itself becomes dissolved into something corresponding to the "movement" of a symphony. Masterpieces like William Vaughn
Moody's "Ode in Time of Hesitation" and
Francis Thompson's "Hound of Heaven"
reveal of course a firm intellectual grasp upon
the underlying theme of the ode and upon the
logical processes of its development. But
although we may follow with keen intellectual
delight these large, free handlings of a lyrical
theme, there are few readers of poetry whose
susceptibility to complicated combinations of
rhyme-sound allows them to perceive the full
verbal beauty of the great irregular odes.
Even in such regular strophes as those of
Keats's "Grecian Urn," who remembers that
the rhyme scheme of the first stanza is unlike
that of the following stanzas? Or that the
second stanza of the "Ode to a Nightingale"
runs on four sounds instead of five? Let the
reader test his ear by reading aloud the intricate sound-patterns employed in such elegies
as Arnold's "Scholar Gypsy" (*Oxford*, No.
751) or Swinburne's "Ave atque Vale" (*Ox-*

ford, No. 810), and then let him go back to
"Lycidas" (*Oxford*, No. 317), the final test of
one's responsiveness to the blending of the intellectual and the sensuous elements in poetic
beauty.   If he is honest with himself, he will
probably confess that neither his ear nor his
mind can keep full pace with the swift and
subtle demands made upon both by the masters of sustained lyric energy.   But he will
also become freshly aware that the ode is a
supreme example of that union of excitement
with a sense of order, of liberty with law,
which gives Verse its immortality.

7. *The Sonnet*

The sonnet, likewise, is a lyric form which
illustrates the delicate balance between freedom and restraint.   Let us look first at its
structure, and then at its capacity for expressing thought and feeling.

Both name and structure are Italian in
origin, "sonetto" being the diminutive of
"suono," sound.   Dante and Petrarch knew it
as a special lyric form intended for musical accompaniment.   It must have fourteen lines,
neither more nor less, with five beats or
"stresses" to the line.   Each line must end

with a rhyme. In the arrangement of the rhymes the sonnet is made up of two parts, or rhyme-systems: the first eight lines forming the "octave," and the last six the "sestet." The octave is made up of two quatrains and the sestet of two tercets. There is a main pause in passing from the octave to the sestet, and frequently there are minor pauses in passing from the first quatrain to the second, and from the first tercet to the last.

Almost all of Petrarch's sonnets follow this rhyme-scheme: for the octave, *a b b a a b b a;* for the sestet, either *c d e c d e* or *c d c d c d.* This strict "Petrarchan" form has endured for six centuries. It has been adopted by poets of every race and language, and it is used to-day as widely or more widely than ever. While individual poets have constantly experimented with different rhyme-schemes, particularly in the sestet, the only really notable invention of a new sonnet form was made by the Elizabethans. Puttenham's *Arte of English Poesie* (1589) declares that "Sir Thomas Wyatt the elder and Henry Earl of Surrey, having travelled into Italy and there tasted the sweet and stately measures and style of the Italian poesie, . . . greatly pol-

ished our rude and homely manner of vulgar
poesie. . . . Their conceits were lofty, their
style stately, their conveyance cleanly, their
terms proper, their metre sweet and well-pro-
portioned, in all imitating very naturally and
studiously their Master Francis Petrarch."

This is charming, but as a matter of fact
both Wyatt and Surrey, with natural English
independence, broke away from the strict
Petrarchan rhyme form.   Wyatt liked a final
couplet, and Surrey used a rhyme-scheme
which was later adopted by Shakspere and
is known to-day as the "Shaksperean" form
of sonnet: namely, three quatrains made up
of alternate rhymes — a separate rhyme-
scheme for each quatrain — and a closing
couplet.   The rhymes consequently run thus:
a b a b c d c d e f e f g g.   To the Petrarchan
purist this is clearly no sonnet at all, in spite of
its fourteen five-beat, rhyming lines.   For the
distinction between octave and sestet has
disappeared, there is a threefold division of
the first twelve lines, and the final couplet
gives an epigrammatic summary or "point"
which Petrarch took pains to avoid.

The difference will be still more clearly
manifest if we turn from a comparison of

rhyme-structure to the ordering of the thought in the Petrarchan sonnet. Mark Pattison, a stout "Petrarchan," lays down these rules in the Preface to his edition of Milton's Sonnets:[1]

"a. A sonnet, like every other work of art, must have its unity. It must be the expression of one, and only one, thought or feeling.

"b. This thought or mood should be led up to, and opened in the early lines of the sonnet; strictly, in the first quatrain; in the second quatrain the hearer should be placed in full possession of it.

"c. After the second quatrain there should be a pause, not full, nor producing the effect of a break, as of one who had finished what he had got to say, and not preparing a transition to a new subject, but as of one who is turning over what has been said in the mind to enforce it further.

"d. The opening of the second system, strictly the first tercet, should turn back upon the thought or sentiment, take it up and carry it forward to the conclusion.

"e. The conclusion should be a resultant, summing the total of the suggestion in the preceding lines, as a lakelet in the hills gathers into a still pool the running waters contributed by its narrow area of gradients.

"f. While the conclusion should leave a sense of finish and completeness, it is necessary to avoid anything like epigrammatic point. By this the sonnet is distinguished from the epigram. In the epigram the conclusion is everything; all that goes

[1] D. Appleton & Co., New York, 1883.

before it is only there for the sake of the surprise of the end, or *dénouement*, as in a logical syllogism the premises are nothing but as they necessitate the conclusion. In the sonnet the emphasis is nearly, but not quite, equally distributed, there being a slight swell, or rise, about its middle. The sonnet must not advance by progressive climax, or end abruptly; it should subside, and leave off quietly."

Miss Lockwood, in the Introduction to her admirable collection of English sonnets,[1] makes a still briefer summary of the thought-scheme of the regular Italian sonnet: it "should have a clear and unified theme, stated in the first quatrain, developed or proved in the second, confirmed or regarded from a new point of view in the first tercet, and concluded in the second tercet. It had thus four parts, divided unevenly into two separate systems, eight lines being devoted to placing the thought before the mind, and six to deducing the conclusion from that thought."

A surprisingly large number of sonnets are built upon simple formulas like "As" — for the octave — and "So" — for the sestet — (see Andrew Lang's "The Odyssey," *Oxford*, No. 841); or "When" and "Then" (see

[1] *Sonnets, English and American*, selected by Laura E. Lockwood. Houghton Mifflin Company, 1916.

Keats's "When I have fears that I may cease to be," *Oxford*, No. 635). A situation plus a thought gives a mood; or a mood plus an event gives a mental resolve, etc. The possible combinations are infinite, but the law of logical relation between octave and sestet, premise and conclusion, is immutable.

Let the reader now test these laws of sonnet form and thought by reading aloud one of the most familiarly known of all English sonnets — Keats's "On First Looking into Chapman's Homer":

"Much have I travell'd in the realms of gold,
  And many goodly states and kingdoms seen;
  Round many western islands have I been
  Which bards in fealty to Apollo hold.
  Oft of one wide expanse had I been told
  That deep-brow'd Homer ruled as his demesne;
  Yet did I never breathe its pure serene
  Till I heard Chapman speak out loud and bold:
  Then felt I like some watcher of the skies
  When a new planet swims into his ken;
  Or like stout Cortez when with eagle eyes
  He stared at the Pacific — and all his men
  Look'd at each other with a wild surmise —
  Silent, upon a peak in Darien."

Read next another strictly Petrarchan sonnet, where the thought divisions of quatrains and tercets are marked with exceptional clear-

ness, Eugene Lee-Hamilton's disillusioned
"Sea-Shell Murmurs":

"The hollow sea-shell that for years hath stood
　　On dusty shelves, when held against the ear
　　Proclaims its stormy parent; and we hear
The faint far murmur of the breaking flood.

"We hear the sea.　The sea?　It is the blood
　　In our own veins, impetuous and near,
　　And pulses keeping pace with hope and fear
And with our feelings' every shifting mood.

"Lo, in my heart I hear, as in a shell,
　　The murmur of a world beyond the grave,
Distinct, distinct, though faint and far it be.

"Thou fool; this echo is a cheat as well, —
　　The hum of earthly instincts; and we crave
A world unreal as the shell-heard sea."

And now read aloud one of the best-known
of Shakspere's sonnets, where he follows his
favorite device of a threefold statement of his
central thought, using a different image in
each quatrain, and closing with a personal
application of the idea:

"That time of year thou mayst in me behold
When yellow leaves, or none, or few, do hang
Upon those boughs which shake against the cold,
Bare ruin'd choirs, where late the sweet birds
　　sang.

In me thou see'st the twilight of such day
As after sunset fadeth in the west;
Which by and by black night doth take away,
Death's second self, that seals up all in rest.
In me thou see'st the glowing of such fire,
That on the ashes of his youth doth lie,
As the death-bed whereon it must expire,
Consumed with that which it was nourish'd by.
This thou perceivest, which makes thy love more
    strong,
To love that well which thou must leave ere
    long."

Where there is beauty such as this, it is an impertinence to insist that Shakspere has not conformed to the special type of beauty represented in the Petrarchan sonnet. He chose not to conform. He won with other tactics. If the reader will analyse the form and thought of the eighty sonnets in the *Oxford Book*, or the two hundred collected by Miss Lockwood, he will feel the charm of occasional irregularity in the handling of both the Petrarchan and the Shaksperean sonnet. But he is more likely, I think, to become increasingly aware that whatever restraints are involved in adherence to typical forms are fully compensated by the rich verbal beauty demanded by the traditional arrangement of rhymes.

For the sonnet, an intricately wrought model of the reflective lyric, requires a peculiarly intimate union of thinking and singing. It may be, as it often was in the Elizabethan period, too full of thought to allow free-winged song, and it may also be too full of uncontrolled, unbalanced emotion to preserve fit unity of thought. Conversely, there may not be enough thought and emotion to fill the fourteen lines: the idea not being of "sonnet size." The difficult question as to whether there is such a thing as an "average-sized" thought and lyrical reflection upon it has been touched upon in an earlier chapter. The limit of a sentence, says Mark Pattison, "is given by the average capacity of human apprehension. . . . The limit of a sonnet is imposed by the average duration of an emotional mood. . . . May we go so far as to say that fourteen lines is the average number which a thought requires for its adequate embodiment before attention must collapse?"

The proper distribution of thought and emotion, that is, the balance of the different parts of a sonnet, is also a very delicate affair. It is like trimming a sailboat. Wordsworth defended Milton's frequent practice of letting the thought of the octave overflow somewhat into the sestet, believing it "to aid in giving that pervading sense of intense unity in which the excellence of the sonnet has always seemed to me mainly to consist."   Most lovers of the sonnet would differ here with these masters of the art.   Whether the weight of thought and feeling can properly be shifted to a final couplet is another debatable question, and critics will always differ as to the artistic value of the "big" line or "big" word which marks the culmination of emotion in many a sonnet. The strange or violent or sonorous word, however splendid in itself, may not fit the curve of the sonnet in which it appears: it may be like a big red apple crowded into the toe of a Christmas stocking.

Nor must the sonnet lean towards either obscurity — the vice of Elizabethan sonnets, or obviousness — the vice of Wordsworth's sonnets after 1820.   The obscure sonnet, while it may tempt the reader's intellectual ingenuity, affords no basis for his emotion, and the obvious sonnet provides no stimulus for his thought. Conventionality of subject and treatment, like the endless imitation of Italian and French sonnet-motives and sonnet-sequences, sins against the law of lyric sincerity. In no lyric form does mechanism so easily obtrude itself. A sonnet is either, like Marlowe's raptures, "all air and fire," or else it is a wooden toy.

CHAPTER IX

RACE, EPOCH AND INDIVIDUAL

"Unless there is a concurrence between the contemporary idioms and rhythms of a period, with the individual idiom of the lyrist, half the expressional force of his ideas will be lost."

ERNEST RHYS, Foreword to *Lyric Poetry*

WE have been considering the typical qualities and forms of lyric poetry. Let us now attempt a rapid survey of some of the conditions which have given the lyric, in certain races and periods and in the hands of certain individuals, its peculiar power.

1. *Questions that are involved*

A whole generation of so-called "scientific" criticism has come and gone since Taine's brilliant experiments with his formula of "race, period and environment" as applied to literature. Taine's *English Literature* remains a monument to the suggestiveness and to the dangers of his method. Some of his countrymen, notably Brunetière in the *Evolution de la Poésie Lyrique en France au XIX Siècle*, and Legouis in the *Défense de la Poésie Française*, have discussed more cautiously and

delicately than Taine himself the racial and
historic conditions affecting lyric poetry in
various periods.

The tendency at present, among critics of
poetry, is to distrust formulas and to keep
closely to ascertainable facts, and this tendency is surely more scientific than the most
captivating theorizing. For one thing, while
recognizing, as the World War has freshly
compelled us to recognize, the actuality of
racial differences, we have grown sceptical
of the old endeavors to classify races in simple terms, as Madame de Staël attempted
to do, for instance, in her famous book on
Germany. We endeavor to distinguish, more
accurately than of old, between ethnic, lin-
guistic and political divisions of men. We
try to look behind the name at the thing itself: we remember that "Spanish" architecture is Arabian, and a good deal of "Gothic"
is Northern French. We confess that we are
only at the beginning of a true science of
ethnology. "It is only in their degree of
physical and mental evolution that the races
of men are different," says Professor W. Z.
Ripley, author of *Races in Europe*. The late
Professor Josiah Royce admitted: "I am

baffled to discover just what the results of
science are regarding the true psychological
and moral meaning of race differences. . . . All
men in prehistoric times are surprisingly alike
in their minds, their morals and their arts.
. . . We do not scientifically know what the
true racial varieties of mental type really
are."[1]

I have often thought of these utterances of
my colleagues, as I have attempted to teach
something about lyric poetry in Harvard
classrooms where Chinese, Japanese, Jewish,
Irish, French, German, Negro, Russian,
Italian and Armenian students appear in be-
wildering and stimulating confusion.   Precisely what is their racial reaction to a lyric of
Sappho?   To an Anglo-Saxon war-song of the
tenth century?   To a Scotch ballad?   To one
of Shakspere's songs?   Some specific racial
reaction there must be, one imagines, but such
capacity for self-expression as the student
commands is rarely capable of giving more
than a hint of it.

And what real response is there, among the
majority of contemporary lovers of poetry, to
the delicate shades of feeling which color the

[1] See Royce's *Race-Questions*.   New York, 1908.

verse of specific periods in the various national literatures? We all use catch-words,
and I shall use them myself later in this chapter, in the attempt to indicate the changes in
lyric atmosphere as we pass, for instance, from
the Elizabethan to the Jacobean age, or from
the "Augustan" to the Romantic epoch in
English literature. Is this sensitiveness to
the temper of various historic periods merely
the possession of a few hundred professional
scholars, who have trained themselves, like
Walter Pater, to live in some well-chosen
moment of the past and to find in their hyper-
sensitized responsiveness to its voices a sort of
consolation prize for their isolation from the
present? Race-mindedness is common, no
doubt, but difficult to express in words: his-
toric-mindedness, though more capable of
expression, is necessarily confined to a few.
Is the response to the poetry of past epochs,
then, chiefly a response of the individual
reader to an individual poet, and do we cross
the frontiers of race and language and historic periods with the main purpose of finding
a man after our own heart? Or is the secret
of our pleasure in the poetry of alien races and
far-off times simply this: that nothing human

is really alien, and that poetry through its generalizing, universalizing power, reveals to us the essential oneness of mankind?

2. Graphic Arts and the Lyric

A specific illustration may suggest an answer. An American collector of Japanese prints recognizes in these specimens of Oriental craftsmanship that mastery of line and composition which are a part of the universal language of the graphic arts. Any human being, in fact, who has developed a sensitiveness to artistic beauty will receive a measure of delight from the work of Japanese masters. A few strokes of the brush upon silk, a bit of lacquer work, the decoration of a sword-hilt, are enough to set his eye dancing. But the expert collector soon passes beyond this general enthusiasm into a quite particular interest in the handicraft of special artists, — a Motonobu, let us say, or a Sesshiu. The collector finds his pleasure in their individual handling of artistic problems, their unique faculties of eye and hand. He responds, in a word, both to the cosmopolitan language employed by every practitioner of the fine arts, and to the local idiom, the personal accent, of, let us say, a certain Japanese draughtsman of the eighteenth century.

And now take, by way of confirmation and also of contrast, the attitude of an American lover of poetry toward those specimens of Japanese and Chinese lyrics which have recently been presented to us in English translations. The American's ignorance of the Oriental languages cuts him off from any appreciation of the individual handling of diction and metre. A Lafcadio Hearn may write delightfully about that special seventeen syllable form of Japanese verse known as the *hokku*. Here is a *hokku* by Bashō, one of the most skilled composers in that form. Hearn prints it with the translation,[1] and explains that the verses are intended to suggest the joyous feeling of spring-time:

> "Oki, oki yo!
> Waga tomo ni sen
> Néru — kochō!"

(Wake up! Wake up! — I will make thee my comrade, thou sleeping butterfly.) An Occidental reader may recognize, through the translation, the charm of the poetic image, and he may be interested in a technical lyric

[1] *Kwaidan*, p. 188. Houghton Mifflin Company, 1904.

form hitherto new to him, but beyond this, in his ignorance of Japanese, he cannot go. Here is a lyric by Wang Ch'ang-Ling, a Chinese poet of the eighth century:

Tears in the Spring [1]

"Clad in blue silk and bright embroidery
  At the first call of Spring the fair young bride,
On whom as yet Sorrow has laid no scar,
Climbs the Kingfisher's Tower. Suddenly
She sees the bloom of willows far and wide,
And grieves for him she lent to fame and war."

And here is another spring lyric by Po Chü-I (A.D. 772–846), as clear and simple as anything in the Greek Anthology:

The Grass [1]

"How beautiful and fresh the grass returns!
  When golden days decline, the meadow burns;
Yet autumn suns no hidden root have slain,
The spring winds blow, and there is grass again.

"Green rioting on olden ways it falls:
  The blue sky storms the ruined city walls;
Yet since Wang Sun departed long ago,
When the grass blooms both joy and fear I know."

The Western reader, although wholly at the mercy of the translator, recognizes the pathos and beauty of the scene and thought expressed

[1] These Chinese lyrics are quoted from *The Lute of Jade*, London, 1909. The translations are by L. Cranmer-Byng.

by the Chinese poet.   But all that is specifically Chinese in lyric form is lost to him.

I have purposely chosen these Oriental types of lyric because they represent so clearly the difference between the universal language of the graphic arts and the more specialized language of poetry.   The latter is still able to convey, even through translation, a suggestion of the emotions common to all men; and this is true of the verse which lies wholly outside the line of that Hebrew-Greek-Roman tradition which has affected so profoundly the development of modern European literature. Yet to express "*ce que tout le monde pense*" — which was Boileau's version of Horace's "*propria communia dicere*" — is only part of the function of lyric poetry.   To give the body of the time the form and pressure of individual feeling, of individual artistic mastery of the language of one's race and epoch; — this, no less than the other, is the task and the opportunity of the lyric poet.

3. Decay and Survival

To appreciate the triumph of whatever lyrics have survived, even when sheltered by the protection of common racial or cultural

traditions, one must remember that the overwhelming majority of lyrics, like the majority
of artistic products of all ages and races and
stages of civilization, are irretrievably lost.
Weak-winged is song! A book like Gummere's *Beginnings of Poetry*, glancing as it
does at the origins of so many national literatures and at the rudimentary poetic efforts of
various races that have never emerged from
barbarism, gives one a poignant sense of the
prodigality of the song-impulse compared
with the slenderness of the actual survivals.
Autumn leaves are not more fugitive. Even
when preserved by sacred ritual, like the
Vedas and the Hebrew Psalter, what we possess is only an infinitesimal fraction of what
has perished. The Sibyl tears leaf after leaf
from her precious volume and scatters them to
the winds. How many glorious Hebrew war-
songs of the type presented in the "Song of
Deborah" were chanted only to be forgotten!
We have but a handful of the lyrics of Sappho
and of the odes of Pindar, while the fragments
of lyric verse gathered up in the *Greek Anthology* tantalize us with their reminder of
what has been lost beyond recall.

Yet if we keep to the line of Hebrew-Greek-

Roman tradition, we are equally impressed
with the enduring influence of the few lyrics
that have survived. The Hebrew lyric, in its
diction, its rhythmical patterns, and above all
in its flaming intensity of spirit, bears the
marks of racial purity, of mental vigor and
moral elevation. It became something even
more significant, however, than the spiritual
expression of a chosen race. The East met
the West when these ancient songs of the
Hebrew Psalter were adopted and sung by
the Christian Church. They were translated,
in the fourth century, into the Latin of the
Vulgate. Many an Anglo-Saxon gleeman
knew that Latin version. It moulded century
after century the liturgy of the European
world. It influenced Tyndale's English version of the Psalms, and this has in turn affected
the whole vocabulary and style of the modern
English lyric. There is scarcely a page of the
Oxford Book of English Verse which does not
betray in word or phrase the influence of the
Hebrew Psalter.

Or take that other marvelous example of
the expression of emotion in terms of bodily
sensation, the lyric of the Greeks. Its clarity and unity, its dislike of vagueness and

excess, its finely artistic restraint, are characteristic of the race.   The simpler Greek
lyrical measures were taken over by Catullus, Horace and Ovid, and though there
were subtle qualities of the Greek models
which escaped the Roman imitators, the
Greco-Roman or "classic" restraint of over-
turbulent emotions became a European heritage. It is doubtless true, as Dr. Henry
Osborn Taylor has pointed out,[1] that the
Greek and Roman classical metres became in
time inadequate to express the new Christian
spirit "which knew neither clarity nor measure." "The antique sense of form and proportion, the antique observance of the mean
and avoidance of extravagance and excess,
the antique dislike for the unlimited or the
monstrous, the antique feeling for literary
unity, and abstention from irrelevancy, the
frank love for all that is beautiful or charming,
for the beauty of the body and for everything
connected with the joy of mortal life, the
antique reticence as to hopes or fears of what
was beyond the grave, — these qualities cease
in medieval Latin poetry."

[1] See his *Classical Heritage of the Middle Ages*, chap. 9, and
particularly the passage quoted in the "Notes and Illustrations" to chap. v of this volume.

4. Lyrics of Western Europe

The racial characteristics of the peoples of Western Europe began to show themselves even in their Latin poetry, but it is naturally in the rise of the vernacular literatures, during the Middle Ages, that we trace the signs of ethnic differentiation. Teuton and Frank and Norseman, Spaniard or Italian, betray their blood as soon as they begin to sing in their own tongue. The scanty remains of Anglo-Saxon lyrical verse are colored with the love of battle and of the sea, with the desolateness of lonely wolds, with the passion of loyalty to a leader. Read "Deor's Lament," "Widsith," "The Wanderer," "The Sea-farer," or the battle-songs of Brunanburh and Maldon in the Anglo-Saxon *Chronicle*.[1] The last strophe of "Deor's Lament," our oldest English lyric, ends with the line:

> "*þæs ofereode, þisses swa mæg*"
> "*That he surmounted, so this may I!*"

The wandering Ulysses says something like this, it is true, in a line of the *Odyssey*, but to

[1] See Cook and Tinker, *Select Translations from Old English Poetry* (Boston, 1902), and Pancoast and Spaeth, *Early English Poems* (New York, 1911).

feel its English racial quality one has only to read after it Masefield's "To-morrow":

"Oh yesterday our little troop was ridden through
  and through,
Our swaying, tattered pennons fled, a broken
  beaten few,
And all a summer afternoon they hunted us and
  slew;
   But to-morrow,
By the living God, we 'll try the game again!"

When Taillefer, knight and minstrel, rode in front of the Norman line at the battle of Hastings, "singing of Charlemagne and of Roland and of Oliver and the vassals who fell at Roncevaux," he typified the coming triumphs of French song in England.[1] French lyrical fashions would have won their way, no doubt, had there been no battle of Hastings. The banners of William the Conqueror had been blessed by Rome. They represented Europe, and the inevitable flooding of the island outpost of "Germania" by the tide of European civilization. *Chanson* and *carole*, dance-songs, troubadour lyrics, the *ballade*, *rondel* and *Noël*, amorous songs of French courtiers, pious hymns of French monks, began to sing themselves in England. The new

[1] See E. B. Reed, *English Lyrical Poetry*, chap. 2. 1912.

grace and delicacy is upon every page of
Chaucer. What was first Provençal and
then French, became English when Chaucer
touched it. From the shadow and grimness
and elegiac pathos of Old English poetry we
come suddenly into the light and color and
gayety of Southern France.[1] In place of
Caedmon's terrible picture of Hell — "ever
fire or frost" — or Dunbar's "Lament for
the Makers" (*Oxford*, No. 21) with its refrain:

> "*Timor Mortis conturbat me*,"

or the haunting burden of the "Lyke-Wake
Dirge" (*Oxford*, No. 381),

> "This ae nighte, this ae nighte,
> — *Every nighte and alle*,
> Fire and sleet and candle-lighte,
> *And Christe receive thy saule*,"

we now find English poets echoing *Aucassin
and Nicolette*:

"In Paradise what have I to win? Therein I
seek not to enter, but only to have Nicolette, my
sweet lady that I love so well. For into Paradise
go none but such folk as I shall tell thee now:
Thither go these same old priests, and halt old men
and maimed, who all day and night cower con-
tinually before the altars and in the crypts; and

[1] See the passage from Legouis quoted in the "Notes and
Illustrations" for this chapter.

such folk as wear old amices and old clouted
frocks, and naked folk and shoeless, and covered
with sores, perishing of hunger and thirst and of
cold, and of little ease. These be they that go
into Paradise; with them I have naught to make.
But into Hell would I fain go; for into Hell fare
the goodly clerks, and goodly knights that fall in
tourneys and great wars, and stout men at arms,
and all men noble. With these would I liefly go.
And thither pass the sweet ladies and courteous
that have two lovers or three, and their lords also
thereto. Thither goes the gold and the silver, the
cloth of vair and cloth of gris, and harpers and
makers, and the prince of this world. With these
I would gladly go, let me but have with me Nicolette, my sweetest lady."

5. The Elizabethan Lyric

The European influence came afresh to
England, as we have seen, with those "courtly
makers" who travelled into France and Italy
and brought back the new-found treasures of
the Renaissance. Greece and Rome renewed,
as they are forever from time to time renewing,
their hold upon the imagination and the art
of English verse. Sometimes this influence of
the classics has worked toward contraction,
restraint, acceptance of human limitations
and of the "rules" of art. But in Elizabethan poetry the classical influence was on

the side of expansion. In that release of vital energy which characterized the English Renaissance, the rediscovery of Greece and Rome and the artistic contacts with France and Italy heightened the confidence of Englishmen, revealed the continuity of history and gave new faith in human nature. It spelled, for the moment at least, liberty rather than authority. It stimulated intellectual curiosity and enthusiasm. Literary criticism awoke to life in the trenchant discussions of the art of poetry by Gascoigne and Sidney, by Puttenham, Campion and Daniel. The very titles of the collections of lyrics which followed the famous *Tottel's Miscellany* of 1557 flash with the spirit of the epoch: *A Paradise of Dainty Devices, A Gorgeous Gallery of Gallant Inventions, A Handfull of Pleasant Delights, The Phœnix Nest, England's Helicon*, Davison's *Poetical Rhapsody*.

Bullen, Schelling, Rhys, Braithwaite, and other modern collectors of the Elizabethan lyric have ravaged these volumes and many more, and have shown how the imported Italian pastoral tallied with the English idyllic mood, how the study of prosody yielded rich and various stanzaic effects, how the

diffusion of the passion for song through all
classes of the community gave a marvelous
singing quality to otherwise thin and mere
"dildido" lines. Mr. Arnold Dolmetsch and
his friends have revived the music of the
Elizabethan song-books, and John Erskine
and other scholars have investigated the
relation of the song-books — especially the
songs composed by musicians such as Byrd,
Dowland and Campion — to the form and
quality of the surviving lyric verse. But one
does not need a knowledge of the Elizabethan
lute and viol, and of the precise difference
between a "madrigal" and a "catch" or
"air" in order to perceive the tunefulness of
a typical Elizabethan song:

> "I care not for these ladies,
> That must be woode and praide:
> Give me kind Amarillis,
> The wanton countrey maide.
> Nature art disdaineth,
> Here beautie is her owne.
>   Her when we court and kisse,
>   She cries, Forsooth, let go:
>   But when we come where comfort is,
>   She never will say No."

It is not that the spirit of Elizabethan lyric
verse is always care-free, even when written by

prodigals such as Peele and Greene and Marlowe. Its childlike grasping after sensuous pleasure is often shadowed by the sword, and by quick-coming thoughts of the brevity of mortal things. Yet it is always spontaneous, swift, alive. Its individual voices caught the tempo and cadence of the race and epoch, so that men as unlike personally as Spenser, Marlowe and Donne are each truly "Elizabethan." Spenser's "vine-like" luxuriance, Marlowe's soaring energy, Donne's grave realistic subtleties, illustrate indeed that note of individualism which is never lacking in the great poetic periods. This individualism betrays itself in almost every song of Shakspere's plays. For here is English race, surely, and the very echo and temper of the Renaissance, but with it all there is the indescribable, inimitable *timbre* of one man's singing voice.

6. The Reaction

If we turn, however, from the lyrics of Shakspere to those of Ben Jonson and of the "sons of Ben" who sang in the reigns of James I and Charles I, we become increasingly conscious of a change in atmosphere. The moment of expansion has passed. The "first fine careless rapture" is over. Classical "authority" resumes its silent, steady pressure. Scholars like to remember that the opening lines of Ben Jonson's "Drink to me only with thine eyes" are a transcript from the Greek. In his "Ode to Himself upon the Censure of his *New Inn*" in 1620 Jonson, like Landor long afterward, takes scornful refuge from the present in turning back to Greece and Rome:

> "Leave things so prostitute,
>   And take the Alcaic lute;
> Or thine own Horace, or Anacreon's lyre;
>   Warm thee by Pindar's fire."

The reaction in lyric form showed itself in the decay of sonnet, pastoral and madrigal, in the neglect of blank verse, in the development of the couplet. Milton, in such matters as these, was a solitary survival of the Elizabethans. Metrical experimentation almost ceased, except in the hands of ingenious recluses like George Herbert. The popular metre of the Caroline poets was the rhymed eight and six syllable quatrain:

> "Yet this inconstancy is such
>   As thou too shalt adore;
> I could not love thee, Dear, so much
>   Loved I not Honour more."

The mystics like Crashaw, Vaughan and Traherne wished and secured a wider metrical liberty, and it is, in truth, these complicated patterns of the devotional lyric of the seventeenth century that are of greatest interest to the poets of our own day. But contemporary taste, throughout the greater portion of that swiftly changing epoch, preferred verse that showed a conservative balance in thought and feeling, in diction and versification. Waller, with his courtier-like instinct for what was acceptable, took the middle of the road, letting Cowley and Quarles experiment as fantastically as they pleased. Andrew Marvell, too, a Puritan writing in the Restoration epoch, composed as "smoothly" as Waller. Herrick, likewise, though fond of minor metrical experiments, celebrated his quiet garden pleasures and his dalliance with amorous fancies in verse of the true Horatian type. "Intensive rather than expansive, fanciful rather than imaginative, and increasingly restrictive in its range and appeal": that is Professor Schelling's expert summary of the poetic tendencies of the age.

And then the lyric impulse died away in England. Dryden could be magnificently

sonorous in declamation and satire, but he
lacked the singing voice. Pope likewise,
though he "lisped in numbers," could never,
for all of his cleverness, learn to sing. The
age of the Augustans, in the first quarter of the
eighteenth century, was an age of prose, of
reason, of good sense, of "correctness." The
decasyllabic couplet, so resonant in Dryden,
so admirably turned and polished by Pope, was
its favorite measure. The poets played safe.
They took no chances with "enthusiasm,"
either in mood or metrical device. What
could be said within the restraining limits of
the couplet they said with admirable point,
vigor and grace. But it was speech, not song.

7. *The Romantic Lyric*

The revolt came towards the middle of the
century, first in the lyrics of Collins, then in
Gray. The lark began to soar and sing once
more in English skies. New windows were
opened in the House of Life. Men looked out
again with curiosity, wonder and a sense of
strangeness in the presence of beauty. They
saw Nature with new eyes; found a new richness in the Past, a new picturesque and savor
in the life of other races, particularly in the

wild Northern and Celtic strains of blood.
Life grew again something mysterious, not to
be comprehended by the "good sense" of the
Augustans, or expressible in the terms of the
rhymed couplet.   Instead of the normal,
poets sought the exceptional, then the strange,
the far-away in time or place, or else the
familiar set in some unusual fantastic light.
The mood of poetry changed from tranquil
sentiment to excited sentiment or "sensibility," and then to sheer passion.   The forms
of poetry shifted from the conventional to
the revival of old measures like blank verse
and the Spenserian stanza, then to the invention of new and freer forms, growing ever more
lyrical.   Poetic diction rebelled against the
Augustan conventions, the stereotyped epi-
thets, the frigid personifications.   It aban-
doned the abstract and general for the specific
and the picturesque.   It turned to the language of real life, and then, dissatisfied, to the
heightened language of passion.   If one reads
Cowper, Blake, Burns and Wordsworth, to
say nothing of poets like Byron and Shelley
who wrote in the full Romantic tide of feeling,
one finds that this poetry has discovered new
themes.   It portrays the child, the peasant,

the villager, the outcast, the slave, the solitary person, even the idiot and the lunatic.   There is a new human feeling for the individual, and for the endless, the poignant variety of "states of soul."   Browning, by and by, is to declare that "states of soul" are the only things worth a poet's attention.

Now this new individuality of themes, of language, of moods, assisted in the free expression of lyricism, the release of the song-impulse of the "single, separate person." The Romantic movement was revelatory, in a double sense.   "Creation widened in man's view"; and there was equally a revelation of individual poetic energy which gave the Romantic lyric an extraordinary variety and beauty of form.   There was an exaggerated individualism, no doubt, which marked the weak side of the whole movement: a deliberate extravagance, a cultivated egoism. Vagueness has its legitimate poetic charm, but in England no less than in Germany or France lyric vagueness often became incoherence.   Symbolism degenerated into meaninglessness.   But the fantastic and grotesque side of Romantic individualism should not blind us to the central fact that a rich person-

ality may appear in a queer garb. Victor
Hugo, like his young friends of the 1830's,
loved to make the gray-coated citizens of
Paris stare at his scarlet, but the personality
which could create such lyric marvels as the
Odes et Ballades may be forgiven for its eccen-
tricities.   William Blake was eccentric to the
verge of insanity, yet he opened, like Whitman
and Poe, new doors of ivory into the wonder-
world.

Yet a lyrist like Keats, it must be remembered, betrayed his personality not so much
through any external peculiarity of the Romantic temperament as through the actual
texture of his word and phrase and rhythm.
Examine his brush-work microscopically, as
experts in Italian painting examine the brush-
strokes and pigments of some picture attrib-
uted to this or that master: you will see that
Keats, like all the supreme masters of poetic
diction, enciphered his lyric message in a language peculiarly his own.   It is for us to de-
cipher it as we may.   He used, of course,
particularly in his earlier work, some of the
stock-epithets, the stock poetic "properties"
of the Romantic school, just as the young
Tennyson, in his volume of 1827, played

with the "owl" and the "midnight" and the "solitary mere," stock properties of eighteenth-century romance. Yet Tennyson, like Keats, and for that matter like Shakspere, passed through this imitative phase into an artistic maturity where without violence or extravagance or eccentricity he compelled words to do his bidding. Each word bears the finger-print of a personality.

Now it is precisely this revelation of personality which gave zest, throughout the Romantic period, to the curiosity about the poetry of alien races. It will be remembered that Romanticism followed immediately upon a period of cosmopolitanism, and that it preceded that era of intense nationalism which came after the Napoleonic wars. Even in that intellectual "United States of Europe," about 1750 — when nationalistic differences were minimized, "enlightenment" was supreme and "propria communia dicere" was the literary motto — there was nevertheless a rapidly growing curiosity about races and literatures outside the charmed circle of Western Europe. It was the era of the Oriental tale, of Northern mythology.   Then the poets of England, France and Germany began their fruitful interchange of inspiration. Walter Scott turned poet when he translated Bürger's "Lenore." Goethe read Marlowe's *Dr. Faustus.* Wordsworth and Coleridge visited Germany not in search of general eighteenth-century "enlightenment," but rather in quest of some peculiar revelation of truth and beauty. In the full tide of Romanticism, Protestant Germany sought inspiration in Italy and Spain, as Catholic France sought it in Germany and England. A new sense of race-values was evident in poetry. It may be seen in Southey, Moore, and Byron, in Hugo's *Les Orientales* and in Leconte de Lisle's *Poèmes Barbares.* Modern music has shown the same tendency: Strauss of Vienna writes waltzes in Arab rhythms, Grieg composes a Scotch symphony, Dvořák writes an American national anthem utilizing negro melodies. As communication between races has grown easier, and the interest in race-characteristics more intense, it would be strange indeed if lovers of lyric poetry did not range far afield in their search for new complexities of lyric feeling.

8. *The Explorer's Pleasure*

This explorer's pleasure in discovering the lyrics of other races was never more keen than it is to-day.   Every additional language that one learns, every new sojourn in a foreign country, enriches one's own capacity for sharing the lyric mood.   It is impossible, of course, that any race or period should enter fully into the lyric impulses of another.   Educated Englishmen have known their Horace for centuries, but it can be only a half-knowledge, delightful as it is.   France and England, so near in miles, are still so far away in instinctive comprehension of each other's mode of poetical utterance!   No two nations have minds of quite the same "fringe."   No man, however complete a linguist, has more than one real mother tongue, and it is only in one's mother tongue that a lyric sings with all its over-tones.   And nevertheless, life offers few purer pleasures than may be found in listening to the half-comprehended songs uttered by alien lips indeed, but from hearts that we know are like our own.

"This moment yearning and thoughtful sitting alone,

It seems to me there are other men in other lands
    yearning and thoughtful,
It seems to me I can look over and behold them in
    Germany, Italy, France, Spain,
Or far, far away, in China, or in Russia or Japan,
    talking other dialects,
And it seems to me if I could know those men I
    should become attached to them as I do to
    men in my own lands,
O I know we should be brethren and lovers,
I know I should be happy with them."

9. *A Test*

If the reader is willing to test his own
responsiveness, not to the alien voices, but to
singers of his own blood in other epochs, let
him now read aloud — or better, recite from
memory — three of the best-known English
poems: Milton's "Lycidas," Gray's "Elegy"
and Wordsworth's "Ode to Immortality."
The first was published in 1638, the second in
1751, and the third in 1817. Each is a "central" utterance of a race, a period and an individual. Each is an open-air poem, written by
a young Englishman; each is lyrical, elegiac —
a song of mourning and of consolation. "Lycidas" is the last flawless music of the English
Renaissance, an epitome of classical and pastoral convention, yet at once Christian, political

and personal.   Beneath the quiet perfection
of Gray's "Elegy" there is the undertone of
passionate sympathy for obscure lives: passionate, but restrained.   Wordsworth knows
no restraint of form or feeling in his great
"Ode"; its germinal idea is absurd to logic,
but not to the imagination.   This elegy, like
the others, is a "lyric cry" of a man, an age,
and a race; "enciphered" like them, with all
the cunning of which the artist was capable;
and decipherable only to those who know the
language of the English lyric.

There may be readers who find these immortal elegies wearisome, staled by repetition,
spoiled by the critical glosses of generations of
commentators.   In that case, one may test
his sense of race, period and personality by a
single quatrain of Landor, who is surely not
over-commented upon to-day:

"From you, Ianthe, little troubles pass
  Like little ripples down a sunny river;
  Your pleasures spring like daisies in the grass,
  Cut down, and up again as blithe as ever."

Find the classicist, the aristocrat, the Englishman, and the lover in that quatrain!

Or, if Landor seems too remote, turn to
Amherst, Massachusetts, and read this amaz-

ing elegy in a country churchyard written
by a New England recluse, Emily Dickinson:

"This quiet Dust was Gentlemen and Ladies,
    And Lads and Girls;
Was laughter and ability and sighing,
    And frocks and curls.
This passive place a Summer's nimble mansion,
    Where Bloom and Bees
Fulfilled their Oriental Circuit,
    Then ceased like these."

CHAPTER X

THE PRESENT STATUS OF THE LYRIC

"And the same may be said of lust and anger and all the other affections, of desire and pain and pleasure which are held to be inseparable from every action — in all of them poetry feeds and waters the passions instead of withering and starving them; she lets them rule instead of ruling them as they ought to be ruled, with a view to the happiness and virtue of mankind."

PLATO's *Republic*, Book 10

"A man has no right to say to his own generation, turning quite away from it, 'Be damned!' It is the whole Past and the whole Future, this same cotton-spinning, dollar-hunting, canting and shrieking, very wretched generation of ours."

CARLYLE *to* EMERSON, *August 29, 1842*

LET us turn finally to some phases of the contemporary lyric. We shall not attempt the hazardous, not to say impossible venture of assessing the artistic value of living poets. "Poets are not to be ranked like collegians in a class list," wrote the wise John Morley long ago. Certainly they cannot be ranked until their work is finished. Nor is it possible within the limits of this chapter to attempt, upon a smaller scale, anything like the task which has been performed so interestingly by books like Miss Lowell's *Tendencies in Modern American Poetry*, Mr. Untermeyer's *New Era in American Poetry*, Miss Wilkinson's *New*

Voices, and Mr. Lowes's *Convention and Revolt*. I wish rather to remind the reader, first, of the long-standing case against the lyric, a case which has been under trial in the court of critical opinion from Plato's day to our own; and then to indicate, even more briefly, the lines of defence. It will be clear, as we proceed, that contemporary verse in America and England is illustrating certain general tendencies which not only sharpen the point of the old attack, but also hearten the spirit of the defenders of lyric poetry.

1. *Plato's Moralistic Objection*

Nothing could be more timely, as a contribution to a critical battle which is just now being waged,[1] than the passage from Plato's *Republic* which furnishes the motto for the present chapter. It expresses one of those eternal verities which each generation must face as best it may: "Poetry feeds and waters the passions instead of withering and starving them; she lets them rule instead of ruling them." "Did we not imply," asks the Athenian Stranger in Plato's *Laws*, "that

[1] See the Introduction and the closing chapter of Stuart P. Sherman's *Contemporary Literature*. Holt, 1917.

the poets are not always quite capable of
knowing what is good or evil?" "There is
also," says Socrates in the *Phædrus*, "a third
kind of madness, which is the possession of
the Muses; this enters into a delicate and
virgin soul, and there inspiring frenzy, awakens lyric and all other members." This
Platonic notion of lyric "inspiration" and
"possession" permeates the immortal passage
of the *Ion*:

"For all good poets, epic as well as lyric, compose their beautiful poems not as works of art, but
because they are inspired and possessed. And as
the Corybantian revellers when they dance are
not in their right mind, so the lyric poets are not
in their right mind when they are composing their
beautiful strains: but when falling under the power
of music and metre they are inspired and possessed; like Bacchic maidens who draw milk and
honey from the rivers, when they are under the
influence of Dionysus, but not when they are in
their right mind. And the soul of the lyric poet
does the same, as they themselves tell us; for they
tell us that they gather their strains from honied
fountains out of the gardens and dells of the Muses;
thither, like the bees, they wing their way. And
this is true. For the poet is a light and winged
and holy thing, and there is no invention in him
until he has been inspired and is out of his senses,
and the mind is no longer in him: when he has not
attained to this state, he is powerless and is unable

to utter his oracles. Many are the noble words in which poets speak of actions like your own words about Homer; but they do not speak of them by any rules of art: only when they make that to which the Muse impels them are their inventions inspired; and then one of them will make dithyrambs, another hymns of praise, another choral strains, another epic or iambic verses — and he who is good at one is not good at any other kind of verse: for not by art does the poet sing, but by power divine. Had he learned by rules of art, he would have known how to speak not of one theme only, but of all; and therefore God takes away the minds of poets, and uses them as his ministers, as he also uses diviners and holy prophets, in order that we who hear them may know that they speak not of themselves who utter these priceless words in a state of unconsciousness, but that God is the speaker, and that through them he is conversing with us."[1]

The other Platonic notion about poetry being "imitation" colors the well-known section of the third book of the *Republic*, which warns against the influence of certain effeminate types of lyric harmony:

"I answered: Of the harmonies I know nothing, but I want to have one warlike, which will sound the word or note which a brave man utters in the hour of danger and stern resolve, or when his cause is failing and he is going to wounds or death or is

[1] Plato's *Ion*. Jowett's translation.

overtaken by some other evil, and at every such crisis meets fortune with calmness and endurance; and another which may be used by him in times of peace and freedom of action, when there is no pressure of necessity — expressive of entreaty or persuasion, of prayer to God, or instruction of man, or again, of willingness to listen to persuasion or entreaty and advice; and which represents him when he has accomplished his aim, not carried away by success, but acting moderately and wisely, and acquiescing in the event. These two harmonies I ask you to leave; the strain of necessity and the strain of freedom, the strain of the unfortunate and the strain of the fortunate, the strain of courage, and the strain of temperance; these, I say, leave."

So runs the famous argument for "the natural rhythms of a manly life," and conversely, the contention that "the absence of grace and rhythm and harmony is closely allied to an evil character." While it is true that the basis for this argument has been modified by our abandonment of the Greek æsthetic theories of "inspiration" and "imitation," Plato's moralistic objection to lyric effeminacy and lyric naturalism is widely shared by many of our contemporaries. They do not find the "New Poetry," lovely as it often is, altogether "manly." They find on the contrary that some of it is what Plato

calls "dissolute," i.e. dissolving or relaxing
the fibres of the will, like certain Russian
dance-music.　I asked an American composer the other day: "Is there anything at all
in the old distinction between secular and sacred music?"　"Certainly," he replied; "secular music excites, sacred music exalts."　If
this distinction is sound, it is plain that much
of the New Poetry aims at excitement of the
senses for its own sake — or in Plato's words,
at "letting them rule, instead of ruling them
as they ought to be ruled."　Or, to use the
severe words of a contemporary critic: "They
bid us be all eye, no mind; all sense, no
thought; all chance, all confusion, no order,
no organization, no fabric of the reason."

However widely we may be inclined to
differ with such moralistic judgments as
these, it remains true that plenty of idealists
hold them, and it is the idealists, rather than
the followers of the senses, who have kept the
love of poetry alive in our modern world.

2. *A Rationalistic Objection*

But the Philistines, as well as the Plato-
nists, have an indictment to bring against
modern verse, and particularly against the

lyric. They find it useless and out of date. Macaulay's essay on Milton (1825) is one of the classic expressions of "Caledonian" rationalism:

"We think that as civilization advances, poetry almost necessarily declines. . . . Language, the machine of the poet, is best fitted for his purpose in its rudest state. Nations, like individuals, first perceive and then abstract. They advance from particular images to general terms. Hence the vocabulary of an enlightened society is philosophical, that of a half-civilized people is poetical. . . . In proportion as men know more and think more, they look less at individuals, and more at classes. They therefore make better theories and worse poems. . . . In an enlightened age there will be much intelligence, much science, much philosophy, abundance of just classification and subtle analysis, abundance of wit and eloquence, abundance of verses and even of good ones, but little poetry." In the essay on Dryden (1828) Macaulay renews the charge: "Poetry requires not an examining but a believing freedom of mind. . . . As knowledge is extended and as the reason develops itself, the imitative arts decay."

Even Macaulay, however, is a less pungent and amusing advocate of rationalism than Thomas Love Peacock in *The Four Ages of Poetry*.[1]

[1] Reprinted in A. S. Cook's edition of Shelley's *Defense of Poetry*. Boston, 1891.

A few sentences must suffice:

"A poet in our times is a semi-barbarian in a
civilized community. He lives in the days that
are past. His ideas, thoughts, feelings, associations, are all with barbarous manners, obsolete
customs, and exploded superstitions. The march
of his intellect is like that of a crab, backward.
... The highest inspirations of poetry are resolv-
able into three ingredients: the rant of unregu-
lated passion, the whining of exaggerated feeling,
and the cant of factitious sentiment; and can
therefore serve only to ripen a splendid lunatic
like Alexander, a puling driveler like Werter, or
a morbid dreamer like Wordsworth. It can never
make a philosopher, nor a statesman, nor in any
class of life a useful or rational man. It cannot
claim the slightest share in any one of the com-
forts and utilities of life, of which we have witnessed so many and so rapid advances. ... We
may easily conceive that the day is not distant
when the degraded state of every species of poetry
will be as generally recognized as that of dramatic
poetry has long been; and this not from any de-
crease either of intellectual power or intellectual
acquisition, but because intellectual power and
intellectual acquisition have turned themselves
into other and better channels, and have aban-
doned the cultivation and the fate of poetry to the
degenerate fry of modern rimesters, and their
Olympic judges, the magazine critics, who continue to debate and promulgate oracles about
poetry as if it were still what it was in the Homeric
age, the all-in-all of intellectual progression, and as

if there were no such things in existence as mathematicians, historians, politicians, and political economists, who have built into the upper air of intelligence a pyramid, from the summit of which they see the modern Parnassus far beneath them, and knowing how small a place it occupies in the comprehensiveness of their prospect, smile at the little ambition and the circumscribed perceptions with which the drivelers and mountebanks upon it are contending for the poetical palm and the critical chair."

No one really knows whether Peacock was wholly serious in this diatribe, but inasmuch as it produced Shelley's *Defense of Poetry* " as an antidote" — as Shelley said — we should be grateful for it. Both Peacock and Macaulay wrote nearly a century ago, but their statements as to the uselessness of poetry, as compared with the value of intellectual exertion in other fields, is wholly in the spirit of twentieth-century rationalism. Few readers of this book may hold that doctrine, but they will meet it on every side; and they will need all they can remember of Sidney and Shelley and George Woodberry "as an antidote."

3. An Æsthetic Objection

In Aristotle's well-known definition of Tragedy in the fifth section of the *Poetics*,

there is one clause, and perhaps only one,
which has been accepted without debate.
"A Tragedy, then, is an artistic imitation of
an action that is serious, complete in itself,
and of an adequate magnitude." Does a lyric
possess "an adequate magnitude?" As the
embodiment of a single aspect of feeling, and
therefore necessarily brief, the lyric certainly
lacks "mass." As an object for æsthetic contemplation, is the average lyric too small
to afford the highest and most permanent
pleasure? "A long poem," remarks A. C.
Bradley in his *Oxford Lectures on Poetry,*[1]
"requires imaginative powers superfluous in
a short one, and it would be easy to show that
it admits of strictly poetic effects of the highest value which the mere brevity of a short
one excludes." Surely the lyric, like the
short story, cannot see life steadily and whole.
It reflects, as we have seen, a single situation
or desire. "Short swallow-flights of song";
piping "as the linnet sings"; have not the
lyric poets themselves confessed this inherent
shortcoming of their art in a thousand similes?
Does not a book of lyrics often seem like

[1] London, 1909. The passage cited is from the chapter on
"The Long Poem in the Age of Wordsworth."

a plantation of carefully tended little trees,
rather than a forest? The most ardent collector of butterflies is aware that he is hunt-
ing only butterflies and not big game. Mr.
John Gould Fletcher's *Japanese Prints* is a
collection of the daintiest lyric fragments,
lovely as a butterfly's wing. But do such
lyrics lack "adequate magnitude"?

It seems to the present writer that this old
objection is a real one, and that it is illustrated afresh by contemporary poetry, but
that it is not so much an argument against
the lyric as such, as it is an explanation of the
ineffectiveness of certain lyric poems. This
defect is not primarily that they lack "magnitude," but rather that they lack an adequate basis in our emotional adjustment to
the fact or situation upon which they turn.
The reader is not prepared for the effect
which they convey. The art of the drama
was defined by the younger Dumas as the art
of preparation. Now the lyrics which are
most effective in primarily dramatic compositions, let us say the songs in "Pippa
Passes" or Ariel's songs in *The Tempest*, are
those where the train of emotional association or contrast has been carefully laid and

is waiting to be touched off. So it is with the markedly lyrical passages in narrative verse — say the close of "Sohrab and Rustum." When a French actress sings the "Marseillaise" to a theatre audience in war-time, or Sir Harry Lauder, dressed in kilts, sings to a Scottish-born audience about "the bonny purple heather," or a marching regiment strikes up "Dixie," the actual song is only the release of a mood already stimulated. But when one comes upon an isolated lyric printed as a "filler" at the bottom of a magazine page, there is no train of emotional association whatever. There is no lyric mood waiting to respond to a "lyric cry." To overcome this obstacle, Walter Page and other magazine editors, a score of years ago, made the experiment of printing all the verse together, instead of scattering it according to the exigencies of the "make-up." Miss Monroe's *Poetry*, *Contemporary Verse*, and the other periodicals devoted exclusively to poetry, easily avoid this handicap of intruding prose. One turns their pages as he turns leaves of music until he finds some composition in accordance with his mood of the moment. The long poem or the drama creates

an undertone of feeling in which the lyrical
mood may easily come to its own, based and
reinforced as it is by the larger poetical structure. The isolated magazine lyric, on the
other hand, is like one swallow trying to make
a summer. Even the lyrics collected in anthologies are often "mutually repellent particles," requiring through their very brevity
and lack of relation with one another, a per-
petual re-focussing of the attention, a constant re-creation of lyric atmosphere. These
conditions have been emphasized, during the
last decade, by that very variety of technical
experimentation, that increased range and
individualism of lyric effort, which have renewed the interest in American poetry.

4. Subjectivity as a Curse

I have often thought of a conversation with
Samuel Asbury, a dozen years ago, about a
friend of ours, a young Southern poet of distinct promise, who had just died. Like many
Southern verse-writers of his generation, he
had lived and written under the inspiration of
Poe. Asbury surprised me by the almost
bitter remark that Poe's influence had been
a blight upon the younger Southern poets, in-

asmuch as it had tended to over-subjectivity, to morbid sensibility, and to a pre-occupation with purely personal emotions. He argued, as he has since done so courageously in his *Texas Nativist*,[1] that more objective forms of poetry, particularly epic and dramatic handling of local and historic American material, was far healthier stuff for a poet to work with.

This objection to the lyric as an encourager of subjective excitement, of egoistic introspection, like the other objections already stated, is one of old standing. Goethe remarked that the subjectivity of the smaller poets was of no significance, but that they were interested in nothing really objective. But though this indictment of over-individualism has often been drawn, our own times are a fresh proof of its validity. If the revelation of personality unites men, the stress upon mere individuality separates them, and there are countless poets of the day who glory in their eccentric individualism without remembering that it is only through a richly developed personality that poetry gains any universal values. "Nothing in literature is so perishable as eccentricity, with regard to

[1] Published by the author at College Station, Texas.

which each generation has its own requirements and its own standard of taste; and the
critic who urges contemporary poets to make
their work as individual as possible is delib-
erately inviting them to build their structures
on sand instead of rock."[1] Every reader of
contemporary poetry is aware that along with
its exhilarating freshness and force there has
been a display of singularity and of silly
nudity both of body and mind. Too intimate
confidences have been betrayed in the lyric
confessional. It is a fine thing to see a Var-
sity eight take their dip in the river at the
end of an afternoon's spin. Those boys strip
well. But there are middle-aged poets who
strip very badly. Nature never intended
them to play the rôle of Narcissus. Dickens
wrote great novels in a room so hung with
mirrors that he could watch himself in the act
of composition. But that is not the best sort
of writing-room for lyric poets, particularly
in a decade when acute self-consciousness,
race-consciousness and even coterie-conscious-
ness are exploited for commercial purposes,
and the "lutanists of October" are duly pho-
tographed at their desks.

[1] Edmond Holmes, *What is Poetry*, p. 68.

5. Mere Technique

There is one other count in the old indictment of the lyric which is sure to be emphasized whenever any generation, like our own, shows a new technical curiosity about lyric forms. It is this: that mere technique will "carry" a lyric, even though thought, passion and imagination be lacking. This charge will inevitably be made from time to time, and not merely by the persons who naturally tend to stress the content-value of poetry as compared with its form-value. It was Stedman, who was peculiarly susceptible to the charm of varied lyric form, who remarked of some of Poe's lyrics, "The libretto (i.e. the sense) is nothing, the score is all in all." And it must be admitted that the "libretto" of "Ulalume," for instance, is nearly or quite meaningless to many lovers of poetry who value the "score" very highly. In a period marked by enthusiasm for new experiments in versification, new feats of technique, the borderland between real conquests of novel territory and sheer nonsense verse becomes very hazy. The *Spectra* hoax, perpetrated so cleverly in 1916 by Mr. Ficke and Mr. Witter Bynner, fooled

many of the elect.[1] I have never believed
that Emerson meant to decry Poe when he
referred to him as "the jingle-man." Emerson's memory for names was faulty, and he
was trying to indicate the author of the

"tintinnabulation of the bells."

That Poe was a prestidigitator with verse, and
may be regarded solely with a view to his
professional expertness, is surely no ground
for disparaging him as a poet. But it is the
kind of penalty which extraordinary technical
expertness has to pay in all the arts. Many
persons remember Paganini only as the violinist who could play upon a single string.
Every *"amplificator imperii"* — every wid-
ener of the bounds of the empire of poetry,
like Vachel Lindsay with his experiments in
chanted verse, Robert Frost with his subtle
renderings of the cadences of actual speech,
Miss Amy Lowell with her doctrine of "curves"
and "returns" and polyphony — runs the risk
of being regarded for a while as a technician
and nothing more. Ultimately a finer balance
is struck between the claims of form and content: the ideas of a poet, his total vision of

[1] See Untermeyer's *New Era*, etc., pp. 320–23.

life, his contribution to the thought as well
as to the craftsmanship of his generation, are
thrown into the scale.   Victor Hugo is now
seen to be something far other than the mere
amazing lyric virtuoso of the *Odes et Ballades*
of 1826.   Walt Whitman ultimately gets
judged as Walt Whitman, and not merely as
the inventor of a new type of free verse in
1855.   A rough justice is done at last, no
doubt, but for a long time the cleverest and
most original manipulators of words and
tunes are likely to be judged by their vir-
tuosity alone.

6. *The Lines of Defence*

The objections to lyric poetry which have
just been rehearsed are of varying degrees of
validity.   They have been mentioned here
because they still affect, more or less, the
judgment of the general public as it endeavors
to estimate the value of the contemporary
lyric.   I have little confidence in the taste of
professed admirers of poetry who can find no
pleasure in contemporary verse, and still less
confidence in the taste of our contemporaries
whose delight in the "new era" has made
them deaf to the great poetic voices of the

past. I am sorry for the traditionalist who cannot enjoy Robert Frost and Edwin Arlington Robinson and Edgar Lee Masters and Carl Sandburg. He is, in my opinion, in a parlous state. But the state of the young rebel who cannot enjoy "Lycidas" and "The Progress of Poesy" and the "Ode to Dejection" is worse than parlous. It is hopeless.

It is not for him, therefore, that these final paragraphs are written, but rather for those lovers of poetry who recognize that it transcends all purely moralistic and utilitarian, as it does all historical and technical considerations, — that it lifts the reader into a serene air where beauty and truth abide, while the perplexed generations of men appear and disappear. Sidney and Campion and Daniel pleaded its cause for the Elizabethans, Coleridge and Wordsworth and Shelley defended it against the Georgian Philistines, Carlyle, Newman and Arnold championed it through every era of Victorian materialism. In the twentieth century, critics like Mackail and A. C. Bradley and Rhys, poets like Newbolt and Drinkwater and Masefield — to say nothing of living poets and critics among our own countrymen — have spoken out for poetry

with a knowledge, a sympathy and an eloquence unsurpassed in any previous epoch.
The direct "Defence of Poetry" may safely be
left to such men as these.

I have chosen, rather, the line of indirect
vindication of poetry, and particularly of the
lyric, which has been attempted in this book.
We have seen that the same laws are perpetually at work in poetry as in all the other
arts; that we have to do with the transmission
of a certain kind of feeling through a certain
medium; that the imagination remoulds the
material proffered by the senses, and brings
into order the confused and broken thoughts
of the mind, until it presents the eternal aspect of things through words that dance to
music. We have seen that the study of poetry
leads us back to the psychic life of primitive
races, to the origins of language and of society,
and to the underlying spirit of institutions and
nationalities, so that even a fragment of surviving lyric verse may be recognized as a part of
those unifying and dividing forces that make
up the life of the world. We have found
poetry, furthermore, to be the great personal
mode of literary expression, a revelation of
noble personality as well as base, and that this

personal mode of expression has continued to hold its own in the modern world. The folk-epic is gone, the art-epic has been outstripped by prose fiction, and the drama needs a theatre. But the lyric needs only a *poet*, who can compose in any of its myriad forms. No one who knows contemporary literature will deny that the lyric is now interpreting the finer spirit of science, the drift of social progress, and above all, the instincts of personal emotion. Through it to-day, as never before in the history of civilization, the heart of a man can reach the heart of mankind. It is inconceivable that the lyric will not grow still more significant with time, freighted more and more deeply with thought and passion and touched with a richer and more magical beauty. Some appreciation of it, no matter how inadequate, should be a part of the spiritual possessions of every civilized man.

> "*Die Geisterwelt ist nicht verschlossen;*
> *Dein Sinn ist zu, dein Herz ist todt!*
> *Auf! bade, Schüler, unverdrossen*
> *Die ird'sche Brust im Morgenroth!*"

NOTES AND ILLUSTRATIONS

I ADD here some suggestions to teachers who may wish to use this book in the classroom. In connection with each chapter I have indicated the more important discussions of the special topic. There is also some additional illustrative material, and I have indicated a few hints for classroom exercises, following methods which have proved helpful in my own experience as a teacher.

I have tried to keep in mind the needs of two kinds of college courses in poetry. One of them is the general introductory course, which usually begins with the lyric rather than with the epic or the drama, and which utilizes some such collection as the *Golden Treasury* or the *Oxford Book of English Verse*. Any such collection of standard verse, or any of the anthologies of recent poetry, like those selected by Miss Jessie B. Rittenhouse or Mr. W. S. Braithwaite, should be constantly in use in the classroom as furnishing concrete illustration of the principles discussed in books like mine.

The other kind of course which I have had in mind is the one dealing with the works of a single poet. Spenser, Milton, Wordsworth, Tennyson, Browning, are among the poets most frequently chosen for this sort of study. I have found it an advantage to carry on the discussion of the general principles of poetic imagination and expression in connection with the close textual study of the complete work of any one poet. It is hoped that this book may prove helpful for such a purpose.

CHAPTER I

This chapter aims to present, in as simple a form as possible, some of the fundamental questions in æsthetic theory as far as they bear upon the study of poetry. James Sully's article on "Æsthetics" in the *Encyclopædia Britannica*, and Sidney Colvin's article on "The Fine Arts," afford a good preliminary survey of the field. K. Gordon's *Æsthetics*, E. D. Puffer's *Psychology of Beauty*, Santayana's *Sense of Beauty*, Raymond's *Genesis of Art Form*, and Arthur Symons's *Seven Arts*, are stimulating books. Bosanquet's *Three Lectures on Æsthetic* is commended to those advanced students who have not time to read his voluminous *History of Æsthetic*, just as Lane Cooper's translation of *Aristotle on the Art of Poetry* may be read profitably before taking up the more elaborate discussions in Butcher's *Aristotle's Theory of Poetry and Fine Art*. In the same way, Spingarn's *Creative Criticism* is a good preparation for Croce's monumental *Æsthetics*. The student should certainly make some acquaintance with Lessing's *Laokoon*, and he will find Babbitt's *New Laokoon* a brilliant and trenchant survey of the old questions.

It may be, however, that the teacher will prefer to pass rapidly over the ground covered in this chapter, rather than to run the risk of confusing his students with problems admittedly difficult. In that case the classroom discussions may begin with chapter II. I have found, however, that the new horizons which are opened to many students in connection with the topics touched upon in chapter I more than make up for some temporary bewilderment.

CHAPTER II

The need here is to look at an old subject with fresh eyes. Teachers who are fond of music or painting or sculpture can invent many illustrations following the hint given in the Orpheus and Eurydice passage in the text. Among recent books, Fairchild's *Making of Poetry* and Max Eastman's *Enjoyment of Poetry* are particularly to be commended for their unconventional point of view. See also Fairchild's pamphlet on *Teaching of Poetry in the High School*, and John Erskine's paper on "The Teaching of Poetry" (*Columbia University Quarterly*, December, 1915). Alfred Hayes's "Relation of Music to Poetry" (*Atlantic*, January, 1914) is pertinent to this chapter. But the student should certainly familiarize himself with Theodore Watts-Dunton's famous article on "Poetry" in the *Encyclopædia Britannica*, now reprinted with additions in his *Renascence of Wonder*. He should also read A. C. Bradley's chapter on "Poetry for its Own Sake" in the *Oxford Lectures on Poetry*, Neilson's *Essentials of Poetry*, Stedman's *Nature and Elements of Poetry*, as well as the classic "Defences" of Poetry by Philip Sidney, Shelley, Leigh Hunt and George E. Woodberry. For advanced students, R. P. Cowl's *Theory of Poetry in England* is a useful summary of critical opinions covering almost every aspect of the art of poetry, as it has been understood by successive generations of Englishmen.

CHAPTER III

This chapter, like the first, will be difficult for some students. They may profitably read, in connection with it, Professor Winchester's chapter on "Imagination" in his *Literary Criticism*, Neilson's discussion of "Imagination" in his *Essentials of Poetry*, the first four chapters of Fairchild, chapters 4, 13, 14, and 15 of Coleridge's *Biographia Literaria*, and Wordsworth's Preface to his volume of Poems of 1815. See also Stedman's chapter on "Imagination" in his *Nature and Elements of Poetry*.

Under section 2, some readers may be interested in

Sir William Rowan Hamilton's account of his famous discovery of the quaternion analysis, one of the greatest of all discoveries in pure mathematics:

"Quaternions started into life, or light, full grown, on Monday, the 16th of October, 1843, as I was walking with Lady Hamilton to Dublin, and came up to Brougham Bridge, which my boys have since called the Quaternion Bridge. That is to say, I then and there felt the galvanic circuit of thought *close*, and the sparks which fell from it were the *fundamental equations between i, j, k; exactly such* as I have used them ever since. I pulled out on the spot a pocket-book, which still exists, and made an entry on which, *at the very moment*, I felt that it might be worth my while to expend the labor of at least ten (or it might be fifteen) years to come. But then it is fair to say that this was because I felt a *problem* to have been at that moment *solved* — an intellectual want relieved — which had *haunted* me for at least *fifteen years before. Less than an hour* elapsed before I had asked and obtained leave of the Council of the Royal Irish Academy, of which Society I was, at that time, the President — to *read* at the *next General Meeting* a *Paper* on Quaternions; which I accordingly *did*, on November 13, 1843."

The following quotation from Lascelles-Abercrombie's study of Thomas Hardy presents in brief compass the essential problem dealt with in this chapter. It is closely written, and should be read more than once.

"Man's intercourse with the world is necessarily formative. His experience of things outside his consciousness is in the manner of a chemistry, wherein some energy of his nature is mated with the energy brought in on his nerves from externals, the two combining into something which exists only in, or perhaps we should say closely around, man's consciousness. Thus what man knows of the world is what has been *formed* by the mixture of his own nature with the streaming in of the external world. This formative energy of his, reducing the in-coming world into some constant manner of appearance which may be appreciable by consciousness, is most conveniently to be described, it seems, as an unaltering imaginative desire: desire which accepts as its material, and fashions itself forth upon, the many random powers sent by the world to invade man's mind. That there is this formative energy in man may easily be seen by thinking of certain dreams; those dreams, namely, in which some disturbance outside the sleeping brain (such as a sound of knocking or a bodily discomfort) is completely formed into vivid trains of imagery, and in that form only is presented to the dreamer's consciousness. This, however, merely shows the presence of the active desire to shape sensation into what consciousness can accept; the dream is like an experiment done in the isolation of a laboratory; there are so many conflicting factors when we are awake that the events of sleep must only serve as a symbol or diagram of the intercourse of mind with that which is not mind — intercourse which only takes place in a region where the outward radiations of man's nature combine with the irradiations of the world. Perception itself is a formative act; and all the construction of sensation into some orderly, coherent idea of the world is a further activity of the central imaginative desire. Art is created, and art is enjoyed, because in it man may himself completely express and exercise those inmost desires which in ordinary experience are by no means to be completely expressed. Life has at last been perfectly formed and measured to man's requirements; and in art man knows himself truly the master of his existence. It is this sense of mastery which gives man that raised and delighted consciousness of self which art provokes."

CHAPTER IV

I regret that Professor Lowes's brilliant discussion of "Poetic Diction" in his *Convention and Revolt* did not appear until after this chapter was written. There are stimulating remarks on Diction in Fairchild and Eastman, in Raleigh's *Wordsworth*, in L. A. Sherman's *Analytics of Literature*, chapter 6, in Raymond's *Poetry as a Representative Art*, and in Hudson Maxim's *Science of Poetry*. Coleridge's description of Wordsworth's theory of poetic diction in the *Biographia Literaria* is famous. Walt Whitman's *An American Primer*, first published in the *Atlantic* for April, 1904, is a highly interesting contribution to the subject.

No theoretical discussion, however, can supply the place of a close study, word by word, of poems in the classroom. It is advisable, I think, to follow such analyses of the diction of Milton, Keats and Tennyson by a scrutiny of the diction employed by contemporary poets like Edgar Lee Masters and Carl Sandburg.

The following passages in prose and verse, printed without the authors' names, are suggested as an exercise in the study of diction:

1. "The falls were in plain view about a mile off, but very distinct, and no roar — hardly a murmur. The river tumbling green and white, far below me; the dark, high banks, the plentiful umbrage, many bronze cedars, in shadow; and tempering and arching all the immense materiality, a clear sky overhead, with a few white clouds, limpid, spiritual, silent. Brief, and as quiet as

brief, that picture — a remembrance always afterward."

2. "If there be fluids, as we know there are, which, conscious of a coming wind, or rain, or frost, will shrink and strive to hide themselves in their glass arteries; may not that subtle liquor of the blood perceive, by properties within itself, that hands are raised to waste and spill it; and in the veins of men run cold and dull as his did, in that hour!"

3. "On a flat road runs the well-train'd runner,
    He is lean and sinewy with muscular legs,
    He is thinly clothed, he leans forward as he runs,
    With lightly closed fists and arms partially rais'd."

4. "The feverish heaven with a stitch in the side,
        Of lightning."

5. "Out of blue into black is the scheme of the skies,
        and their dews are the wine of the bloodshed of
        things."

6. "Dry clash'd his harness in the icy caves
    And barren chasms, and all to left and right
    The bare black cliff clang'd round him, as he based
    His feet on juts of slippery crag that rang
    Sharp-smitten with the dint of armed heels."

7. "As for the grass, it grew as scant as hair
        In leprosy; their dry blades pricked the mud
        Which underneath looked kneaded up with blood.
    One stiff blind horse, his every bone a-stare,
    Stood stupefied, however he came there:
        Thrust out past service from the devil's stud."

8. " For the main criminal I have no hope
   Except in such a suddenness of fate.
   I stood at Naples once, a night so dark
   I could have scarce conjectured there was earth
   Anywhere, sky or sea or world at all:
   But the night's black was burst through by a
      blaze —
   Thunder struck blow on blow, earth groaned and
      bore,
   Through her whole length of mountain visible:
   There lay the city thick and plain with spires,
   And, like a ghost disshrouded, white the sea.
   So may the truth be flashed out by one blow,
   And Guido see, one instant, and be saved."

CHAPTER V

A fresh and clear discussion of the principles governing Rhythm and Metre may be found in C. E. Andrews's *Writing and Reading of Verse.* The well-known books by Alden, Corson, Gummere, Lewis, Mayor, Omond, Raymond and Saintsbury are indicated in the Bibliography. Note also the bibliographies given by Alden and Patterson.

I have emphasized in this chapter the desirability of compromise in some hotly contested disputes over terminology and methods of metrical notation. Perhaps I have gone farther in this direction than some teachers will wish to go. But all classroom discussion should be accompanied by oral reading of verse, by the teacher and if possible by pupils, and the moment oral interpretations begin, it will be evident that "a satisfied ear" is more important than an exact agreement upon methods of notation.

I venture to add here, for their suggestiveness, a few

passages about Rhythm and Metre, and finally, as an exercise in the study of the prevalence of the "iambic roll" in sentimental oratory, an address by Robert G. Ingersoll.

1. "Suppose that we figure the nervous current which corresponds to consciousness as proceeding, like so many other currents of nature, in *waves* — then we do receive a new apprehension, if not an explanation, of the strange power over us of successive strokes. . . . Whatever things occupy our attention — events, objects, tones, combinations of tones, emotions, pictures, images, ideas — our consciousness of them will be heightened by the rhythm as though it consisted of waves."

EASTMAN, *The Enjoyment of Poetry*, p. 93.

2. "Rhythm of pulse is the regular alternation of units made up of beat and pause; rhythm in verse is a measured or standardized arrangement of sound relations. The difference between rhythm of pulse and rhythm in verse is that the one is known through touch, the other through hearing; as rhythm, they are essentially the same kind of thing. Viewed generally and externally, then, verse is language that is beaten into measured rhythm, or that has some type of uniform or standard rhythmical arrangement."

FAIRCHILD, *The Making of Poetry*, p. 117.

3. "A Syllable is a body of sound brought out with an independent, single, and unbroken breath (Sievers). This syllable may be *long* or *short*, according to the time it fills; compare the syllables in *merrily* with the syllables in *corkscrew*. Further, a syllable may be *heavy* or *light* (also called *accented* or *unaccented*) according as it

receives more or less force or *stress* of tone: compare the two syllables of *streamer*. Lastly, a syllable may have increased or diminished *height* of tone, — *pitch: cf.* the so-called 'rising inflection' at the end of a question. Now, in spoken language, there are infinite degrees of length, of stress, of pitch. . . .

"It is a well-known property of human speech that it keeps up a ceaseless change between accented and unaccented syllables. A long succession of accented syllables becomes unbearably monotonous; a long succession of unaccented syllables is, in effect, impossible. Now when the ear detects at regular intervals a recurrence of accented syllables, varying with unaccented, it perceives *Rhythm*. Measured intervals of time are the basis of all verse, and their *regularity* marks off poetry from prose; so that Time is thus the chief element in Poetry, as it is in Music and in Dancing. From the idea of measuring these time-intervals, we derive the name Metre; Rhythm means pretty much the same thing, — 'a flowing,' an even, measured motion. This rhythm is found everywhere in nature: the beat of the heart, the ebb and flow of the sea, the alternation of day and night. Rhythm is not artificial, not an invention; it lies at the heart of things, and in rhythm the noblest emotions find their noblest expression."

GUMMERE, Handbook of Poetics, p. 133.

4. "It was said of Chopin that in playing his waltzes his left hand kept absolutely perfect time, while his right hand constantly varied the rhythm of the melody, according to what musicians call *tempo rubato*, 'stolen' or distorted time. Whether this is true in fact, or even physically possible, has been doubted; but it represents a perfectly familiar possibility of the mind. Two streams

of sound pass constantly through the inner ear of one who understands or appreciates the rhythm of our verse: one, never actually found in the real sounds which are uttered, is the absolute rhythm, its equal time-intervals moving on in infinitely perfect progression; the other, represented by the actual movement of the verse, is constantly shifting by quickening, retarding, strengthening or weakening its sounds, yet always hovers along the line of the perfect rhythm, and bids the ear refer to that perfect rhythm the succession of its pulsations."

ALDEN, *An Introduction to Poetry*, p. 188.

5. "Many lines in Swinburne cannot be scanned at all except by the Lanier method, which reduces so-called feet to their purely musical equivalents of time bars. What, for instance, can be made by the formerly accepted systems of prosody of such hexameters as

'Full-sailed, wide-winged, poised softly forever asway?'

The usual explanation of this line is that Mr. Swinburne, carelessly, inadvertently, or for some occult purpose, interjected one line of five feet among his hexameters and the scansion usually followed is by arrangement into a pentameter, thus:

'Full-sailed | wide-winged | poised softly | forever | asway,'

the first two feet being held to be spondees, and the third and fourth amphibrachs. It has also been proposed to make the third foot a spondee or an iambus, and the remaining feet anapæsts, thus:

'Full-sailed | wide-winged | poised soft- | ly forev- | er asway.'

" The confusion of these ideas is enough to mark them
as unscientific and worthless, to say nothing of the severe
reflection they cast on the poet's workmanship.   We
have not so known Mr. Swinburne, for, if there be anything he has taught us about himself it is his strenuous
and sometimes absurd particularity about immaculate
form.   He would never overlook a line of five feet in
a poem of hexameters.   But — as will, I think, appear
later and conclusively — the line is really of six feet,
and is not iambic, trochaic, anapæstic, the spurious
spondaic that some writers have tried to manufacture
for English verse, or anything else recognized in Coleridge's immortal stanza, or in text-books.   It simply
cannot be scanned by classical rules; it cannot be
weighed justly, and its full meaning extracted, by any
of the 'trip-time' or 'march-time' expedients of other
investigators.   It is purely music; and when read by
the method of music appears perfectly designed and
luminous with significance.   Only a poet that was at
heart a composer could have made such a phrase, based
upon such intimate knowledge of music's rhythmical
laws."

C. E. RUSSELL, "Swinburne and Music"
North American Review, November, 1907.

6. Dr. Henry Osborn Taylor has kindly allowed me
to quote this passage from his *Classical Heritage of the
Middle Ages*, pp. 246, 247:

"Classic metres expressed measured feelings.   Hexameters had given voice to many emotions beautifully,
with unfailing modulation of calm or storm.   They had
never revealed the infinite heart of God, or told the
yearning of the soul responding; nor were they ever
to be the instrument of these supreme disclosures in

Christian times. Such unmeasured feelings could not be held within the controlled harmonies of the hexameter nor within sapphic or alcaic or Pindaric strophes. These antique forms of poetry definitely expressed their contents, although sometimes suggesting further unspoken feeling, which is so noticeable with Virgil. But characteristic Christian poetry, like the Latin mediæval hymn, was not to express its meaning as definitely or contain its significance. Mediæval hymns are childlike, having often a narrow clearness in their literal sense; and they may be childlike, too, in their expressed symbolism. Their significance reaches far beyond their utterance; they suggest, they echo, and they listen; around them rolls the voice of God, the infinitude of His love and wrath, heaven's chorus and hell's agonies; *dies irae, dies illa* — that line says little, but mountains of wrath press on it, from which the soul shall not escape.

"Christian emotion quivers differently from any movement of the spirit in classic measures. The new quiver, the new shudder, the utter terror, and the utter love appear in mediæval rhymed accentual poetry:

> Desidero te millies,
> Mê Jesu; quando venies?
> Me laetum quando facies,
> Ut vultu tuo saties?

> Quo dolore
> Quo moerore
> Deprimuntur miseri,
> Qui abyssis
> Pro commissis
> Submergentur inferi.

Recordare, Jesu pie,
Quod sum causa tuae viae;
Ne me perdas illa die.

. . . . . .

Lacrymosa dies illa
Qua resurget ex favilla,
Judicandus homo reus;
Huic ergo parce, Deus!
Pie Jesu, Domine,
Dona eis requiem.

"Let any one feel the emotion of these verses and then
turn to some piece of classic poetry, a passage from
Homer or Virgil, an elegiac couplet or a strophe from
Sappho or Pindar or Catullus, and he will realize the
difference, and the impossibility of setting the emotion
of a mediæval hymn in a classic metre."

7. "*Friends:* I know how vain it is to gild a grief with
words, and yet I wish to take from every grave its fear.
Here in this world, where life and death are equal things,
all should be brave enough to meet what all the dead
have met. The future has been filled with fear, stained
and polluted by the heartless past. From the wondrous
tree of life the buds and blossoms fall with ripened fruit,
and in the common bed of earth, the patriarchs and
babes sleep side by side.

"Why should we fear that which will come to all
that is?

"We cannot tell, we do not know, which is the greater
blessing — life or death. We do not know whether the
grave is the end of this life, or the door of another, or
whether the night here is not somewhere else at dawn.

Neither can we tell which is the more fortunate — the child dying in its mother's arms, before its lips have learned to form a word, or he who journeys all the length of life's uneven road, painfully taking the last slow steps with staff and crutch.

"Every cradle asks us, 'Whence?' and every coffin, 'Whither?' The poor barbarian, weeping above his dead, can answer these questions as intelligently as the robed priest of the most authentic creed. The tearful ignorance of the one is just as consoling as the learned and unmeaning words of the other. No man, standing where the horizon of a life has touched a grave, has any right to prophesy a future filled with pain and tears. It may be that death gives all there is of worth to life. If those we press and strain against our hearts could never die, perhaps that love would wither from the earth. Maybe this common fate treads from out the paths between our hearts the weeds of selfishness and hate, and I had rather live and love where death is king, than have eternal life where love is not. Another life is naught, unless we know and love again the ones who love us here.

"They who stand with aching hearts around this little grave need have no fear. The larger and the nobler faith in all that is and is to be tells us that death, even at its worst, is only perfect rest. We know that through the common wants of life — the needs and duties of each hour — their griefs will lessen day by day, until at last this grave will be to them a place of rest and peace — almost of joy. There is for them this consolation. The dead do not suffer. And if they live again, their lives will surely be as good as ours. We have no fear. We are all children of the same mother, and the same fate awaits us all.

"We, too, have our religion, and it is this: Help for the living, hope for the dead."

> Robert G. Ingersoll, "Address over a Little Boy's Grave."

Chapter VI

I have not attempted in this chapter to give elaborate illustrations of the varieties of rhyme and stanza in English poetry. Full illustrations will be found in Alden's *English Verse*. A clear statement of the fundamental principles involved is given in W. H. Carruth's *Verse Writing*.

Free verse is suggestively discussed by Lowes, *Convention and Revolt*, chapters 6 and 7, and by Andrews, *Writing and Reading of Verse*, chapters 5 and 19. Miss Amy Lowell has written fully about it in the Prefaces to *Sword Blades and Poppy Seed* and *Can Grande's Castle*, in the final chapter of *Tendencies in Modern American Poetry*, in the Prefaces to *Some Imagist Poets*, and in the *North American Review* for January, 1917. Mr. Braithwaite's annual *Anthologies of American Verse* give a full bibliography of special articles upon this topic.

An interesting classroom test of the difference between prose rhythm and verse rhythm with strongly marked metre and rhyme may be found in comparing Emerson's original prose draft of his "Two Rivers," as found in volume 9 of his *Journal*, with three of the stanzas of the finished poem:

"Thy voice is sweet, Musketaquid, and repeats the music of the rain, but sweeter is the silent stream which flows even through thee, as thou through the land.

"Thou art shut in thy banks, but the stream I love flows in thy water, and flows through rocks and through the air and through rays of light as well, and through darkness, and through men and women.

"I hear and see the inundation and the eternal spending of the stream in winter and in summer, in men and animals, in passion and thought. Happy are they who can hear it."

"Thy summer voice, Musketaquit,
  Repeats the music of the rain;
But sweeter rivers pulsing flit
  Through thee, as thou through Concord plain.

"Thou in thy narrow banks are pent;
  The stream I love unbounded goes
Through flood and sea and firmament;
  Through light, through life, it forward flows.

"I see the inundation sweet,
  I hear the spending of the stream
Through years, through men, through nature fleet,
  Through love and thought, through power and dream."

I also suggest for classroom discussion the following brief passages from recent verse, printed without the authors' names:

1. "The milkman never argues; he works alone and no one speaks to him; the city is asleep when he is on his job; he puts a bottle on six hundred porches and calls it a day's work; he climbs two hundred wooden stairways; two horses are company for him; he never argues."

2. "Sometimes I have nervous moments —
    there is a girl who looks at me strangely
    as much as to say,
    You are a young man,

and I am a young woman,
and what are you going to do about it?
And I look at her as much as to say,
I am going to keep the teacher's desk
        between us, my dear,
as long as I can."

3. "I hold her hands and press her to my breast.

"I try to fill my arms with her loveliness, to plunder her sweet smile with kisses, to drink her dark glances with my eyes.

"Ah, but where is it?   Who can strain the blue from the sky?

"I try to grasp the beauty; it eludes me, leaving only the body in my hands.

"Baffled and weary, I came back.   How can the body touch the flower which only the spirit may touch?"

4. "Child, I smelt the flowers,
        The golden flowers . . . hiding in crowds like
            fairies at my feet,
        And as I smelt them the endless smile of the
            infinite broke over me, and I knew that
            they and you and I were one.
        They and you and I, the cowherds and the cows,
            the jewels and the potter's wheel, the moth-
            ers and the light in baby's eyes.
        For the sempstress when she takes one stitch
            may make nine unnecessary;
        And the smooth and shining stone that rolls and
            rolls like the great river may gain no moss,
        And it is extraordinary what a lot you can do
            with a platitude when you dress it up in
            Blank Prose.
        Child, I smelt the flowers."

Chapter VII

Recent criticism has been rich in its discussions of the lyric. John Drinkwater's little volume on *The Lyric* is suggestive. See also C. E. Whitmore's article in the *Pub. Mod. Lang. Ass.*, December, 1918. Rhys's *Lyric Poetry*, Schelling's *English Lyric*, Reed's *English Lyrical Poetry* cover the whole field of the historical English lyric. A few books on special periods are indicated in the "Notes" to chapter IX.

An appreciation of the lyric mood can be helped greatly by adequate oral reading in the classroom. For teachers who need suggestions as to oral interpretation, Professor Walter Barnes's edition of Palgrave's *Golden Treasury* (Row, Petersen & Co., Chicago) is to be commended.

The student's ability to analyse a lyric poem should be tested by frequent written exercises. The method of criticism may be worked out by the individual teacher, but I have found it useful to ask students to test a poem by some or all of the following questions:

(*a*) What kind of experience, thought or emotion furnishes the basis for this lyric? What kind or degree of sensitiveness to the facts of nature? What sort of inner mood or passion? Is the "motive" of this lyric purely personal? If not, what other relationships or associations are involved?

(*b*) What sort of imaginative transformation of the material furnished by the senses? What kind of imagery? Is it true poetry or only verse?

(*c*) What degree of technical mastery of lyric structure? Subordination of material to unity of "tone"? What devices of rhythm or sound to heighten the intended effect? Noticeable words or phrases? Does the author's power of artistic expression keep pace with his feeling and imagination?

Chapter VIII

For a discussion of narrative verse in general, see Gummere's *Poetics* and *Oldest English Epic*, Hart's *Epic and Ballad*, Connell's *Study of Poetry*, and Matthew Arnold's essay "On Translating Homer."

For the further study of ballads, note G. L. Kittredge's one volume edition of Child's *English and Scottish Popular Ballads*, Gummere's *Popular Ballad*, G. H. Stempel's *Book of Ballads*, J. A. Lomax's *Cowboy Songs and other Frontier Ballads*, and Hart's summary of Child's views in *Pub. Mod. Lang. Ass.*, vol. 21, 1906. The *Oxford Book of English Verse*, Nos. 367–389, gives excellent specimens.

All handbooks on *Poetics* discuss the Ode. Gosse's *English Odes* and William Sharp's *Great Odes* are good collections.

For the sonnet, note Corson's chapter in his *Primer of English Verse*, and the Introduction to Miss Lockwood's collection. There are other well-known collections by Leigh Hunt, Hall Caine and William Sharp. Special articles on the sonnet are noted in Poole's *Index*.

The dramatic monologue is well discussed by Claude Howard, *The Dramatic Monologue*, and by S. S. Curry, *The Dramatic Monologue in Tennyson and Browning*.

Chapter IX

The various periods of English lyric poetry are covered, as has been already noted, by the general treatises of Rhys, Reed and Schelling. Old English lyrics are well translated by Cook and Tinker, and by Pancoast and Spaeth. W. P. Ker's *English Literature; Mediæval*, is excellent, as is C. S. Baldwin's *English Mediæval Literature*. John Erskine's *Elizabethan Lyric* is a valuable study. Schelling's introduction to his Selections from the Elizabethan Lyric should also be noted, as well as his similar book on the Seventeenth-Century Lyric. Bernbaum's *English Poets of the Eighteenth Century* is a careful selection, with a scholarly introduction. Studies of the English poetry of the Romantic period are very numerous: Oliver Elton's *Survey of English Literature, 1780–1830,* is one of the best. Courthope's *History of English Poetry* and Saintsbury's *History of Criticism* are full of material bearing upon the questions discussed in this chapter.

Professor Legouis's account of the change in atmosphere as one passes from Old English to Old French poetry is so delightful that I refrain from spoiling it by a translation:

"En quittant *Beowulf* ou la *Bataille de Maldon* pour le *Roland,* on a l'impression de sortir d'un lieu sombre pour entrer dans la lumière. Cette impression vous vient de tous les côtés à la fois, des lieux décrits, des sujets, de la manière de raconter, de l'esprit qui anime, de l'intelligence qui ordonne, mais, d'une façon encore plus immédiate et plus diffuse, de la différence des deux langues. On reconnaît sans doute généralement à nos vieux écrivains ce mérite d'être clairs, mais on est trop habitué à ne voir dans ce don que ce qui découle des tendances analytiques et des aptitudes logiques de leurs esprit. Aussi plusieurs critiques, quelques-uns français, ont-ils fait de cet attribut une manière de prétexte pour leur assigner en partage la prose et pour leur retirer la faculté poétique. Il n'en est pas ainsi. Cette clarté n'est pas purement abstraite. Elle est une véritable lumière qui rayonne même des voyelles et dans

laquelle les meilleurs vers des trouvères — les seuls qui
comptent — sont baignés.   Comment dire l'éblouisse-
ment des yeux longtemps retenus dans la pénombre du
Codex Exoniensis et devant qui passent soudain avec
leurs brillantes syllables 'Halte-Clere,' l'épée d'Olivier,
'Joyeuse' celle de Charlemagne, 'Monjoie' l'étendard
des Francs?   Avant toute description on est saisi
comme par un brusque lever de soleil.   Il est tels vers
de nos vieilles romances d'où la lumière ruisselle sans
même qu'on ait besoin de prendre garde à leur sens:

> "'Bele Erembors a la fenestre au jor
>   Sor ses genolz tient paile de color,'[1]

ou bien

> "'Bele Yolanz en chambre coie
>   Sor ses genolz pailes desploie
>   Coust un fil d'or, l'autre de soie. . . .'[2]

C'est plus que de la lumière qui s'échappe de ces mots,
c'est de la couleur et de la plus riche." [3]

CHAPTER X

While this chapter does not attempt to comment upon
the work of living American authors, except as illustrating certain general tendencies of the lyric, I think
that teachers of poetry should avail themselves of the
present interest in contemporary verse.   Students of a
carefully chosen volume of selections, like the *Oxford
Book*, should be competent to pass some judgment upon

[1] "Fair Erembor at her window in daylight
    Holds a coloured silk stuff on her knees."
[2] "Fair Yoland in her quiet bower
    Unfolds silk stuffs on her knees
    Sewing now a thread of gold, now one of silk."
[3] Emile Legouis, *Défense de la Poésie Française*, p. 44.

strictly contemporary poetry, and I have found them keenly interested in criticizing the work that is appearing, month by month, in the magazines. The temperament and taste of the individual teacher must determine the relative amount of attention that can be given to our generation, as compared with the many generations of the past.

APPENDIX

BELIEVING as I do that a study of the complete work of some modern poet should accompany, if possible, every course in the general theory of poetry, I venture to print here an outline of topical work upon the poetry of Tennyson. Tennyson's variety of poetic achievement is so great, and his technical resources are so remarkable, that he rewards the closest study, even on the part of those young Americans who cannot forget that he was a "Victorian":

TOPICAL WORK UPON TENNYSON

I

THE METHOD OF CRITICISM

[The scheme here suggested for the study of poetry is based upon the methods followed in this book. The student is advised to select some one poem, and to analyse its content and form as carefully as possible, in accordance with the outline printed below. The thought and feeling of the poem should be thoroughly comprehended as a whole before the work of analysis is begun; and after the analysis is completed, the student should endeavor again to regard the poem synthetically, i. e., in its total appeal to the æsthetic judgment, rather than mechanically and part by part.]

CONTENT	**A** "IMPRESSION"	*Of Nature.* What sort of observation of natural phenomena is revealed in this poem? Impressions of movement, form, color, sound, hours of the day or night, seasons of the year; knowledge of scientific facts, etc.? *Of Man.* What evidence of the poet's direct knowledge of men? Of knowledge of man gained through acquaintance with Biblical, classical, foreign or English literature? Self-knowledge? *Of God.* Perception of spiritual laws? Religious attitude? Is this poem consistent with his other poems?
FORM	**B** "TRANSFORMING IMAGINATION"	Does the "raw material" presented by "sense impressions" undergo a real "change in kind" as it passes through the mind of the poet? Do you feel in this poem the presence of a creative personality? What evidence of poetic instinct in the selection of characteristic traits? In power of representation through images? In idealization?
	C "EXPRESSION"	What is to be said of the range and character of the poet's vocabulary? Employment of figurative language? Selection of metre? Use of rhymes? Modification of rhythm and sound to suggest the idea conveyed? Imitative effects? In general, is there harmony between form and content, or is there evidence of the artist's caring for one rather than the other?

II

TENNYSON'S LYRIC POETRY

[Write a criticism of the distinctively lyrical work of Tennyson, based upon an investigation at first hand of the topics suggested below. Do not deal with any poems in which the narrative or dramatic element seems to you the predominant one, as those forms of expression will be made the subject of subsequent papers.]

A. "IMPRESSION" (i. e., experience, thought, emotion).

General Characteristics.

Does the freshness of the lyric mood seem in Tennyson's case dependent upon any philosophical position? Upon sensitiveness to successive experiences?

Is his lyric egoism a noble one? How far does he identify himself with his race? With humanity?

Is his lyric passion always genuine? If not, give examples of lyrics that are deficient in sincerity. Is the lyric passion sustained as the poet grows old?

Of Nature.

What part does the observation of natural phenomena — such as form, color, sound, hours of the day or night, seasons, the sky, the sea — play in these poems? To what extent is the lyrical emotion called forth by the details of nature? By her composite effects? Give instances of the poetic use of scientific facts.

Of Man.

What human relationships furnish the themes for his lyrics? In the love-lyrics, what different relationships of men and women? To what extent does he find a lyric motive in friendship? In patriotism? How much of his lyric poetry seems to spring from direct contact with men? From introspection? From contact with men through the medium of books? How clearly do his lyrics reflect the social problems of his own time? In his later lyrics are there traces of deeper or shallower interest in men and women? Of greater or less faith in the progress of society?

Of God.

Mention lyrics whose themes are based in such conceptions as freedom, duty, moral responsibility. Does Tennyson's lyric poetry reveal a sense of spiritual law? Is the poet's own attitude clearly evident?

B. "TRANSFORMING IMAGINATION."

What evidence of poetic instinct in the selection of characteristic traits? In power of representation through images? Distinguish between lyrics that owe their poetic quality to the Imagination, and those created by the Fancy. (Note Alden's discussion of this point; "Introduction to Poetry," pp. 102–112.) How far is Tennyson's personality indicated by these instinctive processes through which his poetical material is transformed?

C. "EXPRESSION."

What may be said in general of his handling of the lyric form: as to unity, brevity, simplicity of structure? Occasional use of presentative rather than representative language? Choice of metres? Use of rhymes? Modification of rhythm and sound to suit the idea conveyed? Evidence of the artist's caring for either form or content to the neglect of the other? Note whatever differences may be traced, in all these respects, between Tennyson's earlier and later lyrics.

III

TENNYSON'S NARRATIVE POETRY

[Write a criticism of the distinctively narrative work of Tennyson, based upon the questions suggested below.]

A. "IMPRESSION" (i. e., experience, thought, emotion).

General Characteristics.

After classifying Tennyson's narrative poetry, how many of his themes seem to you to be of his own invention? Name those based, ostensibly at least, upon the poet's own experience. To what extent do you find his narrative work purely objective, i. e., without admixture of reflective or didactic elements? What themes are of mythical or legendary origin? Of those having a historical basis, how many are drawn from English sources? Does his use of narrative material ever show a deficiency of emotion; i. e., could the story have been better told in prose? Has he the story-telling gift?

Of Nature.

How far does the description of natural phenomena, as outlined in Topic II, A, enter into Tennyson's narrative poetry? Does it always have a subordinate place, as a part of the setting of the story? Does it overlay the story with too ornate detail? Does it ever retard the movement unduly?

Of Man. (Note that some of the points mentioned under *General Characteristics* apply here.)

What can you say of Tennyson's power of observing character? Of conceiving characters in complication and collision with one another or with circumstances? Give illustrations of the range of human relationships touched upon in these poems. Do the later narratives show an increased proportion of tragic situations? Does Tennyson's narrative poetry throw any light upon his attitude towards contemporary English society?

Of God. (See Topic II, A.)

B. "Transforming Imagination."

Adjust the questions already suggested under Topic II, B, to narrative poetry. Note especially the revelation of Tennyson's personality through the instinctive processes by which his narrative material is transformed.

C. "Expression."

What may be said in general of his handling of the narrative form, i. e., his management of the setting, the characters and the plot in relation to one another? Have his longer poems, like the "Idylls," and "The Princess," the unity, breadth, and sustained elevation of style that are usually associated with epic poetry? What can you say of Tennyson's mastery of distinctly narrative metres? Of his technical skill in suiting rhythm and sound to the requirements of his story?

IV

Tennyson's Dramas

[Reference books for the study of the technique of the drama are easily available. As preparatory work it will be well to make a careful study of Tennyson's dramatic monologues, both in the earlier and later periods. These throw a good deal of light upon his skill in making characters delineate themselves, and they reveal incidentally some of his methods of dramatic narrative. For this paper, however, please confine your criticism to "Queen Mary," "Harold," "Becket," "The Cup," "The Falcon," "The Promise of May," and "The Foresters." In studying "Becket," compare Irving's stage version of the play (Macmillan).]

A. Classify the themes of Tennyson's dramas. Do you think that these themes offer promising dramatic material? Do you regard Tennyson's previous literary experience as a help or a hindrance to success in the drama?

Nature. Apply what is suggested under this head in Topics I, II, and III, to drama.

Man. Apply to the dramas what is suggested under this head in Topics II and III, especially as regards the observation of character, the conception of characters in collision, and the sense of the variety of human relationships. Do these plays give evidence of a genuine comic sense? What tragic forces seem to have made the most impression upon Tennyson? Give illustrations, from the plays, of the conflict of the individual with institutions.

God. Comment upon Tennyson's doctrine of necessity and retribution. Does his allotment of poetic justice show a sympathy with the moral order of the world? Are these plays in harmony with Tennyson's theology, as indicated elsewhere in his work? Do they contain any clear exposition of the problems of the religious life?

B. Compare Topic II, B. In the historical dramas, can you trace the influence of the poet's own personality in giving color to historical personages? Compare Tennyson's delineation of any of these personages with that of other poets, novelists, or historians. Do you think he has the power of creating a character, in the same sense as Shakespeare had it? How much of his dramatic work do you consider purely objective, i. e., untinged by what was called the lyric egoism?

C. What may be said in general of Tennyson's handling of the dramatic form? Has he "the dramatic sense"? Of his management of the web of circumstance in which the characters are involved and brought into conflict? Comment upon his technical skill as displayed in the different "parts" and "moments" of his dramas. Does his exhibition of action fulfill dramatic requirements? Is his vocabulary suited to stage purposes? Give instances of his purely lyric and narrative gifts as incidentally illustrated in his dramas. Instance passages that cannot in your opinion be successfully acted. In your reading of these plays, or observation of any of them that you have seen acted, are you conscious of the absence of any quality or qualities that would heighten the pleasure they yield you? Taken as a whole, is the form of the various plays artistically in harmony with the themes employed?

BIBLIOGRAPHY

THIS list includes the more important books and articles in English which have been discussed or referred to in the text. There is an excellent bibliography in Alden's *Introduction to Poetry*, and Patterson's *Rhythm in Prose* contains a full list of the more technical articles dealing with rhythms in prose and verse.

ALDEN, RAYMOND M.
    English Verse. New York, 1903.
    An Introduction to Poetry. New York, 1909.
    "The Mental Side of Metrical Form," in *Mod. Lang. Review*, July, 1914.
ALEXANDER, HARTLEY B.
    Poetry and the Individual. New York, 1906.
ANDREWS, C. E.
    The Writing and Reading of Verse. New York, 1918.
ARISTOTLE.
    Theory of Poetry and Fine Art, edited by S. H. Butcher. New York, 1902.
    On the Art of Poetry, edited by Lane Cooper. Boston, 1913.
BABBITT, IRVING.
    The New Laokoon. Boston and New York, 1910.
BERNBAUM, ERNEST, *editor.*
    English Poets of the 18th Century. New York, 1918.
BOSANQUET, BERNARD.
    A History of Æsthetic. New York, 1892.
    Three Lectures on Æsthetic. London, 1915.
BRADLEY, A. C.
    Oxford Lectures on Poetry. London, 1909.

BRAITHWAITE, WILLIAM S., *editor*.

The Book of Elizabethan Verse. Boston, 1907.

Anthology of Magazine Verse 1913–19. New York, 1915.

BRIDGES, ROBERT.

Ibant Obscuræ. New York, 1917.

BUTCHER, S. H.

(See Aristotle.)

CHILD, F. G.

English and Scottish Popular Ballads, 5 vols., 1882–1898.

CLARK, A. C.

Prose Rhythm in English. Oxford, 1913.

COLERIDGE, S. T.

Biographia Literaria. Everyman edition.

CONNELL, F. M.

A Text-Book for the Study of Poetry. Boston, 1913.

COOK, ALBERT S., *editor*.

The Art of Poetry. Boston, 1892.

COOK, A. S., *and* TINKER, C. B.

Select Translations from Old English Poetry. Boston, 1902.

CORSON, HIRAM.

A Primer of English Verse. Boston, 1892.

COURTHOPE, WILLIAM J.

A History of English Poetry. London, 1895.

Life in Poetry: Law in Taste. London, 1901.

COWL, R. P.

The Theory of Poetry in England. London, 1914.

CROCE, B.

Æsthetics. London, 1909.

CROLL, MORRIS W.

"The Cadence of English Oratorical Prose," in *Studies in Philology*, January, 1919.

See also Croll and Clemons, Preface to *Lyly's Euphues*.
New York, 1916.

DRINKWATER, JOHN.
The Lyric. New York (n.d.).

EASTMAN, MAX.
Enjoyment of Poetry. New York, 1913.

ELTON, OLIVER W.
"English Prose Numbers," in *Essays and Studies*,
by members of the English Association, 4th Series.
Oxford, 1913.

ERSKINE, JOHN.
The Elizabethan Lyric. New York, 1916.

FAIRCHILD, ARTHUR H. R.
The Making of Poetry. New York, 1912.

GARDINER, J. H.
The Bible as English Literature. New York, 1906.

GATES, LEWIS E.
Studies and Appreciations. New York, 1900.

GAYLEY, C. M., and SCOTT, F. N.
Methods and Materials of Literary Criticism. Boston,
1899.

GORDON, K.
Æsthetics. New York, 1909.

GOSSE, EDMUND W.
English Odes. London, 1881.

GUMMERE, FRANCIS B.
A Handbook of Poetics. Boston, 1885.
The Beginnings of Poetry. New York, 1901.
The Popular Ballad. Boston and New York, 1907.
Democracy and Poetry. Boston and New York, 1911.

HART, WALTER M.
Epic and Ballad. Harvard Studies, etc., vol. 11, 1907.
See also his summary of Child's views in *Pub. Mod.
Lang. Ass.*, 21, 1906.

HAYES, ALFRED.
"Relation of Music to Poetry," in *Atlantic*, January, 1914.

HEARN, LAFCADIO.
Kwaidan. Boston and New York, 1904.

HOLMES, EDMOND.
What is Poetry? New York, 1900.

HUNT, LEIGH.
What is Poetry? edited by Albert S. Cook. Boston, 1893.

JAMES, WILLIAM.
Psychology. New York, 1909.

KITTREDGE, G. L., *editor*.
English and Scottish Popular Ballads. Boston, 1904.

LA FARGE, JOHN.
Considerations on Painting. New York, 1895.

LANIER, SIDNEY.
Science of English Verse. New York, 1880.
Poem Outlines. New York, 1908.

LEGOUIS, ÉMILE.
Défense de la Poésie Française. London, 1912.

LEWIS, CHARLTON M.
The Foreign Sources of Modern English Versification. Halle, 1898.
The Principles of English Verse. New York, 1906.

LIDDELL, M. H.
Introduction to the Scientific Study of English Poetry. New York, 1912.

LOCKWOOD, LAURA E., *editor*.
English Sonnets. Boston and New York, 1916.

LOMAX, JOHN A.
Cowboy Songs and Other Frontier Ballads. New York, 1916.

LOWELL, AMY.

Tendencies in Modern American Poetry. New York, 1917.

Men, Women and Ghosts. New York, 1916.

Can Grande's Castle. New York, 1918.

LOWES, JOHN L.

Convention and Revolt in Poetry. Boston and New York, 1919.

LYLY, JOHN.

Euphues, edited by Croll, M. W., and Clemons, H. New York, 1916.

MACKAIL, J. W.

The Springs of Helicon. New York, 1909.

MARSHALL, HENRY R.

Æsthetic Principles. New York, 1895.

MAYOR, J. B.

Chapters on English Metre. London, 1886.

MILL, J. S.

"Thoughts on Poetry," in *Dissertations,* vol. 1.

MOORE, J. ROBERT.

"The Songs in the English Drama" (Harvard Dissertation, unpublished).

MORSE, LEWIS K., *editor.*

Melodies of English Verse. Boston and New York, 1910.

NEILSON, WILLIAM A.

Essentials of Poetry. Boston and New York, 1912.

NEWBOLT, SIR HENRY.

A New Study of English Poetry. New York, 1919.

OMOND, T. S.

A Study of Metre. London, 1903.

PALGRAVE, FRANCIS T.

The Golden Treasury. London, 1882.

PANCOAST, H. S. and SPAETH, J. D.
  Early English Poems. New York, 1911.
PATTERSON, WILLIAM M.
  The Rhythm of Prose. New York, 1916.
PATTISON, MARK, *editor.*
  Milton's Sonnets. New York, 1883.
PHELPS, WILLIAM L.
  The Beginnings of the English Romantic Movement.
  Boston, 1893.
POUND, LOUISE.
  "The Ballad and the Dance," *Pub. Mod. Lang. Ass.,*
  September, 1919.
QUILLER-COUCH, A. T., *editor.*
  The Oxford Book of English Verse. Oxford, 1907.
RALEIGH, WALTER.
  Wordsworth. London, 1903.
RAYMOND, GEORGE L.
  Poetry as a Representative Art. New York, 1886.
  The Genesis of Art-Form. New York, 1893.
  Rhythm and Harmony in Poetry and Music. New
  York, 1895.
REED, EDWARD B.
  English Lyrical Poetry. New Haven, 1912.
RHYS, ERNEST.
  Lyric Poetry. New York, 1913.
RHYS, ERNEST, *editor.*
  The New Golden Treasury of Songs and Lyrics. New
  York (n.d.).
RIBOT, T.
  Essay on the Creative Imagination. Chicago,
  1906.
RUSSELL, C. E.
  "Swinburne and Music," in *North American Review,*
  November, 1907.

SAINTSBURY, GEORGE.
History of English Prosody. London, 1906–10.
History of English Prose Rhythm. London, 1912.

SANTAYANA, GEORGE.
The Sense of Beauty. New York, 1896.
Interpretation of Poetry and Religion. New York, 1900.

SCHELLING, F. E., *editor.*
A Book of Elizabethan Lyrics. Boston, 1895.
Seventeenth Century Lyrics. Boston, 1899.

SCHELLING, F. E.
The English Lyric. Boston and New York, 1913.

SHACKFORD, MARTHA H.
A First Book of Poetics. Boston, 1906.

SHELLEY, PERCY B.
A Defense of Poetry, edited by Albert S. Cook. Boston, 1891.

SHERMAN, L. A.
Analytics of Literature. Boston, 1893.

SHERMAN, STUART P.
Contemporary Literature. New York, 1917.

SIDNEY, SIR PHILIP.
The Defense of Poesy, edited by Albert S. Cook. Boston, 1890.

SNELL, ADA F.
"Syllabic Quantity in English Verse," in *Pub. Mod. Lang. Ass.,* September, 1918.

SPINGARN, J. E.
Creative Criticism. New York, 1917.

STEDMAN, EDMUND C.
The Nature and Elements of Poetry. Boston and New York, 1892.

STEMPEL, G. H.
A Book of Ballads. New York, 1917.

STEWART, J. A.
  The Myths of Plato.   London, 1905.
SYMONS, ARTHUR.
  The Seven Arts.   London, 1906.
TAYLOR, HENRY O.
  The Classical Heritage of the Middle Ages.   New York, 1901.
TOLMAN, A. H.
  Hamlet and Other Essays.   Boston, 1904.
TOLSTOY, L.
  What is Art?   New York (n.d.).
UNTERMEYER, LOUIS.
  The New Era in American Poetry.   New York, 1919.
WATTS-DUNTON, THEODORE.
  Poetry and the Renascence of Wonder.   New York, (n.d.).
WELLS, CAROLYN.
  A Parody Anthology.   New York, 1904.
WHITMORE, C. E.
  Article on the Lyric in *Pub. Mod. Lang. Ass.*, December, 1918.
WHITNEY, W. D.
  Language and the Study of Language.   New York, 1867.
WILKINSON, MARGUERITE.
  The New Voices.   New York, 1919.

INDEX